*Torches Rekindled*

*Third edition, expanded*

# TORCHES REKINDLED

*The Bruderhof's Struggle for Renewal*

*told by*
*Merrill Mow*

*a word from Tom Sine*
*foreword by John M. Perkins*

**PLOUGH PUBLISHING HOUSE**
**HUTTERIAN BRETHREN**
Ulster Park, NY, USA
Robertsbridge, England

Rifton, NY 12471, USA
Robertsbridge, East Sussex TN32 5DR, England

Printing history
First edition, Oct. 1989
Second edition, Jan. 1990
(Epilogue expanded)
Third edition, Jan. 1991
(Expanded and Index added)

*Many of the photographs in this book were taken before the Bruderhof communities were reunited with the Hutterian Brethren in 1974. The photographs of brothers, sisters, and children may therefore not all show our united dress.*

*The editors wish to express our gratitude for the essential help and advice of Don Mosley.*

Library of Congress Cataloging-in-Publication Data

Mow, Merrill.
    Torches rekindled: the Bruderhof's struggle for renewal/told by
Merrill Mow; a word from Tom Sine; foreword by John M. Perkins. —
3rd ed., expanded.
343 p. 15 × 20 cm.
    ISBN 0-87486-032-6:   $13.00
    1. Hutterian Brethren—History.    I. Title.
BX8129.B63M68   1991
289.7'3—dc20                             90-49626
                                           CIP
                                           AC

Printed at Thomson-Shore, Inc.
Dexter, Mich., USA

# Contents

Wherefore burn poor and lonely
As one needy brand?
Torches together, hand to hand!

He who feels deep within him
A fire burning bright
Must through that glow
With his brothers unite.

Wherefore burn poor and lonely
As one needy brand?
Torches together, hand to hand!

*Otto Salomon*

If one sets out to live a life according to *God's* will, there are going to be problems and the problems must be faced, and facing the problems *always* means *struggle—always*!

Merrill Mow

# A Word from Tom Sine

Coming Home. Deep within the human spirit is a longing for home. We all long to come back home again. *Torches Rekindled* is a story about coming home. ... To a home and a community we have never known before. *Torches Rekindled* is the compelling story of a Bruderhof Community planted, struggling, and experiencing the renewal of God in a new land.

Merrill Mow begins by remembering the green lumber and the hot days of June 1955 at Woodcrest, New York, as the seed was planted. We are invited to come home to the Bruderhof and, for a few pages, to be a part of the life of this unusual family of God's planting. As we journey with these brothers and sisters, we will experience what we experience in all families. ... The tragic losses and the joyous celebrations. ... The rending conflicts and the loving reconciliations.

But what makes this family unique is that they are struggling in their brokenness and joys to live out an authentic expression of another story. ... The story of God. They have come from many different families to create a new family that has a single purpose: to seek to follow Jesus Christ in every aspect of their lives together.

So as you read *Torches Rekindled*, you will meet a very unusual family. As you join them on their journey, you will see them set aside personal autonomy, materialism, and ambitions. ... You will see them seek to faithfully and courageously live out the rightside-up values of the Kingdom in an upside-down world. And, of course, you will find, like all of us who seek to follow God, there are setbacks.

On this journey, we will get to know some of the family very intimately. We will see them through a freezing winter with no insulation or heat. We will watch them dressing up in outlandish costumes to raise the spirits of some that were down. Intense seriousness of purpose, festive celebrations, and times of out-rageous hilarity all characterize this family. And Merrill Mow relates the story in a straightforward, unassuming style that draws the reader in like a letter from home.

In a society where many of us have attempted to replace our profound sense of alienation from community by seeking to find intimacy and security in things, you will find this book a breath of fresh air. In a world where families seem to know more of alienation than mutual loving relationships, this book will give you hope. And, in a day in which the American church has unquestionably embraced the secular values of society, *Torches Rekindled* will introduce you to a large and growing family who march to a different drumbeat.

One cannot help but ask as we journey with the Bruderhof through these pages, "How does God call me to live out the values of his rightside-up Kingdom in an upside-down world?" In prayerfully struggling with that question, we will, like the Bruderhof, begin to come home to all that God intends for our lives and his world.

Tom Sine
Seattle, Washington

# Foreword

Whenever I'm at the Bruderhof, I feel I belong. I feel a great sense of unity, of love and acceptance. Of kinship. This, I believe, is the Bruderhof testimony. Theirs is a prophetic witness of what it means to live in community.

Through the Bruderhof, God is showing us a model of what we need in our day, especially what we need in our nation's growing ghettos. Today's materialism and individualism are creating a larger and larger underclass less and less able to function in the rest of society. It's going to take communities—people in community, working together to care for "the least of these" not just socially and spiritually but economically as well, as the New Testament teaches and the Bruderhof practices—to make a difference.

I once joined a group called Community of Communities, since they tried to form communities all around the world. There was something that felt good and right about trying to love God, not just on a theoretical level, but with all your heart and soul and strength. So coming to the Bruderhof and meeting the Bruderhof people was wonderful for me. I fell in love with the whole idea instantly.

But I also felt the great struggle: I, like the Bruderhof, heartily believe that to be the people of God we must be in community, but since being in community can in a great sense isolate you from reality, how can you be in community and still reach the world? So I am excited when I am with the Bruderhof as they struggle to keep their identity as God's people, a separate community yet at the same time obedient to whatever God may have in mind for them as their witness to the world. I consider the Bruderhof to be one of the greatest expressions of God's love on earth, certainly an expression far greater than most of ours.

We as God's people have got to go beyond individual conversion! American evangelicals now number seventy million, but so what? More abortions, more divorce, and lotteries and gambling legal in every state, and what do we talk about? Church growth. More conversions. But what difference do church growth and conversion make when the Christianity of today is little more than a shameless exhibition of selfishness and greed, an extension of individualism? "Yes! I'll send money to radio preachers if they'll help me lead a better—better-off—life." People use God to get what they want from life, not to make a difference in society. We don't see ourselves as salt in the world, and we aren't.

What we need to do is re-create community. A strange idea in our individualistic church today, but it wasn't so strange in earlier days. In fact, it was assumed that people would worship and work together. That was parish life; you *lived* in such and such a parish, you didn't just attend services there. What happened to the parish idea? The me-God worship—God helping *me* to do *my* will, God keeping me from suffering—that's what happened recently in the church; the charismatic movement has made undeniable contributions (for one thing, they've brought the joy of Christ back into the church) but parts of that movement are responsible for making us as a church believe that suffering is not of God, that suffering is evil. But that's just more selfish individualism. More health, wealth, and prosperity—"God wants me rich!"

Suffering—not self-inflicted suffering—is a virtue we have to restore in society, as well as in the church. Suffering that is fully accepted suffering can give us stamina and courage. It can make us grow to be the kind of people who cherish life in a day when life's so cheap that a fourteen-year-old can knock an old lady in the head and grab her purse, and her life is worth nothing more than to help him buy something shiny. Suffering will help us value life.

I have been privileged to share suffering with the Bruderhof. I suffered with them when two of their members were dying. Hard as it was, it was good for us because it called us to cherish the life all around us. You know, there is something good about having the older people right with you, caring for old and young together in their illnesses, and having their burials right in your midst, not isolating the suffering but accepting it. All that should be part of parish life, part of the church's life together as community, as it used to be. As it still is for the Bruderhof.

I think of the Bruderhof as the highest form of community. Maybe it can be the salvation of a lot of people, because of the need everywhere for community. When I say community I am also talking about neighborhoods. I'm also talking about people living within a geographical area who worship within that area— like the earlier parish idea, a sort of church neighborhood we have to rebuild. We will never restructure society until we first restructure the family and then the neighborhood.

What has happened in the ghettos is that all the black folks that used to be there, who used to worship God and serve God and care for their neighbors there, got themselves upward mobility! Now they can move to the suburbs. Sure, they commute back to church every Sunday morning and hope things will get better in the old neighborhood, but things can't get anything but worse. The killing is going to continue and the gangs are going to rule because there are no men-people there, no real families. The people of the neighborhood have no control.

And a bunch of individual conversions might only make the matter worse. Individual conversions might lift those people right out of there. Once they clean up and get a little ahead and start tithing and doing good, they might just find a house in another part of town. Individual conversion might just remove the people who could make a difference. So we have to do something more than make individual converts. We have to rebuild community wherever we happen to be.

How do we start? First of all, we need to bring faith back into our communities, our neighborhoods. We need to come back to the Word of God, to give people his Word. After all, "Heaven and earth may pass away . . ."—his Word is the only sure thing we have.

And it cannot be that kind of faith that is evangelical but only theoretical. It must be belief that works itself out in meeting human needs. Faith without works is dead. Abraham is the father of our faith because he lived it. And faith came through the *living* Word of God. Faith comes from obedience to the Word—to love our neighbor. Real faith meets real human needs.

Something we can relearn from the Bruderhof is understanding the whole idea of the forgiveness of sin, so that God's love flows back through us as we forgive others and learn to live in community relationships. I don't think we understand the impact of our sins on the community—the greater the sense of community, the greater the sin. That is why restoration and healing are so important, although we try to circumvent them.

I know that I find the most difficult thing for me in my day-to-day life is to be able to talk honestly to people. I mean, telling the truth, speaking up when I hurt, and saying what's on my heart. But when we reduce Christianity to ourselves we can never get outside ourselves; we can't make a witness because we're too caught up in our own emotions. Our emotions need to be cleansed. We need the cleanliness so we can forgive each other and talk to each other. Then we can have pure thoughts and relationships that restore forgiveness.

My encouragement to the Bruderhof would be that it continue to carry on in community, but more visibly. That is its witness.

Why is *Torches Rekindled* inspiring? It reflects that long struggle, the deep and necessary struggle, to be a truly united community in Christ. The very fact that the Bruderhof is growing and developing is a testimony that God wants it to be here now, to light the way.

It means much to me to know personally of the struggle of the Bruderhofs both to express their faith and to maintain their identity as a separate community of God's people, to really believe that the Gospel can burn through racial and cultural barriers to unite people for a justice that has no racial or cultural bias. The Gospel calls us to be reconciled—God's reconciliation of us to himself already having taken place through Jesus—across racial, economic, and social barriers. We have to acknowledge that we are failing a little. But all the more, as my son says, "Stay the course!"

John M. Perkins
Pasadena, California

# 1
# Torches Rekindled

*Merrill Mow is telling the Bruderhof communities at mealtimes about their history, beginning with his arrival in 1955, with a flashback to 1935. The big dining room is filled with older and newer members, guests, and children. There is something for everybody in his account: for many it is new and enlightening, for others it adds an important new perspective, for all it has flashes of humor. You are invited to take a chair and listen . . .*

The first house was being built. The outer shell was completed: the inside was bare studding, you could look right through. In my first weeks at the Woodcrest Bruderhof I joined the building crew. That summer of 1955 five carpenters from Western Hutterite colonies were having a wonderful time working together. The green lumber made conditions a bit odd. If you missed the nail head and your hammer struck the wood, it would squirt water in your eye. After the attic was closed in, I saw a brother come crawling out of it where he was doing electric wiring. He was absolutely soaked, as if he had been swimming, with water all over his glasses; under the hot June sun that attic was full of steam from this green lumber. But it had been the cheapest lumber

1

available, and there wasn't money to buy anything better.

The dining room and kitchen for this new Bruderhof near Rifton, New York, were being pushed to completion in the old Carriage House (of the original Dimmick estate). The first meal in the new dining room was a lovemeal, and at that communal mealtime a married couple made their novice vows. Now my wife Kathy and I had heard about the novitiate, but we had never heard the novice questions. That evening was a very strong—I could even say wrenching—experience for me.

For one thing, I had had a very negative experience that afternoon. Mac, the Rifton village postman—who was a very good friend of the community and had gotten to know the Western brothers—wanted to do something very special for them; he asked permission to come up our hill with a keg of cold beer to celebrate with them before they went home. On Wednesday afternoon—a very hot afternoon—at snack time a pickup came up the hill with a keg of beer in the back. What I did not know, and heard only years later, was that Heini Arnold (as the one responsible for this Bruderhof), had been very concerned about that snack time. He did not want to hurt the love that Mac was expressing, but he did not want the celebrating to get out of hand. There were many guests, including people from Rifton. So he had particularly asked certain brothers to do the serving, and they were to limit the quantity. The beer was drawn off into pitchers and served.

In those days we members of the Church of the Brethren were very strong in our opposition to any kind of beverage containing any amount of alcohol, including beer. I don't know how much the Brethren are still like that. I sat off to one side, pretty glum and depressed, not taking part at all, and I felt terrible. I think I felt even worse because it was just the responsible brothers here who were doing the serving.

Now I return to the communal supper that evening, which was

also the farewell for the five carpenters from the Western communities. Each of them rose and said how moved he was by the whole visit. Next, James and Harriet Alexander were asked to stand while Heini read out the novice questions. Those questions are so all-encompassing in covering this first step into Christian community that it swept away completely my whole negative reaction to the afternoon. The atmosphere at that suppertime was even stronger than the words used. I had never experienced anything like it in my whole life, and I remember being very deeply moved. With great sensitivity to what was moving in another person, Heini came straight over to me after supper and shook my hand. I don't remember what he said, but I do remember feeling, "This is it. There are no more questions, this way of life is the only possible life for me, I am called by God to this."

Kathy has told how she experienced this in a quite different way:

> Over the years Heini has teased us about that barrel of beer, and we have had some good laughs over it, but at the time, it was not funny to me at all. In our own Church of the Brethren we had been taught that if a person drank beer, he was not a Christian. We also knew with our heads that we could not be that rigid, but with our emotions we didn't, and suddenly we came face to face with the question just days after our arrival. At that lovemeal I hadn't gotten over the shock. But Merrill had, and he felt and experienced the lovemeal and what James and Harriet promised in their novice vows, while I was still trying to cope with that keg of beer. I actually missed the main experience of that whole lovemeal, and it was another shock to me when afterwards Merrill said he was going to ask to be a novice—he was ready to stay and I was ready to go!

> I remember taking a long walk, trying to cope with this completely new thing, and with the fact that Merrill and I saw things differently. Heini led us through all this to see something

greater and to see how a thing like that could blind you so
much that you couldn't experience something greater. It was
a real pain for us then, but now we can look back and laugh
at the whole incident.

What I said about the novice vows in that first lovemeal answering
all my questions certainly didn't mean that there weren't others
like them coming up later on. Sometimes they were questions
we had a real struggle to understand.

Our first contact with Heini had been in February 1954 through
a letter from him in Paraguay. He was a servant of the Word at
the Ibaté Bruderhof (one of the three in Primavera, Paraguay),
and lived there with his wife and helper Annemarie.*

In August of the previous year some very close friends of ours,
Bob and Shirley Wagoner, had gone to Paraguay and had stayed
there until the next January. The Wagoners experienced the
community life at the Bruderhof where Heini and Annemarie
Arnold lived in Primavera, the large estancia in Paraguay. The
Wagoners came back very much on fire with the inner call and
reality of this brotherly life in Christ, as first witnessed to by
Eberhard Arnold in Germany in 1920. Later on we were to learn
that there had also been dark powers at work after Eberhard's
death, along with a real grace from God that had kept alive the
original flame, especially through the faithfulness of those
inwardly close to Eberhard's widow Emmy and to their children
Heini and Annemarie. Bob and Shirley had had some questions,
but when they came back, they would not even share them with
our little circle of Chicago friends. They wouldn't do it because
they were concerned that we experience the Bruderhof directly.

*Servant of the Word is the old Hutterian designation for minister or pastor. To
support this service, witness brothers are also chosen by the whole church. A
Chronology and a Glossary at the back of the book may help with "Bruderhof"
and with the terms and dates used.

When they returned from their trip to Primavera, they were determined to live in community, but they were not clear about uniting with the Hutterian brothers. They had in mind, rather, something more related to the Church of the Brethren.

While in Primavera, Bob and Shirley had spoken about the seeking and longing in our circle in Chicago. So Heini and Annemarie and others knew of us. I wrote to Primavera, introducing myself and saying that we hoped to visit the Bruderhof, that we didn't have any money but were raising it towards a trip. I asked whether we should try to go to the Bruderhof in Primavera or to the Wheathill Bruderhof in England. On February 26, 1954, Heini wrote to us:

> It is quite true that Paraguay would be a much better place to get a true impression of the Bruderhof life. Wheathill has a great problem with housing, because it is so difficult and expensive to build there, but it is a possibility. Because there are so many interrelated questions, it would be very good if you could talk matters over with one of our brothers now traveling in the States, rather than try to work the whole thing out by correspondence. It is good that you have introduced yourselves and that we are now in direct contact. Do please let us know how things are developing. With warm interest,
>
> Heinrich Arnold

Coming from a church and seminary background, I was very much accustomed to examine all the different philosophies of life and then to develop one and hold to it. This was very much on a human level of deciding what one's own personal belief and theology are going to be. But we had been subscribing to the little Bruderhof quarterly, *The Plough*, and had read in it of the absolute call of God, the absolute call of Jesus, which demands everything; it isn't a question of choosing what you are going to follow, but a question of responding to a call.

When we came to Woodcrest the summer of 1955, we didn't see all this so clearly. We had very much to learn, and it was thrilling to see it even in small ways. In one of our first meetings I was so impressed by what Heini was saying that I pulled out a piece of paper and jotted it down. In those days guests would ask questions after the reading, and answers would be given by Heini or other brotherhood members. Someone had asked the question, "What does the Bruderhof teach about the devil and hell?" According to my notes, Heini answered, "God is God, and we are not to make our own teachings. What the Bruderhof teaches about hell or anything else is of no importance whatsoever. In the final judgment we can only stand trembling before God in our weakness. What the Bruderhof teaches, or anyone else teaches, will not change the perfect will of God a bit; we have no right to interpret God. What is important are the words of Jesus: first, sell what thou hast and give it to the poor; second, go and sin no more; third, love thy neighbor as thyself." And then Heini said, "Do it. Don't interpret it, don't write papers about it, do it."

We could never have dreamed of what we experienced at Advent and Christmas 1955—it was that special. We know how Christmas is usually celebrated in the States. Ours, as Brethren, wasn't as crassly commercialized. But we were unfamiliar with the German customs. And the Brethren Church historically had very little of the church-year feasts, which is a reaction against the institutional church. We knew nothing of "Advent." For us Christmas began very close to Christmas Day, and the whole idea of the four Sundays of Advent was foreign to our thinking. But that first Advent Sunday eve, when the angels (our youth group) came around and sang, when the communal Advent breakfast followed with more Advent songs and the reading of the Messianic prophecies—well, all this was very deep and shaking for us.

That Advent Sunday evening we also experienced our first Bruderhof baptism. Heini spoke about the meaning of baptism, dedication, and surrender. Again I tried unobtrusively to take a few notes:

> In such a life one stands by the church community—with God and in God—faithful to all who give themselves to that same way. The old life and its ideals, even its good ideals, must be surrendered to God with complete willingness to change them however he leads. The new life will always be a life of love, especially to the poor. In any persecution, suffering, or trial, nothing can separate us from the peace of God if we are true to him. The tongue and the lips must be watched: no slandering, no talk about sins that are forgiven, no talking behind someone's back, no gossip. All we do must point to unity with God. There must be nothing of a selfish, egotistical surrender just to be saved; this leads us astray. We must live in God and for him.
>
> Baptism is a special act of faith. It means: a break with the sin and injustice of this age, a break with all unfaithfulness and lust, a break with the murderous power of abortion and war, a break with false piety and with any church organization or religion that tries to mix the teachings of Jesus or the love of God with war, injustice, race discrimination, or mammon. It means a break with all these, and *complete* repentance.
>
> Baptism is a practical dedication to Christ. The form was set by him. Water symbolizes purity and cleanliness and is in common use by men. Baptism means to be born again from *above*. Baptism also symbolizes burial and resurrection, thus many practice immersion. We lay no special emphasis on any one form, and use several, according to what is practical. As the Lord's Supper must be bread and wine (as was commonly used), so water for baptism must be water as commonly used,

by pouring or by immersion. It testifies that the person is giving
himself to Christ's death and resurrection for all time. We
identify ourselves with the shame that Jesus took upon himself;
we want to be one with him and spread his message to the world.

Out of that experience and out of the days that followed, Kathy
and I finally—six months after our arrival—decided to make a
life commitment.

On October 21, 1955, Heini had written to Bob and Shirley
Wagoner, who were doing their two years of alternative service
in Puerto Rico. During their time there the inner fire in them
nearly went out. They never did return to the community, but
Heini still had a great love and longing for them. I shared their
letters with Heini, and he wrote:

My dear Bob and Shirley,
   I feel the urge to write a few words about your main question,
so far as I understand it. Certainly, the Bruderhof has specific
characteristics, and some of them are not essential; they arise
partly from background and other circumstances. The same is
true of the Church of the Brethren. I can well understand that
you or anyone coming from this background feel a certain love
and perhaps attachment to the culture, and still more to the
people of this background. The same is the feeling of some of
the Quakers and of former members of other free churches or
small churches.
   Let us for a moment consider the "community of believers"—
I mean this one organism going through the centuries, in all
countries. What is the Bruderhof then with its culture? What
is the Church of the Brethren? Whatever good there may be in
them, it is because they are surrendered to, and gripped by,
this stream of life. Perhaps, dear Bob and Shirley, the stress
is laid too much on the Bruderhof or Brethren. *The Bruderhof*

*movement will pass away as many movements have passed away, but the stream of life to which the Bruderhof is surrendered can never pass away.* That is what matters.

You write in a way that gives me the definite impression that both of you want to surrender your lives to this one great stream of life. You want to do this as much as possible in the framework and background of the Brethren. There can be nothing wrong in this in itself. The Bruderhof also started within the culture of the country in which it began, with the strong influence of the original German Youth Movement. The danger lies in the second step, and I must say that I feel a little that you are at least in danger of taking this second step. If the Bruderhof would have made up its mind to be *only* a Christian community of German culture with the special task to those people whose background was the Youth Movement, then we would be in danger of drying up before we even began. Either we give our life completely to be used wherever God moves the heart and are open to what is simply given, or we are in danger of limiting the truth.

You may answer, "But the Bruderhof and its outreach is also limited; the circles they reach are also limited." This is absolutely right. We are and we will remain very limited, but still we do not make up our minds to limit our dedication to this or that culture, background, or task. We are limited because we are a circle of weak human beings. But the task to which you or we want to give our lives can never be limited. God is without limits.

I am quite sure, dear friends, that those letters Merrill showed me cannot be taken out of context. Therefore I write only about my impressions, and if I should have come to a wrong conclusion, I am more than willing to accept this.

There were one or two sentences in your letters where I had the feeling that you think of the Bruderhof as authoritarian; I am not sure if my impression is right. In a certain way we are authoritarian (with respect to Christ), but never in the sense that certain people dictate; we would refuse that. But we are definitely not democratic, since we believe in a King, and our surrender must be without limitation. You yourself would accept this, because it lies within the idea of the suffering servant.

The idea of the suffering servant is based on the Isaiah passages about Jesus and the suffering of Jesus that were then lived out in Jesus' life—we know them so well from *The Messiah*. "Suffering servant" is a term that we came to know very well before coming to the Bruderhof; Bob Wagoner had written that this was what he wanted somehow to represent.

Since we feel very close to you, you will not mind if I express everything I feel. I do this with the knowledge that I may be mistaken and that I am willing to be corrected. I see in the direction you are taking, dear Bob and Shirley, the danger of limiting. The whole picture you gave of the suffering servant is true; it is true that Jesus was a suffering servant; it is true that all those who want to follow him must be suffering servants. But Jesus is more than this. He is also the Risen One. We cannot do more than give ourselves to him without limitation.

Your picture of Jesus and mine will be limited always—as long as we are on this earth—but he has no limits. I am sure you accept this and did not doubt it for a moment. But in the direction you seem to take, isn't there a danger of stressing a certain truth so much that it could become detached from the Jesus to whom you and we want to surrender? Please take this only as a question; perhaps it is worth considering. Please take all this as written in love.

Heinrich Arnold

When experiences are deep ones of the heart, it is not easy to put them into words, but I want to try. I undertake this story of the Bruderhof's fight for renewal with a strong sense of my own unworthiness to have been part of it in these years since 1955. We all feel a great sorrow for not having listened to our consciences speaking to us in support of the direction that Heini and Annemarie's lives gave us; also for our pride that deliberately worked against the atmosphere of Jesus, which they lived for. But when one thinks of them, and not of oneself, it brings back wonderful memories.

Now in 1986, over thirty years later, it is a wonderful thing to think of our fifth Bruderhof, Pleasant View, coming into being as something new, something that was not there before. The brothers and sisters of Pleasant View (New York) were certainly already part of the whole body of our brotherhood. Still, the specific composition there is a new thing.

I have been struggling over how to explain something that I find very hard to express, how to put it in terms that our children will understand, because the question is a paradox. But I will try. If we look around any one of our dining rooms and see the whole community eating together, we naturally think, "We people, we who sit here and who see each other, are the New Meadow Run Bruderhof, or the Woodcrest, Deer Spring, Pleasant View, or Darvell Bruderhof." And there is a certain truth in it. But there is also a sense in which we can't say that, daren't say it. Each community—or each brotherhood—as a whole is a great deal more than the total of the people who happen to be collected there, or let me say, more than what is represented by the people gathered there.

I remember hearing that Eberhard Arnold was very upset by what was said by a member of the first Bruderhof in Germany. At the end of a time of particular struggle, when the weakness of the community was strongly evident, this member said something like, "Well, we certainly have nothing to boast about, nothing to represent to the world."

I think all of us who have been very long in the brotherhood recollect times in our lives when we could have said the same. The struggles we had been through, either personally or as a group, revealed a spirit so opposite to the way of Jesus that one would get the feeling: "We sure have nothing to represent to the world; there is no reason for us to send people out on mission. It's a good thing we have no guests now, for we have nothing to represent."

What I am saying, or trying to say, is this: *The way of life that we are called to, and what we represent, is more than what we are.* It is something so great that even though in representing it we are total failures, even though we have just been through a crisis and feel rotten because we have so misused it, still, what we are called to and what we are meant to represent comes from heaven. To us it is a calling and a witness that comes from the kingdom of God. We have no right at any time to say, "Well, our life together is nothing to go to anybody else with or to represent to anyone else." If we have been in a sinful situation, what we need to do is to snap out of it and get back to our original calling.

I am thinking of a paradox that belongs to our history. Those who have been in the community for years are very well aware that something had gone terribly wrong in our brotherhood life in Primavera, Paraguay, in Wheathill, England, and in Sinntal, Germany. Looking at the examples and hearing about the things that happened, one would be tempted to say, "Well, my land, rather than living like that, maybe it would have been better if people had gone their own way and lived their own private lives outside."

We have no right to talk like that. In the early 1950s—years when one would not hold up Primavera as an example of all we are trying to represent in the world—people who visited the communities in Paraguay were so struck by what they saw and felt amongst a collection of weak brothers and sisters that it turned their lives upside down. A sense of urgency came to them that something really new could be born, although it was not new at all but simply went back to the Rock and Foundation, upon which Eberhard Arnold's witness and life were based. I refer particularly to the coming of the Wagoners and four Quaker families and three single persons from various backgrounds. What happened in the Wagoners' lives and what happened in these other lives came from God. We should remember through all struggles—no matter what they are—that behind them is a calling from God that does not depend upon us. It is the calling that is perfect; a calling to a life that none of us can, or ever will, really live up to.

The Bruderhof's start in the States (and the beginning of this account) was connected with events in the late 1940s. There were conferences and meetings amongst the brothers and sisters in Europe and in South America, much of it related to the needs of our hospital in Paraguay, which was almost without income. The economy in Primavera—the farm and so on—was not providing the money needed for the communities. The voice of Philip Britts, a young servant of the Word, was one of the few raised in the 1940s in favor of a visit to the United States. A number had to travel there, trying to raise money to help support the communities and the work of the hospital. Out of those journeys, especially that of Heini and Annemarie, came the contacts, the interest, and the spirit that culminated in the establishment of the Woodcrest Bruderhof.

In a July 1953 conference in Paraguay there had been a decision to begin a new Bruderhof in North America and also in Germany. In February 1954 there were meetings between the community of Macedonia in Georgia and a little community called Kingwood in New Jersey. From the Bruderhof in Paraguay were

Hans-Hermann (the youngest of Eberhard's three sons) and Gertrud
Arnold, Gerd Wegner, Will and Kathleen Marchant, and later
Balz Trümpi. Guy Johnson from Wheathill also came later. Out
of these meetings came the definite decision from Paraguay and
Europe that it would be right and good to look for a property for
the new Bruderhof in the northeastern United States. And no
matter what the Bruderhof life may have lacked in representing
what it really should have, still this search took place, and the
result was the purchase of Woodcrest in the month of June, 1954.
Shortly after this, it began to function as a very small community,
but nevertheless as a Bruderhof.

When Kathy and I came in June one year later, there were
many guests. We came thinking that we were pretty typical but
found we were far from that. We met people from all over and
from many different backgrounds. I was able to record in my
diary the composition of the Woodcrest household. Twenty-four
were in the brotherhood, of whom only *ten* were baptized brothers
and sisters from Primavera and Wheathill (that is, experienced
"old sheep who knew the way"). Fourteen were newly baptized
Americans, eighteen were novices, and there were twenty guests
and seventy-three children. (Five of the new members were asked
to teach when school began in the fall.)

One can see in this distribution of the 135 people in the
household that there was a long, long "tail"—very few brotherhood members and many guests. It was said that "the tail wags
the dog." I think you all know what it looks like when a dog is
so happy that instead of wagging his tail he kind of wags from
the middle both ways. Well, when you say the tail wags the dog,
it is as though the tail were standing still and the dog was waving
back and forth. In early Woodcrest this referred to the fact that
there were many guests and that the influence of the guests
sometimes made the brotherhood wave: the brotherhood had to
scramble to know what to do in that situation.

We heard another catch phrase from the world of nature—
"guests of a feather flock together." Amongst the guests at
Woodcrest there was a certain affinity for one another, a certain
freedom to talk with one another that you simply didn't have
when the brotherhood members were around. I remember it very
well when we were guests with the Nobles and some others at
Woodcrest. When a brotherhood member came along, we changed
gears and talked in a different tone of voice.

Gossip is a danger, no matter who is talking, and gossip has
a tremendously destructive power, and if we fight that sort of
thing now, then everybody should realize that we all went through
it ourselves. We have often experienced in our communities the
power of this kind of talking, particularly talking behind the back
of the brotherhood. You see, when you are a guest talking about
the brotherhood, you don't fully know what the brotherhood is
up to, but you wish you did. So speculation comes in, and oh
my, in the summer of 1955 did we guests have reason for
speculation! We will come later to the things that were happening.

For most of the year before Kathy and I arrived, Hans-Hermann
had been there as servant of the Word with his wife Gertrud as
his helper. There had been baptism groups, and the newly baptized
brotherhood circle included Tom and Florrie Potts, who were
baptized by Heini in Paraguay, the Kurtzes, Stanaways, Hazel,
Duffy, Domers, Hinkeys, and Moodys—all very new members
in this life of brotherhood. In March 1955, the time allotted by
the U.S. Immigration and Naturalization Service ran out for Hans-
Hermann and Gertrud. They and others who had left Paraguay
in October 1953 and entered on visitors' visas had to return.

In the meantime the communities in South America and Europe
were able to decide whom to send to Woodcrest on immigrant
visas to become residents and take up the services. As a result,
in February Heini and Annemarie and their family were sent to
Woodcrest, where by God's grace and with the thanks of all of

us, they have lived ever since. Very soon after they arrived, there
was a baptism (March 11, 1955) that Heini and Hans-Hermann
were able to undertake together before Hans-Hermann and Gertrud
had to leave. Soon after this the brotherhood was able to celebrate
the Lord's Supper.

Efforts were being made during these two years to start a
community in Germany. I have a letter that Heini wrote on April
25, 1955, in which he reported that his son and daughter,
Christoph and Anneli (now Maria Maendel), began school at New
Paltz that day and that Woodcrest was looking forward to the
first report from Hohenstein. "Hohenstein" sounds to me like a
rock situated high up somewhere, and I guess that is about what
it was. It was a castle somewhere in Europe where brothers and
sisters had started living in community. But when the Sinntal
property became available later, that became the place where a
beginning was made in Germany instead.

However, the Sinntal community took a different direction
from that of Woodcrest. From the very beginning something
gripped Woodcrest and worked there—and I don't mean only
from the time Heini and Annemarie were there but also from the
very beginning. I believe there was a spirit that worked there and
a will that came from God—a spirit of uniting, a spirit of fighting
for a good atmosphere, a spirit that has been betrayed and has
suffered greatly over the years—a spirit whose fruits we now
enjoy. But what we currently experience of these deepest fruits
is such a mystery and wonderful gift that we cannot explain it.
It is not just for us but for the whole world. This spirit and
message is needed desperately—it burned in the heart of Eberhard
and in the hearts of our early forefathers, the Anabaptists of the
16th and 17th centuries, the early Hutterian Brothers. This witness
depended, not on people, but on the Spirit, who alone can
"rekindle torches."

Even the children understand that in a school group or in a

Heini and Annemarie Arnold visit Macedonia—1953

Pouring Forest River House floor . . .

with the help of five Western
carpenters—1955

Airview of early Woodcrest—spring 1955

Gerd Wegner, Hans-Hermann and Gertrud Arnold seeking Bruderhof site in the United States—1954

Mow family—December 1955

Farm and Carriage Houses
Woodcrest

Immigrants from Primavera . . .
Heini and Annemarie's family
1955

First Woodcrest nursery

classroom a spirit will sometimes get hold of the whole group
and something nasty will come in and run free. Afterwards no
one can say why it happened or what it was. They were not for
it, they didn't want it, they were against it, but there it was,
something just came over them. I think everybody knows of this
and has experienced it.

On the other hand there is another spirit in which one can come
together and seek God, seek the leading of Jesus. Then something
happens in the group that you also cannot explain, but your heart
just glows with joy about it. We have a calling to this second
spirit, this spirit of the early forefathers, the spirit that ruled in
Eberhard and in Sannerz and in the early Rhön, and that also
broke in strongly into early Woodcrest.

Next I will try to tell of things that took place, not all nice
things; there were also struggles.

# 2
# *The Unity Is Broken*

When Kathy and I with our two-year-old girl arrived at Woodcrest in June 1955, there were many guests—long-term and short-term. The dining room was still in what was then our main house—the old mansion. Our first mealtime in that little dining room was Sunday noon, the day after our arrival. For a community of that size, with a high proportion of adults, it was extremely tight. I remember finding a place at a table and seeing Heini sitting over near the hatch, where the food came through from the kitchen. First of all he asked us to stand up and say who we were, where we had come from, and what we had come for, which we did with trembling. We were very warmly welcomed.

We had come with the understanding that it would be for a year's visit—a mighty big risk on the part of the community. But that was the understanding. We were coming out of a school situation where our lives were governed by the school year that always began in September and ended in June. In between you got your bearings. So we were there in June expecting to spend a school year, and expecting to come to a decision during that time: whether following Jesus and living by the Sermon on the

21

Mount meant a life of complete sharing. For us this was not by
any means a clear matter; it was especially unclear to us whether
it was possible.

As I have said, friends of ours, the Wagoners, had come back
from Paraguay with the enthusiastic report that it is not only
possible but absolutely necessary. So we were responding to the
pressure this placed on our own consciences. We walked in on
the visit from the West of five Hutterian carpenters, a crucial
event in the history of Woodcrest. My first work on the
construction of the Forest River House was with these five dear
brothers: Paul and Darius Maendel from Forest River, Sam Hofer
from Bloomfield, Fred Kleinsasser from Sturgeon Creek, and
Dave Waldner from Milltown. As guests we were taking in only
part of what was going on, because we had come out of the small
world of our own little experiences into something affecting a
very large number of people. The five carpenters were deeply
shaken by the movement of spirit present in Woodcrest, not made
or planned by anybody but simply a gift from God.

These brothers returned home, as we heard later, with very
enthusiastic reports of what they had seen and experienced of the
inner vitality of this life together, the unity in the brotherhood,
the outreach so clearly visible through the constant stream of all
sorts of guests. Their reports struck sparks out West in other
longing hearts that were hungering for a new birth of the zeal
and spirit of their forefathers from the time of the Reformation.
Even though in the end it became twisted into something that
worked for the devil and culminated in a break in the unity with
the Western brothers, it was simply true that the brothers were
struck and that all this was the work of God.

Some of those who lived at Forest River said the reports
reminded them of what they had experienced in the early 1930s
in Old Rosedale, where there was a similar spirit, which later
had cooled through the branching out of the different colonies.

Two of the five carpenters had come from Forest River—a descendant colony one might say, of Old Rosedale. They had a very special longing because they felt the Forest River Colony was by then afflicted—as any one of our places (Bruderhofs) can be at times—by other spirits, such as quarreling among brothers, opinionatedness, ambition, gossiping, disunity, and unpeace. Hard feelings would lie unresolved and not be cleared up according to the command of Jesus in the Sermon on the Mount and in Matthew 18.

And here these brothers came back with the story of people from all walks of life—people who had never met each other before—living in harmony and in unity. People were giving up all their property, riches, influence, family, and friends to follow Jesus in a very poor and simple way. (There really was poverty in early Woodcrest, there was no extra money, the place was bought only by going into debt.) Even if one guest said, "Oh, it's simply a rural slum," still here were people coming to give up everything voluntarily in order to seek Jesus and the life of discipleship together.

The five brothers were drawn to our guest meetings that summer of 1955. And my memory is that it was hot and the worst summer for mosquitoes that I have experienced in all the years since. There used to be a meeting with guests every evening, out on one of the verandas or somewhere on the hof.* There would be a circle of eight to fifteen or more guests, most often with Stanley Fletcher but sometimes with other brothers and sisters. The questions flew thick and fast. Not a few of the guests were college intellectuals from New York City and they were full of questions—sharp questions. The needles of the mosquitoes were sharp too. So one would hear the inner battle as well as the slapping of the outer battle! These lively meetings very much

---

*Short for Bruderhof. See Glossary.

affected the five brothers, who came whenever they had the chance.

Our brothers in the West have a deep and abiding longing for outreach and mission, going back to their very earliest times. This longing helped spark something in the visiting carpenters, who wished it could become more alive in their own colonies. Out of this awakening, in response to their reports, came more contact with the East.* It was deeply moving, something given by God, not affected by the later spirits of division.

The home of my parents in Chicago had become a stopping point for the brothers because my mother, Anna Mow, always had a very warm feeling for them. Arnold and Gladys Mason had stayed there as houseguests and had gotten to know my parents quite well. And so it was that for a couple of days in July a certain conference called the Chicago Meeting took place in their home at the request of some of the Forest River brothers. My parents simply left the house to the brothers—mother went shopping downtown or did something to allow them to talk together. Heini and Alan and Nellie Stevenson came from Woodcrest, Hans Meier from England especially for the contact with Forest River, and John Maendel and Alan Baer from Forest River. Arnold and Gladys were already there and living in the house. The purpose of the meeting was just to talk over what to do: When there is a movement of the Spirit, shouldn't one respond to it? And if so, in what way?

Unfortunately, from that meeting onward things happened that were not right—I don't know if anything wrong occurred in the meeting but at least it did from then on. I do know that Heini himself was deeply moved by the inner contact with the five carpenters and by hearing that there was hope for more. He knew

---

*East and West are consistently used to refer to Hutterian brothers or communities— East to "new" Hutterites (also called Bruderhof) and West to "old" Hutterites. See Glossary also.

how much it had meant to his father Eberhard to travel to the United States in 1930 and 1931, to join completely with the movement of the brothers known as Hutterian, and to be commissioned by them as a servant of the Word.* One must remember that in 1930 Eberhard represented a community with a well-defined circle already ten years old, with traditions of its own, and with its own ways of doing things. In any little community where people love one another and live together in harmony, there can often come a feeling to protect it so that it is not damaged in any way.

In his contact with the Brothers, Eberhard had none of this protective feeling that would say, "We don't want something wrong to come from you into our movement, into our Bruderhof." His feeling was entirely the other way round. When Eberhard discovered that the brothers called Hutterian still existed, still lived in community in the Western United States and Canada, he had none of this feeling of caution that says, "We want first to see whether you have what we want." His approach was one of open arms that said: "Please, Brothers, send servants of the Word to us, take over our whole situation, and bring our church life into order. We do not want to be a little movement of our own but to be one with you, the Brothers, and part of that great movement that goes back to Whitsun itself—to Pentecost." He felt that God broke into history; that what happened at Pentecost in Jerusalem resulted in the establishment of the Church; that this living organism of the Church had always been alive and awake in one way or another—and in a particularly strong way during the Reformation time—even though Satan had spent 2,000 years trying to destroy it in every possible way.

All this was in Heini's heart too when he felt the response of

---

*See *Brothers Unite: An Account of the Uniting of Eberhard Arnold and the Rhön Bruderhof with the Hutterian Church*, Plough Publishing House, Ulster Park, N.Y., 1988.

the five carpenters to life in Woodcrest and when he met with
the brothers in Chicago. So his vision was toward an enrichment
that would deepen what was genuinely from the life of the old
Hutterians because it was from the New Testament life revealed
in the Book of Acts. (Especially the Maendel and Hofer families
in Forest River had a longing for a return to genuine early
Hutterianism—I don't know how much this term was in their
minds—which meant a return to what lived in the early church.)

As always, Heini's only concern was that the true Gospel is
preached and that the souls of faithful, searching people are
nurtured; that people who hunger and thirst for righteousness are
filled; that amongst brothers there is peace and unity with no
human honor or influence; that there is no property to divide
brothers and sisters. And he wished and requested that this concern
be openly and mutually brought before a gathering of the elders*
out West—this is what Heini represented.

I want to quote from a letter in which Heini speaks of his
longing for the kind of contact that should begin between the
brothers East and the brothers West. He wrote on July 30, 1955,
two weeks after the meeting in Chicago:

> We feel we should face the elders openly. We are willing
> to answer all the questions they have. What we want to avoid
> is giving the impression that we are starting to bring *Parteiungen*
> or disunity or a split in the communities, since all we want is
> to represent the very opposite, namely, the unity of the true
> church community of Christ. We are not afraid of the meeting,
> since we feel we have nothing to hide and we want rather to
> speak openly with all cards on the table.

If only that wish and prayer had been followed, disunity in this

---

*Older servants of the Word appointed to support the Elder. See Glossary also.

crucial year could have been avoided. Unfortunately the story has to be told differently.

The dissensions that arose in Forest River in 1955 cannot be said to have had their origin in that year or in the outer events that took place then. The roots of the guilt that lay on our side (the Bruderhof or "Eastern" communities) went back nearly two decades. Early in 1937 two Western servants, David Hofer Vetter* and Michael Waldner Vetter, made the very first visit from the West to the Bruderhofs in Europe. In 1950 in September and October two other servants, Samuel Kleinsasser Vetter and John Wipf Vetter, visited the Bruderhofs in Primavera, Paraguay. There was blessing but also much guilt on our side in both of these visits. Sin had come in after Eberhard Arnold's death: arrogant communitarianism based not on Jesus and church unity in his Spirit but on humanistic principles and power politics. In later chapters I tell first the fuller story of this earlier guilt and then the story of the reuniting with the Western brothers in 1974.

Our Western brothers were certainly keenly aware of a big cultural difference between the old Hutterites (a sociologist would say, the ethnic Hutterites of Western United States and Canada) and the new Hutterites of the Bruderhof movement in Germany and later in England. Our differences with the brothers in the West involved such things as traditional patterns of seating for mealtimes and meetings, where sisters were on one side and brothers on the other; the holding of a certain type of meeting on Sunday with children, called Sunday school (different from our family meeting with the whole household); and the exclusive use of the German language for church meetings. Not one of these has been demanded of us within the last decade, in which our love and humility were stronger.

---

*A Hutterian term of respect for an older brother or one carrying a special responsibility in the church.

Now such differences are not so unusual; just read in the Book of Acts of the great difference between the churches in Asia Minor that were established by the apostle Paul, and the church in Jerusalem, where the earliest basis for a pattern of organization was that of the synagogue. (By that time the synagogue existed in Jerusalem.) All of the first Christians in Jerusalem were Jews. What they did together when they met was certainly done as Jews and with Jewish pattern and tradition behind it, things very strange and unusual to the Gentiles of Asia Minor.

There could have been a very serious split, with bitterness and animosity between Gentile and Jewish Christians, had there been pride on either side. But they met together in Jerusalem, and because the Spirit ruled in the hearts of brothers and sisters throughout the churches, both sides were able to come together. They came to an agreement based on two or three very simple points—not only for the sake of principle but out of love, and from this came a complete unity. In 1974 this is what happened between us and our brothers in the West; it should have been maintained throughout the years after the first uniting in 1930.

Our story now returns to Forest River, where there was this longing that culminated in changes in the community life. Consciences were struck: by accumulation of possessions like the yearly allotment of cloth, material, or shoes, which was often more than was needed in a family; by the accumulation of pocket money or little earnings from work done on the side by brothers or sisters; or by having attachment to possessions in the home. Now none of these are temptations that we are exempt from; they come from Mammon and we are all susceptible to them and stand in danger of them in one form or another. The brothers and sisters were struck and brought possessions and turned them in.

Consciences were also struck in connection with the relationship —the all-important relationship—between brothers and sisters as Jesus speaks of it in the Sermon on the Mount and in Matthew

18. We call it the First Law in Sannerz: If there is a difference between brothers and sisters, one speaks directly and comes to unity before bringing a gift to the altar, before coming to prayer together. Thus one maintains a united relationship rather than a silent, cold war relationship, which would otherwise definitely develop.

We heard told very movingly how one of the elderly sisters at Forest River called Rahel Basel* (mother of our Dave Maendel and also of Sarah and Lizzie in Deer Spring) said that in the new time that came to them, "Peter Riedemann† came alive!" I always found that quite a striking testimony. She died in Forest River in February 1957.

After the conference in Chicago, there came many journeys East and West through the relationship with Forest River. Right at the time of the conference, John and Sarah Maendel were not living in Forest River but were down in Koinonia, Georgia, exchanged with Claud and Billie Nelson and their family, who were in Forest River. (Claud and Billie were teachers.) John had come up from Koinonia for the conference. After John's return to Koinonia for the birth of Gladys Georgia Maendel (now Johnson), he came unexpected to Woodcrest in August. He simply phoned from Newark Airport asking if somebody could pick him up. We have a photo of my mother, who was visiting then, standing with John and Arnold Mason.

Then too, quite a few brothers and sisters were sent out to Forest River in 1955, responding to the request for help. After the Chicago Conference in the middle of July a number of responsible brothers and sisters were called together from

---

*Rahel is another form of Rachel, and Basel is a term of respect for an older sister or the wife of one carrying a special responsibility in the church.

†An early servant and Elder whose *Confession of Faith* (written in prison 1540-42) is still today the basic confession of the Hutterian Brethren. Available in English from the Plough Publishing House, Rifton, N.Y. 12471, 1970, 302 pp.

Primavera and Wheathill to go out to Forest River. By the middle
of August there was quite a circle out there to have the contact
with the brothers in the West and to meet with the elders. It
included Heini and his wife Annemarie, Bruce Sumner, Hans
Meier, and Arnold Mason.

On the last day of August, nine more went out to Forest River,
some in the night and some by plane, including two couples who
were novices. It was a very upsetting and disturbing time, as you
can imagine, particularly for those in Forest River. (As I said
before, it could have been completely different if only the attitude
in Paraguay and Europe had been different.) Several members of
this Hutterian colony were seeking a closer relationship with the
Bruderhof, the Eastern Hutterites. Some of the members of Forest
River even felt strongly drawn to "join" the Society of Brothers
(the official name for the Bruderhof 1939-78), more in the sense
of their joining a reawakened Hutterian church. This time (actually
a split) was summarized in 1974 by Hardy Arnold (the oldest of
Eberhard's three sons) in his postcript to our book, *Seeking for
the Kingdom of God\**:

> In the ensuing conflict with our Hutterian Brothers of Manitoba
> and South Dakota, brothers and sisters acted sinfully. We took
> possession of the Forest River Colony for a time. This was
> legally in order, but it violated the love of the Sermon on the
> Mount.

About 60% of the adult members of Forest River wanted to join
us, and about 40% did not, and the latter were obliged to move
out. And that is where the sin and the lovelessness lay. They had
nowhere to go; they simply had to be accepted into other colonies.

---

*Eberhard and Emmy Arnold, Plough Publishing House, Rifton, N.Y., 1974,
pp.280-281.

We accepted some of its members into membership of our own group, and in this way forced those members of Forest River who wanted to stay loyal to the Hutterian Brothers to leave their own colony. We deeply regret this arrogant act, which led to a complete break with the Brothers called Hutterian. This break took more than eighteen years to repair.

Heini and Annemarie had returned (before the division) and brought with them sisters from the West, including Dorothy Maendel (now Kaiser), Lizzie Maendel (now Boller), and Susie Maendel (now Black). It was quite an experience in Woodcrest to welcome these three young sisters from Forest River; they arrived with much joy and enthusiasm.

With reference to this question of struggle and crisis, I want to make another comparison with the Bible. In all the world's national histories that have ever been written, there is none that can compare in one respect with the history of Israel as recorded in the Old Testament. The history of Israel instead of being the history of the glories and wonderful achievements of these people and of their kings and of their leaders, is a history that includes their failures and unfaithfulness. Now that is remarkable and it is unique. If one doubts the authenticity of history, this is the history that one can doubt least of all. Because nations write and also rewrite their history to make it look good, even crooks (who no doubt did something for that country) are later on nothing but heroes. And this goes on all the time and in every country. But when you read the history of Israel and of its greatest kings like King David, there you will find him as he was, as Americans say, "warts and all!"

Our little group of "Eastern" Hutterites has a story too, a part of the far larger story of the Hutterian Brethren told in their

A circle of guests . . . most
often with Stanley Fletcher

Heini reading letters at
communal dinner

Hardy and Martha Arnold
at Forest River

Rachel Maendel Basel at the wedding
of her daughter Lizzie to Hans Uli
Boller, Forest River–1956

*Chronicle.*\* If a history is to be authentic, it must include the struggle and it must tell all sides. The history of Israel was written like that because the important thing wasn't Israel. The important thing was God and his intervention into the lives of sinful men and his constant faithful calling them back to himself and to his way. And that is what our short history is too.

Our history is full of very difficult, even terrible things, which are very hard to hear about, and that is not at all a matter of anyone pointing at someone else. Even though the use of names may be needed to avoid confusion, focusing on the sin, not the sinner, is always of utmost importance. It is first of all a matter of every one of us pointing to our own selves, because none of us can stand before God and say, "Well, the rest were unfaithful, but I was faithful." Instead, our situation is like that of Peter, going out and weeping bitterly—without looking horizontally at others to make comparisons, but looking only to God and what he has done for us through the Cross—and then simply repenting and asking for forgiveness and a new start.

That is our history, and that is also what the history of Israel is all about.

---

\*Volume I of *The Chronicle of the Hutterian Brethren* is now available in English from the Plough Publishing House, Rifton, N.Y. 12471, 1987. Volume II is being translated for print.

# 3
# *What Holds Community Together?*

We have often heard the supposition that our main industry of Community Playthings originated in Woodcrest. Its origin was actually in the Macedonia Cooperative Community in northeast Georgia. Indeed, the very beginning of Woodcrest itself was through a conference at Macedonia in 1954. So the origins of Community Playthings and of Woodcrest go together.

In the fall of 1953, it had been decided in Primavera that journeys would be made to the United States to investigate the possibility of establishing a community. The first reason for this decision was a ground swell of interest in the Bruderhof. People in the States were seeking something radical and new, possibly as a result of World War II (similar to seekers in Germany after World War I). The second reason for the decision was that the hospital in Primavera was not able to function without a lot of outside support, and it was found that America was a good place to get help. Therefore, different brothers and sisters were sent to the United States from Paraguay and also from England, some in late 1953 and some in early 1954.

On February 1, 1954, a conference began at Macedonia Cooperative Community in Georgia—a three-way meeting of the brothers from the Bruderhof, the members of Macedonia Community, and the members of Kingwood Community in New Jersey. This seeking together continued because of the mutual interests of members of Kingwood and Macedonia. But already by the end of March, a group who wanted to commit themselves to Christ were taken into the Bruderhof novitiate, even though there was no Bruderhof existing yet in North America. Those who became novices were Mark and Peggy Kurtz, David and Virginia Newton, Chuck and Carmen Stanaway, Delf and Katie Fransham (all from Macedonia), and Hazel Brownson from Kingwood. Also from Kingwood were Fran and Pearl Hall and Jim and Kore McWhirter, who joined but later did not stay with us.

Very soon after this there began a search for a new site for a community, for a Bruderhof in the eastern United States. The northeast was preferred, something out in the country and yet within easy traveling distance of the major population centers. Balz Trümpi (from Primavera) also came then and was taking part in this search with Guy Johnson (Wheathill) and Duffy Black (who had become a member in Paraguay) and some of the new novices like Fran and Mark. One of the places they looked at—not seriously considered at the time—later became Evergreen and then Deer Spring. One drives past various other sites looked at in that area, like Troutbeck near Amenia, New York.

During this time of searching, the home of Bob and Jane Clement in Haddonfield, New Jersey, became home base and a temporary Bruderhof in the north. Bob was already in Primavera as part of their search for a new life, and Jane joined him in May. At the same time, Hans-Hermann and Gertrud and others went to Celo Community in North Carolina for talks with the Hinkeys, the Domers, and the Moodys, who all came later and joined.

On May 25 a group went up to Woodcrest to have a thorough inspection of the property. They liked what they saw, and a few days later (June 3) a contract was signed to buy the place. One important part of the purchase story belongs here. There was a couple from Kingwood Community, John and Josephine Houssman, who had joined us. John was so ill that although he was a novice, he was never baptized. The total price of Woodcrest with all the land and the buildings was $57,500, which would just about buy a very small house now. The Houssmans had money and contributed the $20,000 needed as a down payment—quite a sum then—which made it possible to purchase Woodcrest.

Four member families had joined from Macedonia, and that left about half the member families: Wisers, Mommsens, and Kneelands, who wanted to stay and keep it going. The Burlesons had not yet joined Macedonia. The whole original community of Macedonia had agreed to this division. Those who wanted to stay had an interfaith basis—not limiting themselves to Christ alone—whereas those who joined the Bruderhof wanted to find the relationship to Jesus that the Bruderhof seeks and stands for. But it was a very harmonious division, and all tried to do it in the best way. Well, on the one hand there was the Macedonia Community (land and buildings, sawmill, dairy barn, and so on), and on the other hand there was Community Playthings, the woodworking business. The latter was the one thing portable, and so it was decided that it would be moved to Woodcrest.

So the origin of Community Playthings really was Macedonia, and the name Community Playthings also came from Macedonia. The inventory and machinery were transported to Woodcrest late in 1954. To get set up and into production, work went on feverishly into the cold winter of 1954-55 (without any heat in the shop). Some of that machinery was pretty good; some of it was amazingly ingenious. For instance, the cutoff saw (now I am speaking to shop brothers), was not one of these fancy things with the blade coming safely up out of the table and completely guarded on all sides. It was a saw blade mounted on the end of a shaft that went up to the rear axle of an old car that was hung up near the ceiling. Where the wheels had been, the axle was rigid, but the whole differential and driveshaft part of it swung back and forth, braced with wooden struts and welded angle irons. It came down to a very heavy motor mounted on a wooden table carrying a great big saw blade. To cut the wood off to the correct sizes, you had to pull toward yourself this monster (hung from the ceiling).

The ripsaw was even more amazing. We have ripsaws today that have a chain down in the table that takes the boards in a perfectly straight line through the blade. Well, that ripsaw had a gigantic motor mounted on it and the rest of it was made out of angle iron—just an open framework of angle iron with some corrugated rollers that pushed the lumber through. Whoever was feeding the lumber through to rip it on this blade had to have a sledgehammer with him to bludgeon the piece through, so that it would get past the blade.

On one occasion at the ripsaw, the brother who was off-bearing (taking off from) the machine noticed that bright colored metal stars were appearing on the floor. On a little closer inspection it was clear that the solder in the joints of the dust extraction system was melting and dropping on the floor, making splashes of hot lead in these star shapes. If it had been dark, one could have seen that the whole pipe going up from the machine was red-hot. A piece of lumber had stuck and burned. Sparks went down and ignited the sawdust caught in the bottom of the machine. And so we had a well-fanned fire going! We quickly shut down the whole air-delivery system, and several of us then went out into the sawdust shed—jumped in—and crawled around looking for sparks. We sprinkled water around to make sure we didn't lose the whole shed.

We did have, though, some good machinery—there was a

very nice little molder. But in those days we made our unit blocks a bit oversize and then sanded them down on a sanding machine. The blocks were laid out on a huge tray table and moved back and forth underneath a large sanding belt. You put pressure downward on the belt to sand the blocks (with a carriage assembly on wheels that was above it). You would sand awhile, stop the machine, take out a block, and measure it with a caliper to see how you were doing. When you had it about right, you would turn them all over and sand again until they calipered to just the right size. An interesting aspect of this machine was that in the winter it generated electricity. If you didn't watch out, you got charged enough to jump a gap of about an inch. And that was a bit dangerous if you came too near to somebody who was operating another machine. It could give the wrong kind of surprise. That was the early Woodcrest shop!

All of this was in what was later called the old shipping building, on the main floor of the original barn. The upper floor had some housing in it (some single men lived up there, maybe Stanley) and the whole CP office. The basement contained the entire assembly department—packing, storage, and shipping of all Community Playthings products.

I cannot remember the exact product run at that time, because we were gradually adding to it. But it surely included the unit blocks, the triangle set, the solid wooden animals and people, maybe the hollow blocks, and the workhorse (a sturdy sawhorse). I think we don't make them anymore, but these workhorses had a hole in the top, not in the side, for picking out your tools. I think the big trucks had just been launched, and there was the pony swing, or pump swing—some growing into middle age will remember—a very wonderful kind of swing to ride on. It had three ropes holding it and you could pump yourself to very nice heights. We had them set up around Woodcrest, but the swing turned out to be a bad bet as far as public schools were

The Barn, Woodcrest's
first shop—1954

Rock and Whirl

Paul Willis helps boat modeler

concerned—schools didn't want the hazard of kids getting hit.

Down in Macedonia's shop the unit blocks and the basic framework of the triangle set were being made of maple. But the other products were made out of wood native to Macedonia, grown in their own stand of trees. They had their own drying system and processed it right through to the final products, also from an idealistic wish to do so. But the wood was yellow pine, a soft wood. It has very prominent grain, more so than Douglas fir, for instance. So it was hard to get things really smooth, and it was hard to avoid splinters. The first big trucks were just the size they are today, but the axles were maple dowels, and the wheels were also of maple. These wheels in turn gave birth to the easel. We cut out the wheels from strips of wood. That left us a row of holes just right for holding paint pots in front of an easel. The early easels all used these wood strips from which the wheels had been cut.

By the time Kathy and I joined in June 1955, more products had been added, and everything was converted to maple. We phased out the soft woods completely. By then there was a child-size cradle big enough for a man to get into and rock. He couldn't lie down, but he could sit up. It seems to me that Stanley Fletcher spent about a month that summer of 1955 working right through a run of twenty-five child-size cradles, from beginning to end. One of these cradles without the rockers was used in the Woodcrest bakery for mixing dough for the whole community.

Don Noble had the idea that it would be wonderful to make a toy with this cradle as basis, but bowl-shaped. It would not just rock back and forth but forward, backward, and in all directions— even spinning round and round. There were discussions about creating such a thing out of fiberglass. Then one day after a shop snack in the afternoon, some of the brothers began talking, "Why not try to make one out of wood?" Ideas started flowing—one of them was to have six cradle rockers meet underneath in the middle of this thing. It would have a diameter of about three feet with sides of some eight or nine inches and a rim round the top.

We made a first model that afternoon and took it up to the Children's House to see what they thought of it; all liked it, the children and the teachers, so we put it on the market. I remember speculating that we might sell a dozen in the first year, and oh, the sales were well over that; we had to make them over and over again. But it died out after another three years. It was known as a "Rock and Whirl"; you could rock in it and you could whirl around in it. And it was guaranteed not to turn over. Sometimes we were surprised—people would order a "Rock and Roll"!

That illustrates how one of our new products came into being out of the general discussion. I think some will remember our son David's old turtle being displayed. It was the prototype for the current "Ride-a-stride." Later we tended more to assign one or two brothers to develop something new. Our other Woodcrest products were a tugboat and a freighter (routed out of solid wood), the floor train we have had for so many years, another small solid train, and later on the furniture.

There was often great fun in the shop. For instance, I was working on a jig—something you clamp material into for machining a product—and went off to snack, having filled a large hole with wood filler. I came back to continue work on it, hoping the wood filler would be dry. Some kind person had dug all the wood filler out and replaced it with peanut butter. By the winter of 1955-56, we did have heat in the shop, there was considerable improvement in the production, and the offices had been moved up on to the hof*. But it took years before the business itself was able to support this Bruderhof completely.

When the division at Macedonia took place in 1954, Macedonia

---

*Hof has two Bruderhof usages. Here it means the area (uphill in Woodcrest) for the main communal buildings other than the workshops. See Glossary also.

was in the process of developing furniture and some other products. So they asked if they couldn't stay in the Community Playthings business and work in cooperation with us. We agreed, and it worked for a few years. The fuller story of what happened to this cooperative working together comes later. Of course in 1957 when Macedonia became a Bruderhof, the whole business from beginning to end became part of our Bruderhof livelihood.

Before this interlude on Community Playthings, I had told the story of the 1955 Forest River rupture of our unity with the Hutterian Brethren. The increased contact East and West had begun with the Bruderhof's first construction of a new house at Woodcrest. The name "Forest River House" was obvious to us.

The house was nearly completed by midsummer—at least one could live in it—but no paint! Paint was not included in the completion of buildings in those days. The outside walls were dark brown masonite, or hardboard. After a year or two of exposure to rain and sun, it warped into all kinds of funny bulges, until finally there was enough money to put asbestos shingles over it. In the following years the buildings were built in the same way—no paint inside or out—using Homosote, a material like Cellotex. If you would start working on it, as children sometimes did during rest time with a fingernail, you just kept on going until pretty soon you were through the stuff. It was like compressed paper.

Since the Forest River House was filled and still more people were wanting to come (and were expected to arrive), the brotherhood decided that summer to buy five little cabins. Somebody in the town of Rifton had them for sale—if he hadn't sold to us, the chances are they would have been torn down. They were just little things, about 15 x 15 feet, and the price on each, depending on the condition, ran between $200 and $300. They were loaded onto a flatbed trailer, hauled up to Woodcrest, and spotted around the hof and used for housing. Later, John

Maendel in his spare time used one of them for a shop. We called it "Siberia" because it was unheated. The last little cabin was used by the night watch for many years.

On September 15, 1955, Wayne and Loretta Shirky arrived as guests. One of the important aspects of their coming was that they brought a car—a great big Buick. Wayne, a young, poor student as we Church of the Brethren all were, had bought it cheap since it was a "gas hog." But because it took long journeys so well, this big car of the Shirkys made many trips back and forth to Forest River. In that same September Welton and Kathleen Snavely made their first one-week visit, and Art Wiser of Macedonia and George Burleson of Tuolumne Farms visited from a nearby conference of an organization in America known as the FIC (Fellowship of Intentional Communities).

In the wave of idealism following World War II, many people were looking for something new, and some were looking in the direction of community. It was not as in more recent years when young people were living in community because they felt it should follow from being a serious Christian. Rather, in this grouping of communities in America, the motives were social concerns, and these communities, or "intentional" communities, were of all sorts. I won't attempt to list their names, but some were anarchistic, some semi-communal, and others simply cooperative. They included Macedonia and Kingwood and Celo. In the beginning, Woodcrest was also part of the FIC. All this was still two years before Art and George with their families asked to join the Bruderhof (by that time Burlesons were also Macedonia members). Bud and Doris Mercer also belonged to this early Woodcrest time until October 1, 1955, when they left for Primavera, where Bud's teaching experience was needed.

There followed a period of family exchanges. For instance, the Guy Johnson family went from Wheathill to reside at Forest River; Hardy Arnold and Martha (in those days we still called

her Sekunda) and their son Eberhard Claus came up from
Primavera, also bound for Forest River. About November the
Hinkey and Alexander children went out from Woodcrest to join
their parents. Ruth Dodd Jr. also moved out, and there were other
trips back and forth. Family exchanges with Woodcrest continued
into 1956. David and Anna Maendel and their family arrived
from Forest River with Sarah Maendel Jr. on February 1, and
the next day the LeBlancs moved to Forest River. At the combined
welcome and farewell lovemeal Rachel Maendel was taken into
the novitiate. In the same month Nicky Maas and her family went
to Paraguay and Josephine Houssman went to Forest River (John
had died the previous year in March).

In mid-December 1955 Joe and Mary Maendel of Forest River
came to Woodcrest for about a month. I worked a lot with Joe
on the shop heating, which was going, but with problems. For
instance, there was a two-inch pipe that came out of the roof over
the furnace room in the old shop, and every day this pipe was
sending out a jet of steam into the air. Nobody thought anything
of it, but Joe said, "Are you trying to heat all of Ulster County?"
It was a bad steam leak and needed to be stopped; he was quite
a help during that time.

That same December Jörg Barth—then single—arrived in the
States to get more education at Pendle Hill; he was in training
as a teacher before going on out to Forest River. Hans Uli Boller,
who had come to Woodcrest from Paraguay in March, had gone
out in November. In 1956 this proved important for him and
Lizzie Maendel, who were engaged on the day Jörg traveled to
Forest River and were married on the 28th of October. The time
at Woodcrest with both Jörg and Hans Uli had been an enrichment
for all of us. Both were young people full of enthusiasm, and
they translated many German songs and *Reigen* (singing circle
games) for us Americans, who didn't know the German customs,
songs, or language.

To be able to use the Carriage House dining room for the first time that winter of 1955, we had installed one of these great square kerosene space heaters with a stovepipe going outside. One Sunday morning in early December some brother went in to light this heater before the family meeting. And it blew up—after he went out. Now that is something I couldn't have imagined before. I guess anyone who lived in England with Coleman stoves knows what these blow-ups are like. They go "poof" and the place is absolutely filled with soot. That was a bitter cold morning. Everybody had to crowd into the former dining room, the Kinderschaft room in the main house, for the meeting. The central heating was hurried up after that.

At Christmas the school put on *Amahl and the Night Visitors*. Peter Maas, then eleven years old, played the part of Amahl. From the play in the Carriage House the community went to the main house (later the Woodcrest House) for a live nativity scene— the first time I had ever experienced one. Open House was a week later, when the neighbors were invited to see the play. I don't know what was thought of it because by then it was a well-known television opera.

The month before in Woodcrest Kathy and I had experienced our first Bruderhof baptism—that of Wilmot and Beth Durgin. Lowell and Norma LeBlanc were taken into the brotherhood at the same time with the laying on of hands, because they had had adult believers' baptism before coming to the Bruderhof. In the early years two young blacks came to the community. One of them arrived about this time, a girl by the name of Rubina Smith (anyone who was there will remember her as a very lively young person). A young man named Walter Morris was already a novice. Although both of them asked for and were taken into the novitiate, they unfortunately decided later on to leave, so we do not have either of them with us anymore.

As Christmas approached, there was another time of baptism

preparation with Bob and Jane Clement, Nicky Maas, and Doris Greaves. Nicky's husband was a novice and was also a member of the group. But unfortunately he was not wanting to face the struggle involved, and he left and never returned. That was a very sad event for all of us. Kathy and I didn't hurry in asking for the novitiate. We wanted first to test ourselves and come as far as we could in our relationship to our families and friends back home, but we did manage to ask in the middle of January, six months after our arrival.

In the previous chapter I told about the Forest River affair. Kathy and I were guests; we were never out there and so were not very much aware of what was happening. However, at Easter time in 1956 there was a struggle there for the unity of the whole church, the first at the Bruderhof since we had come. The result of it was that two servants of the Word at Forest River lost their services and returned to Paraguay. The way that we were introduced to it—we had not yet been taken into the novitiate—was as follows.

Hardy Arnold had been scheduled for months ahead to speak in chapel at Oberlin College before Easter. In his correspondence with Oberlin College and in his contact with somebody there, Hardy had pointed out to them that Eberhard Arnold's great-grandfather John Arnold had been at Oberlin and had worked with Charles D. Finney, who was President of Oberlin College for fifteen years. I guess it is known that Heini and Hardy's forebears were Americans. They came from England and settled in Hartford, Connecticut, in the 1630s, moving near East Haddam in 1662, before going on to Ohio around 1825. Franklin Luther Arnold (their great-grandfather) went to Africa as a missionary and married a German. Their son Carl Franklin—that was Eberhard's father—although born in Ohio was sent with his brother Gottfried to be educated in North Germany in the Bremen area. So Eberhard's father and his uncle, after being Americans, became Germans.

This trip to Oberlin College had been all arranged for Hardy, when he came to me and asked me if I, a Bruderhof *guest*, would take his place and make his chapel speech for him. Well, man alive, what an idea! And the reason was that Hardy had to go out to Forest River to meet with others coming—Hans Zumpe and Arnold Mason from England and Heini and Annemarie. All went to Forest River to fight everything through to unity.

I was told who the contact person was and where to go and was sent off with a car to Oberlin College to take Hardy's place. And I wasn't a novice yet. I didn't know quite how to approach the thing. I studied up a bit on Bruderhof history, and I think I was able to speak more positively about the Bruderhof than I would have dared had I been a member. I could say "they," and I could get as flowery as I wished, and nobody could accuse me of patting my own back. But I didn't know what to think when just before going into the chapel to speak to the student body, they came up to me with a long black robe and said, "Here, you have to wear this." I thought, "Man, is that against the principles of the Bruderhof or not? Do I dare to wear this ornate thing?" I came from a tradition where such things were not worn, or hardly ever, except by choirs. Anyway, I did wear it and hoped it was all right and went in and did my best. On Palm Sunday, after I came back, we were taken into the novitiate. So I guess the brothers hadn't minded when I confessed that I had worn that robe.

One of the important characteristics of true Christian community is the presence of struggle. It's impossible to live a brotherly life together without struggles, which sometimes become "crises." Of course for anyone hurt needlessly through these struggles, crisis is a hated term and one which evokes very painful memories. Yet, I want to make here again the comparison that I made earlier with the candid reporting of the Jews of the Old Testament. If one sets out to live together according to God's will, there are going to be problems and the problems must be faced, and facing the problems always means struggle—*always*.

The struggling process, however, is truly tragic if it is directionless. But if there is clarity in the mind of even one person as to how the struggle should be rightly led—and if that person is under the leadership of God, under his Spirit's leadership—then crises are a gift of God. They are the means by which a derailed train can be gotten back on the rails again, and this has happened in our community life again and again. For this we can only thank God, because if you look at history, communities generally and typically go off the rails and stay off the rails. Before Kathy and I came to the Bruderhof, we had no interest in living in community. It did not attract us in the slightest, because we had studied communities like the Oneida Community, the Shakers, the Amana Community, and many others, which had all gone off in the direction of impurity or in the opposite direction of becoming legalistic and hidebound—so they just died out.

As this account goes on, I am going to come back again and again to the theme of how much it means to struggle through something. But it can't be all struggle; there have to be times of pause for inner recuperation. I remember somebody offering a toast—at a teatime perhaps—"Here's for a nice long period without any struggle, a time of normal, peaceful, nothing happening." In those early years things happened so constantly that one really wished for this. But in looking back, one sees that the struggles were urgently needed and were tremendously important. And the most important thing about them was and is to know what they are about and what they are for. If that is not known, then struggle can be extremely tragic, and people can be hurt very seriously.

# 4
# *Vows For Life*

Our time of baptism preparation took place in May 1956. I think our group was the first to withdraw from the hof for a time of quiet. The earlier groups had had all their preparation right at the hof. And it was a bit unusual how we came into our baptism group. It never occurred to us to ask for baptism; we did not even know one did ask. Kathy has described how it came about:

One afternoon Heini called us to his office, which was in the little tower room in the old Carriage House; he wanted to talk to us about baptism. I remember that Merrill and I started by telling Heini how the Brethren baptize and what we had experienced, not realizing that he had wanted to ask us if we would like to be in a baptism group. Merrill and I talked quite a long time before Heini got around to asking us that question. We were quite unprepared and didn't know what to answer. We were novices but hadn't thought this would be considered yet. We said we just couldn't answer and took a long walk trying to decide. Heini had assured us that it did not mean we would be baptized if it was not God's hour, but would we be willing to be part of the group and see how it was led? We had been in the Brethren Church and had been baptized quite young. We felt that here we could give ourselves in a completely new way, but we did not know what our attitude was to our past experience.

Especially difficult for us was the question, What are we saying to the people we came from, our parents and the people who had meant a lot to us in our lives up till then, who gave us guidance and help, who were themselves deeply dedicated Christians, giving their lives in ways that put ours to shame? What were we saying to them by leaving them and joining something that in their eyes was completely strange and distant, looking very sectarian; and what hurt were we thereby causing to other people? It was mighty hard to face the thought of seeming to reject what God had done in our lives (in spite of ourselves). We struggled with this for months.

Ultimately we found the answer during our baptism preparation. Heini was able to convey to us that when we give our lives to Jesus, we give him everything: not only the bad of which we have to repent, but we also give him whatever may be good; it is safe to give everything of one's past to Jesus in trust. To do this does not carry with it an implication that everybody else is evil or that everything in the past was black, but only that one confesses that from oneself, nothing good has come. "No one is good but One."

It was quite an experience to go out into an isolated place in the Pocono Mountains—just the group and Heini and Annemarie and later a few others—for a concentrated time of seeking. We did not know what to expect; everything just unfolded before us. Our little group consisted of Bob and Kathy Greenwood, Paul and Mary Pappas, Kathy and me. The meetings began in Heini's office and went on for some weeks before we left the hof. I don't remember how frequently we met, maybe not more than once or twice a week, but I do remember that we read 1 Corinthians together. One of us would read a few verses, and then we would stop to think about it or talk about it.

Before coming to the Bruderhof, I had the misfortune of having been in seminary—and I really say that seriously. The seminary I went to was more of a simple Bible school, and I did not go into theology enough to learn either Greek or Hebrew. Yet, "the Bible is closed to the *human* scholarly approach," as Eberhard says in *Inner Land.** And I know that for me the experience of the living, pulsing life of the Bruderhof was Christ-centered— even at a time when we didn't sing Jesus songs like those in the *Reichslieder*. Most people in the community were like those who came from Macedonia, who didn't want to hear any glib religious words. Still, the central thing for them and for all of us was that our life be Christ-centered.

For me personally, when something connected with the Bible was brought up, my mind would work as if I were thumbing through a stack of 3 x 5 cards until I came up with an answer, as if from a commentary. I just couldn't help it. When you are in an academic process of learning, where you are going to be graded on what you have learned—well, to treat the Bible in that way, at least in my experience, does something to your heart, to your innermost perception of the Bible. The approach was too mechanical. I had to try to forget it in order to listen and approach it anew like a child, as though I were hearing it for the first time. Something began to dawn that I had never realized with any amount of study.

There were some who reacted very strongly to my scholarly approach. I had a set of Bible commentaries called *The Inter- preter's Bible*, so I brought the volume on 1 Corinthians along

---

*Eberhard Arnold, Plough Publishing House, Rifton, N.Y., 1976, p.468 (emphasis added; "human," *menschlich* in German, was overlooked in translation).

to our first meeting. I didn't hear this until much, much later, but Paul Pappas had said to Heini, "Either those books go or I go!" Actually the books were of no use to me at that point.

However, the way in which Heini opened the book of 1 Corinthians for us and the way in which we went through it together, brought it to life: it wasn't study, it wasn't taking only words here and there, but it took you right to the depth of what it means, growing out of real life in community. All this struck us very much.

I have to admit that in those days I seldom read the Bible. I had to unlearn a great deal to be able to appreciate it again, afresh. So our baptism preparation was a very new experience for us, also being with Bob and Kathy, and with Paul and Mary in particular, whose background was so completely different from ours. The group started on May 10 and we withdrew on May 31, which probably was arranged to give Heini a chance to be more intimately with the group. That was a marvelous time; I don't even remember exactly how long we were out there together— maybe a week—in a summer house owned by the parents of Tom Potts.

You know how it is with groups that withdraw; the group takes care of everything—all the cleaning, all the dishes, everything— and so we worked out a schedule. There were just the six of us and Heini and Annemarie. Later the witness brothers came out to help. Our mealtimes and every part of every day, even a walk in the woods, had a real meaning. It was a rich experience, and it started something that continued over all the years—of baptism preparation groups being given time to go off and be alone for inner seeking and an intense time together.

Before our group withdrew, we met Emmy Arnold for the first time. She arrived from Wheathill on May 15, accompanied by Burgel, her granddaughter. That trip and subsequent trips also had very important results in our lives that led eventually to real

June 1956
baptism group

Bertha Mills sorts mail

Emmy Arnold in Woodcrest—1956

times of enrichment. At Emmy and Burgel's welcome lovemeal the day after their arrival, Wayne and Loretta Shirky and Aleck and Ruth Dodd were taken into the novitiate. While we were in the Poconos for that week, Bennie and Esther Bargen arrived for their first visit of a few weeks, and Donna Ford came to stay. On June 6 Tante Käthe passed into eternity in Primavera. The following day was the day of our baptism.

Very soon afterwards the next baptism group withdrew—this time in the opposite direction—to the Berkshires near Sheffield, Massachusetts. This group was called the Berkshire group. Anne Gale (later Wiehler) was in it, with Don and Anne Peters, Jim and Jeanette Warren, Josephine Houssman, and Margit Hirschenhauser. (To our great joy Margit returned to New Meadow Run at age ninety-four after a long time away.)

Those early baptism times also involved struggle, which was very necessary because we came from widely different backgrounds. One member of the group had lamented to Heini how very sorry she was that she had no really significant gift to bring to the church, and she wanted so much to bring something that would be an asset. Heini answered and said, "All the others bring nothing but their own sins, and you want to come like Father Christmas!" The actual baptism was only in mid-July, though the group had withdrawn on June 19, as there was a lot going on that month. Heini and the group were called home and finished their time of preparation at the hof. When the baptism did take place on July 13, 1956, our brother Christoph was taken into the novitiate with his sister Roswith, and with Bertha Mills.

Bertha Mills' story warms the heart. She was an elderly sister in her 70s who came to us early in that year from an Episcopal Church and city mission background. In 1960 she had a totally crippling stroke and was called into eternity a few weeks after Easter 1962. She was so incapacitated that there was no communication from her, except perhaps in the expression in her eyes indicating pain or peace. It meant a lot to Woodcrest—taking care of this elderly, beloved sister.

On the 1st of August there was another baptism—this time in Forest River—and Heini went out for it, with Dick Domer and Doug Moody and Christoph Arnold. In this group were Rachel Maendel, Barbara Maendel, Ruth Dodd Jr., and Don and Marilyn Noble. I mentioned earlier that Claud and Billie Nelson were in Forest River, an exchange with John and Sarah. Then came the whole experience with us, the Bruderhof. In July 1956 Nelsons returned briefly to Koinonia before coming to Woodcrest to join the Bruderhof life fully. Later they moved to New Meadow Run.

As I mentioned, Emmy was with us in Woodcrest, having come with Burgel, and in August she went out to Forest River for six weeks. Later she went for an even longer stay. One of the things that we experienced with Emmy in her last years (when she was over ninety)—particularly when brothers from the West visited—was her telling about the time she traveled amongst the colonies with her Eberhard in 1930-31. Because she then had a vivid memory of the colonies through her visits and still a vivid impression through Eberhard's letters of everything he experienced in 1930-31, she was convinced that she had traveled with him and always said so quite clearly. Of course Eberhard had traveled alone, but it was very precious to experience her saying this. Our brothers from the West had such a deep respect for her that whenever she told it, they just listened and nodded and appreciated every word that our dear Emmy could tell them of her "journey with Eberhard." She made two trips to Forest River and was able to visit some of the colonies. I don't know exactly how she was received always, because we were under a church pronouncement forbidding us to go visiting the colonies.

At Forest River everything wasn't always smooth. I didn't experience the problems personally—but we heard about them in 1956 when we were in the brotherhood. There arose problems that one could call "cultural." For instance, at that time indoor plumbing was very rare, perhaps unknown amongst the colonies. There were also questions about safety in regard to the children and about general sanitation. It is quite different today. Amongst the Schmiedeleut there are very few colonies without indoor plumbing, but at that time the question aroused deep feelings—not just something exterior—because some people sincerely felt that it was worldly to go in that direction.

Nowadays if you go West, you will find quite an awareness of a healthy diet. There will be two or three vegetables on the table, and they will urge you to "take some carrots, take some beans and some salad, it is good for you." But back in those days, as I understand, it was a much heavier meat and french fries diet, deep-fat-fried. Some of our folks from the East who went out there were a bit horrified by this unbalanced diet, and so it was changed for a time to be more balanced. Then someone remarked, "Well, at least with the old Hutterian diet one got a square meal even if it did build square people!"

The reason the Snavelys and another Brethren family by the name of Morris went to Forest River was simply that Woodcrest was already full of people from the Church of the Brethren. As I said before, "guests of a feather flock together." Nobody said it to us, but I know it was like that: it was better for them to go to another of our places so we could really all experience this life for ourselves.

In that month of August 1956, we had visits from an elderly man from the Philadelphia area who had no place to live and no one to care for him. I refer, of course, to Paul Willis. That August the brotherhood made the decision that he could stay permanently at Woodcrest. He was there for over 18 years—a very dear old man. He died in January 1975.

When I was storekeeper at Woodcrest, I experienced Paul every week, because he always looked forward to going to town. Riding around in the cab of the truck wherever I went, he just waited when I went in to pick up something. But the place he looked forward to was the supermarket. There he always went to a certain counter and with his own money got himself some soft buns. Then he would go to the 4-oz glass jars of cream cheese, choose the one with pimento in it, and have his lunch consisting of these two items. And I often joined him in that.

He looked forward to asking for the novitiate on a certain birthday—I think his sixtieth—and he kept us very well informed. "When my birthday comes, I am going to ask for the novitiate!" Really something to look forward to. As the date got closer we were becoming more and more concerned, because we knew Paul and knew that he hadn't the slightest idea what he was asking for.

When his birthday was nearly there, Paul Pappas and I had the task of going out and sitting down on a bench on the lawn and having a little talk with Paul. And we told him, "Paul, that is very wonderful if you want to ask for the novitiate, but we do have to tell you a bit of what it means. You have certain privileges that nobody else on the hof has. You can ride to town with the storekeeper and have your own money . . ." There was a string of different things we allowed him to do, quite clearly because he was there as our permanent guest and had actually nowhere else to go. And we said, "As soon as you become a novice all these privileges are going to be given up, because once you are a novice, you don't have privileges and rights any more; then you only have responsibilities, just that you know it." And we said, "Don't answer now, just think about it." Well, he answered in due time, "I think I'll not ask."

Paul was certainly very helpful around the hof. For years we had old chairs that were bought who knows where, auctions or somewhere. They had old woven cane bottoms that of course were always going through, especially if somebody would stand on one. One of Paul Willis's jobs was tightening up the joints of these chairs so that they wouldn't squeak so much and replacing the cane bottom with a piece of flat masonite—straight and uncomfortable, but at least serviceable.

For many years Paul was responsible for little groups of our boys down in the basement workshop of the Farmhouse. It was a crowded little place down there and was at one time the shoe repair shop. He would help the boys build model boats, and other things. We still have one model in the school. Before he came to us, he had been a builder of model trams (streetcars)—the kind that used to run on rails through the cities. There were many different types, each having certain exact characteristics and painted just right and so on. He was very careful about making accurate scale models.

Paul was in our family for a time and once Kathy wanted to give him joy. So she painted a picture of a streetcar, and boy, she really got into a mess on that, because she used her imagination and it wasn't identical to the real thing, and he gave her quite a few instructions on how to straighten that out. Well, dear Paul Willis was one of our Woodcrest legends, and he had quirks that had to do with his diet and the kind of clothes he wore and other things, which in retrospect we love him for. Also his language sometimes became too rich, and we had to speak to him about this and tell him that it doesn't go.

Something else took place in the early fall of 1956 that I don't think many would think of: I have a note that on September 6 the brotherhood decided that there would be no more early breakfast man. When we first arrived in Woodcrest, we lived in the Orchard House—an old, converted chicken house—and you smelt chickens whenever you mopped the concrete floor, you really did. At the end of the first floor corridor there was a wood stove, and every morning—we learned upon our arrival—you were awakened at some early hour, 6:15 or 6:30 a.m., by hearing somebody bang on a pot lid with a spoon, make a big racket, and yell, "Come and get it!" It was time for breakfast, and that would get us out of bed. There was an early breakfast man; he had to get up in time to make porridge, which was fetched from the pot by each family in the house. It was oats or some kind of whole wheat cereal that was supposed to be very healthy. It was like eating sand. So when the decision was made to abolish that duty, I found it important enough to put it down. When we could afford it later, we were able to have enough electricity to give families hot plates and other appliances. In the early years these things did not exist.

When we bought Oak Lake—later renamed New Meadow Run—the wiring in this huge hotel building was so precarious that if you dared to plug in a toaster upstairs you would blow a fuse and cut out the lights on a whole string of people. So there also was a breakfast man there, and everybody met in the kitchen to make their toast. Nowadays we have a lot given to us in our life together and we don't even think twice about it; we certainly have much in the way of creature comforts.

The event known to us as "The 1956 Conference" (for members) occurred in Primavera at the end of that year. In Woodcrest we began to experience something of it when Rudi Hildel arrived in September and we met him for the first time. The departure of the delegates didn't take place until the end of October, so we had a period of about six weeks of getting to know Rudi. I remember that I had a CP exhibit to attend at a hotel in Albany, New York, and Rudi came along to help out at the booth. While we were walking along the street, Rudi was approached by a gentleman who opened his coat, flashed his FBI badge, and questioned Rudi about his alien status and whether everything was in order—which it was. I never did know where this man came from or why he questioned Rudi. We are not used to such things in the States, but it was evidence that the government is active.

At the lovemeal for Rudi's welcome, Claud and Billie Nelson were taken into the novitiate with Donna Ford and Collette Schlatter (now Collette Thomson), the only guest to arrive at Woodcrest on a bicycle. During his stay, Rudi was able to make a ten-day visit to Forest River with Heini, Mark, and Alan Stevenson. In the beginning of October, Hans Zumpe arrived in Woodcrest, en route to this 1956 conference. But first he and Heini flew out to Winnipeg, Manitoba, because we had heard that the Elder* of the Schmiedeleut, Peter Hofer Vetter, was very sick and was in the hospital. The two flew out in an effort to see him and somehow effect reconciliation. They were unsuccessful, not able to see him, and had to return.

On October 2, 1956, John and Sarah Maendel arrived in Woodcrest with their one-year-old Gladys, to begin their brotherhood life in the East. They have been with us ever since. That was also the day on which Dwight and Norann Blough arrived as guests in Woodcrest. I had not met them before, but the previous December when we were still guests, I had received, suddenly out of the blue, my first letter from Dwight (he was in college in Kansas). There were four questions in that letter, which came just before Christmas of 1955:

Are you satisfied with the workings of the Bruderhof?

Is the community really what we read about in *The Plough* and in Sorokin's book (Pitirim A., *The Ways and Power of Love*)?

Is the adjustment that must be made to that way of life a difficult task?

Do you feel that that way of life is something that can be worldwide?

---

*The leading servant of the Word, carrying the main responsibility for all the communities under his service—here all Schmiedeleut colonies. See Glossary also.

Dwight knew about us and the Bruderhof through Dick and Cosette Wareham. Dwight was a student at McPherson College and Dick was a coach and teacher there. Dick had been youth counsellor in Chicago during my high school years; I knew him very well in seminary and had kept in touch over the years. Cosette had been a member of our high school group. The Bloughs and Donna Ford had heard about the Bruderhof through the Warehams in college.

Another letter dated April 19, 1956, tells of the Bloughs' intention to stay:

> We received your letter of April 1 and were overjoyed by the answers to our questions. Norann and I went through a very soul-searching time last Sunday evening after we had come home from a discussion at the church. We simply and determinedly tried to analyze just what we were attempting to avoid or put off in our lives that we knew we must include and act upon. How could we be sincere in visiting the community of brothers if we did not put ourselves in a position of openness of mind, body, and spirit, so that if this was the answer—and we have little doubt about it—we would be in a position to respond?
>
> You have probably guessed what we are about to ask, and that is, may we come to Woodcrest this summer? We feel this must be our course of action if we are ever to live in peace with our own souls. A person can hide from the facts only so long. We pray that soon new skins may be filled with the new wine.

Dwight had promised to finish building a house for his father that summer, and so as it happened, they did not arrive until October 1956. Many of us remember Dwight telling that as he and Norann drove up the hill to Woodcrest, there was something about the atmosphere—simply in coming up the drive—which gave Dwight a sense of inner conviction that this was where God wanted them to be and to stay.

On the day after Christmas Dwight and Norann were taken into the novitiate. During the three months before, Dwight worked with the building crew. After the Forest River House was full, the Sturgeon Creek House, then called Sinntal House, was under construction. No sooner was it finished than the Primavera House was started. As I have said, there was no question of using paint on the buildings; there simply was no time—when the doors were hung, somebody needed to move in. For some years they did not receive their outside shingles. In those days brothers had to do all kinds of different jobs even though not too experienced at them. We had a lot of fun over Dwight's wiring of one of the apartments. When it was ready, we found out that as soon as you pushed the toaster lever down, the lights would come on!

On October 29 the delegation left for the conference in Primavera: Annemarie and Mark Kurtz from the U.S., and Hans Zumpe and Rudi Hildel from Europe. I can well remember the departure from Newark Airport (later the North Terminal and used by People-Express for their domestic flights). As always happened during waits for planes, Annemarie had a stack of postcards and was writing feverishly to different ones whom she had on her mind.

The conference that took place during November and December in Primavera was not a happy event. I was not there—and most of what we know about it is in retrospect. What is all-important in a conference is seeking the will of God—and this conference could not have been on that foundation. A very long-winded, forty-page letter by Hans Zumpe was read out before he arrived. Betty Robinson bravely stood up and said that it was an arrogant letter—an accurate evaluation. But unfortunately it was not a time when others who felt exactly the same dared to agree. At the conference itself almost everyone was shocked when one servant was referred to as a "servant without words."

Nothing was straightened out, because the conference was not under the sign of the crucified Jesus as a gathering of needy, sinful people. At best it was a conference that evaluated the Bruderhof and its tasks from a utilitarian viewpoint. (At that point in our history there were eleven communities—counting the Bruderhof House in Asuncion—four in Paraguay, one in Uruguay, three in the U.S.A., and three in Europe.) Our Bruderhof communities—all of us—did not have enough humility, and so this conference, though historically critical, goes down on the negative side. However, to welcome Mark and Annemarie back home to Woodcrest on the 5th of January was a very joyful and happy event.

In the Easter time (1955) when I had gone to Oberlin College to pinch-hit for Hardy, a crisis had resulted in the laying down of the service of the Word of two servants who had been at Forest River. It had been decided soon after, that Balz Trümpi should come up from Paraguay to replace them. Well, moving families from Paraguay to the States—you couldn't do that overnight! It took cutting through a lot of red tape to immigrate a family, and they only arrived at Forest River in December 1956 while this conference in Primavera was still in process. During this whole interim time Hardy had been at Forest River in the service of the Word.

That December the young people put on a play at Woodcrest, "The Loaf of Bread" by Jane Clement, and I think those who saw it will not forget. It was based on two songs in the *Oxford Book of Carols* that we sing every Christmas (unknown to us then): "If ye would hear the angels sing," and "Neighbor, what was that sound, I pray?" Some of the lines were incorporated into the play, and it was done by our young people—mainly high school and college age.

On New Year's Eve the Snavelys were taken into the novitiate
in Forest River with four other young people. That brings us to
the year 1957, which in Woodcrest started off on January 2 with
the arrival from California of the Huleatt family. They stayed until
the middle of March and then continued on to Primavera.

I want now to go into the very important subject of the struggles
or crises that have been in our communities and that are inevitable
in a Christian life together. What Hans Meier has reported to us
from the Rhön time is important here. As an idealist, Hans had
questioned the need of written orders (*Ordnungen*)* for members:
they should take for granted what the church orders demand and
should do them quite freewillingly. Eberhard Arnold answered
simply, "You just don't know human nature."

On his 50th birthday Eberhard said that the Spirit is given to
those who seek the Spirit and is withdrawn in measure equal to
how much we try to carry the ball ourselves. His words were:

> Only to the degree that all our own power is dismantled will
> God go on effecting the results of his Spirit and the construction
> of his cause through us, in us, and among us—not otherwise.
> If a little power of our own were to rise up among us, the Spirit
> and authority of God would retreat in the same moment and to
> the corresponding degree. In my estimation that is the single
> most important insight with regard to the kingdom of God.

The key to living in community is the Spirit, the leadership of the
Spirit, and our willingness to place ourselves under God and his
sovereignty, our willingness to give up our independence. We
speak of being dependent upon God as a baby is dependent on its

---

*A church discipline that grows out of the unity given constantly afresh by the
Spirit to maintain order and harmony in all areas of the communal life, while
making certain of the freedom and voluntariness of each person.

mother. If you think about it, the word "dependent" means "hanging from"—a chandelier hanging in a room is dependent on the chain that connects it to the ceiling; without that chain it would fall. Our relationship to God should be like that, one of dependence; our natural tendency is to be independent, non-dependent, wanting it our own way. And this will destroy community—always!

Later on as a member, Hans Meier expressed that in a community of idealists you will have as many ideals as there are members, with all of the ideals different. That does not unite. Only when all members listen to the voice of God, and not to their own human ideas, will there be unanimity.

One of the things we know as necessary for the community to function—wanted and needed at all times—is that gifts are there and that they are used: the gift of having somebody to be storekeeper, somebody to be work distributor, somebody to oversee the garden work, someone to teach the children—all the various gifts. Paul goes into it very simply and clearly in 1 Corinthians 12, where he says, speaking of the varieties, "Now there are varieties of gifts, but the same Spirit." How true, thinking of our community life, varieties of gifts but the same Spirit:

> And there are varieties of service, but the same Lord; and there are varieties of working, but it is the same God who inspires them all in every one. To each is given the manifestation of the Spirit for the common good.

That is the purpose of gifts. They are given in order to be used for the common good. "To one is given through the Spirit the utterance of wisdom"—not many of us have that. I don't! But to some it is given to utter wisdom, "and to another the utterance of knowledge according to the same Spirit." Knowledge is something you can accumulate through books and through study, but it doesn't necessarily mean that that is wisdom. "...to another gifts of healing by the one Spirit, to another the working of miracles."

We are now getting into something that was much more powerful in the early church and that we don't see so much anymore: "to another prophecy, to another the ability to distinguish between spirits"—how important that one is—"to another various kinds of tongues, to another the interpretation of tongues." This issue of tongues is quite a controversial one. You are not talking about languages but about what is called "speaking in tongues," which comes today under the Greek term "charismatic." The word "charisma" simply means gift; it is just the word gift in the Greek, and a charismatic person is simply a person who is gifted. It doesn't say how he is gifted—it could be through any of these gifts. "All these are inspired by one and the same Spirit, who apportions to each one individually as he wills." But the important thing is that to each is given a manifestation of the Spirit for the *common good*. That is speaking about the community.

And then, as we know, Paul goes on from speaking of gifts in chapter 12 to speaking in chapter 13 of what he describes as "a still more excellent way." He speaks of faith, hope, and love; actually he speaks of all those other gifts as though they were worthless, and uplifts faith, hope, and love, and especially love, as the greatest of these.

In the fifth chapter of Galatians, after Paul tells about the works of the flesh (impurity, fornication, and so on), he uses another term. He speaks of fruits—not of gifts but of fruits—and it is a different kind of list. He says, "But the fruit of the Spirit is love, joy, peace, patience, kindness, goodness, faithfulness, gentleness, self-control." In this list you don't find the qualities that in themselves suggest a work distributor or an administrator or a teacher, and so on. It is nice to have these things, but they don't point directly to gifts; there is something different in the quality of this list of fruits than in the list of gifts he gives in 1 Corinthians 12.

The relationship of these two lists was once described in an illustration I like. You mustn't take it too far—all illustrations have their limits—but it is an appropriate comparison of fruits and gifts. Jesus says that trees are known by their fruit: if the tree is a good tree, it bears good fruit; if it doesn't bear the fruit it is supposed to bear, then it is cut down. He is quite specific about that. In this illustration he speaks of fruit trees, like apple, orange, or peach trees. But when one is speaking about gifts, one speaks of Christmas trees, you see. Christmas trees bear not fruits but gifts. There they are, they are hanging on the branches, and they are just wonderful; bright, valuable—not speaking about the Bruderhof now—Rolex watches and diamond rings—they could really be very valuable things or very useful things like chainsaws or what-have-you. The tree bears those gifts, but what happens to that tree in January? It is useless because the gifts have been taken off.

Don't carry the picture too far, but for me it illustrates the importance of this difference between gifts and fruits. And we have experienced it in our church life. Even though we are always searching for gifted people—a person with this or that gift—when we have come into a crisis or into difficulties, it is actually because of *gifted people*! It is not because of a lack of gifts, it is because of gifted people. You wouldn't have a dictator unless he were in some way gifted. The gifts that Paul names can be identified as these different abilities: knowledge, wisdom, the ability to teach, the ability of language, and so on. They are very valuable, they are given to us for the common good, and there is no lack of them. But if there is ever a lack of the *fruits*—a lack of love, a lack of joy (meaning the kind of joy that belongs to the joy of the Lord), a lack of peace, patience, kindness, goodness—then that lack *destroys community*.

We have never lacked gifted people. But gifted people often lack these fruits. And what is more, even if you have these fruits,

you can lose them very easily. "Once smart always smart"—
maybe. But as soon as you take to yourself either the gifts you
are given or the fruits you bear and think that makes *you* good,
then right away it brings in a spirit that divides and that often has
tried to destroy our community. I am convinced that it is not the
lack of gifts, but it is this spirit of division that destroys all
community attempts and it is also what destroys churches.

So all this isn't something that has to do only with Bruderhof
history; but Bruderhof history certainly has to do with it because
it all belongs to the whole history of mankind. That is why I drew
the parallel with the Old Testament the first time I spoke of it.
The same struggle was there—sharp, you know—and yet through
it all God was again and again calling his people back with those
things which go to the heart: love, joy, peace, patience, kindness,
goodness, faithfulness, gentleness, and self-control.

Early Woodcrest . . . view north to the Catskills

# 5
# *Fire and Rebuilding: Woodcrest and Macedonia*

On the preceding page is a picture of early Woodcrest with a view to the north. The large building in the background was later called the Woodcrest House and has offices for our Community Playthings. It was the Schoolhouse for most of the years of the community, but in the very beginning just an old, dusty, empty mansion. The small windows on the first floor south (to the left of the lone fir tree) open into what was the original kitchen of the building and also the first communal kitchen at Woodcrest. Just beyond the kitchen, going north toward the Catskill Mountains, is the largest room in the building. At first it was our dining room; much later it was the high school room; but before the new Woodcrest School was finished in 1980, it was mostly referred to as the Kinderschaft room.

The lower level of the two-story bay-window arrangement on the south end (and center) of the building housed our first snuggery. There was an oval table there, a table that came out of the old luxury liner, the *Normandy*. There were built-in benches around the table with just room to slide in, and the watches (those responsible for the small children during a communal meal or meeting) could eat their meals there. A number of big airy rooms in the building served as classrooms for many years.

On the second floor underneath the southeast gable to the right, there is a corner jutting out, a very special spot for a child's desk, with windows on three sides. Later the switchboard for the community was located there. If inquiry was being made for somebody, the operator had a three-way sweep of the center of the hof. This picture shows the building as it was in those days. Later on for safety we added an entrance through the snuggery and fire escapes all around the building.

In what this picture shows of the old Carriage House tower (peeping over the Farm House, left foreground), the oval windows were in Heini's office. It was not a very big place. An old bell was hung inside the cupola (far left), not a very big bell, maybe twelve to fifteen inches in diameter at the bottom. It was the first community bell. Up under the roof at the top of the Carriage House was the housemother room (where all the motherly oversight for the care of the whole community comes together in the housemother service).

The Farm House (in the left foreground) was built along the lines of a typical American farm building. In the first years the whole ground floor was used for all the babies and toddlers. The upstairs had been family housing. Later the bottom floor was used for our medical facilities. It has been added to and is a bit larger than you see in the picture. The perspective is a bit strange here because the largest maple tree has since been replaced by a young maple. And of course many other buildings have been built around the hof.

On February 4, 1957, there were two significant events. Rahel Basel—the mother of our Dave Maendel, Sarah Hofer, Lizzie Boller, and quite a few others—passed into eternity at Forest

River. The Woodcrest Carriage House fire was on that same Monday. (I did not experience the fire except at the end of the day, because I had left early in the morning to go to New York City to look at some woodworking machines.) The snuggery of the Carriage House was just at the head of the old concrete steps to the basement. It was the room where the mailboxes were and the mail was collected. The singles had their breakfast there every morning. One of them was a young man by the name of Vincent Lagano. He happened to go down the steps into the basement—I don't remember what for—and looked through the doorway into the Woodcrest bakery, where he had worked with a guest by the name of Ross Anderson. Just around the corner from the bake oven, he saw flames going up the wall.

To this day I don't think we ever discovered what the actual source of the fire was; perhaps it was electrical, perhaps it had to do with the oil feed to the oven. He said later on, "If I had only used my head!" If he had reached out his left hand right where he was standing when he first saw flames, he would have had his hand on the fire extinguisher. But he turned and dashed upstairs to spread the alarm and to "find the fire extinguisher." But as he grabbed one and started down the steps again, the smoke was already so dense that he couldn't go down.

As our main house at that time, it contained our dining room and kitchen and all of the food stores for the community. In one part of the basement was the garage where car repairs were made and all the tools and equipment were kept. In another part was the maintenance workshop. Upstairs on the second floor were all of the community offices—Heini's office; the steward's office and the accounts; Community Playthings offices with all the records of orders previously sent, orders not yet filled, and accounts receivable. The Kurtz family apartment was up there too, and also a guest room occupied by an elderly lady by the name of Mary Stevens, who was due to leave that day. One level above that—the attic—had been completely refinished into the housemother room, so all clothing and supplies for family needs were in that building too.

The building was what in America is called "balloon frame construction," in which any fire that gets into any of the walls will easily travel up through the wall, all the way up, as through a chimney. Before anyone could do anything, the fire had just taken off. It happened that the fire broke out right by the main phone circuitry, and all the telephones in the building were knocked out as one of the very first consequences. So we couldn't even call the fire department. The board on which the car keys were hung was right at the head of those self-same steps, and by the time anyone thought of getting a car key, the smoke was too dense. The only way to phone the fire department was for someone to run all the way down to the shop, where there was a direct telephone line. When the fire trucks got there, our old fire hydrants didn't work.

By the end of the afternoon, there was nothing to be seen above ground level except the chimney—the stone chimney was still standing. Everything else from all three stories—the ground floor and two stories above that—had all burned to ashes and plunged down into the cavity of the basement area. That included all the metal files from the offices. There were no fireproof files, and for weeks—I would say even months—people were there sifting through the remains of the Community Playthings invoice files. Where an invoice had been on a normal-sized sheet of paper, there might be left a six-inch circular piece from the middle, partly saved by the spraying of water. They would go at it with tweezers, trying to read the name and address of the customer involved.

Of course it meant that customers all over America just didn't hear anything from us. They had put in an order, they had sent in checks, and they got no response. In many cases, there was no way of knowing who on earth they were until their complaint letters came in, and then they got a letter explaining what had happened. Fortunately it was during the time of the joint Woodcrest and Macedonia business relationship. Macedonia was always sent a duplicate of all orders that included any of its products. These were available to us, but that was only a quarter of our orders.

There was a tremendous response of love and help from all over. I wasn't there to experience lunch that day, but Kathy remembers that the community had a real dinner. White "Wonder Bread" tasted especially good for a change—we had been having only homemade bread. There was also a delicious stew. From that day onward streams of neighbors brought in all sorts of things, so that the schoolhouse porch was loaded with donations of furniture, crockery, dishes, chairs, pots and pans, and even pianos. The very next day the local businesses donated for our use their dump trucks, shovels, wheelbarrows, and so on. It was too hot the day of the fire, but the following days we could dig out all the debris from the basement areas—packed full of sodden wet ashes and other things.

Down in the storekeeper's department there had been stacks of cases of canned goods. Well, it turned out that these canned goods weren't harmed; they were buried before they got hot enough to burst. But all the labels had burned, and there was no way of knowing what was in them as the cans were no longer in place in neat stacks. The kitchen would open cans for a meal and the menu would be a surprise!

There were also two chest-type deep freezers down there that were loaded with bologna and various kinds of sausage, liverwurst, and so on. This stuff was still edible but it had been cooked by the smoke and fire—which doesn't put in exactly the right flavors. We were eating this meat for weeks afterwards—until we didn't think we could stand another piece of it. But we did use it up.

In the long run the greatest loss was the books and papers in Heini's office, located in a little round tower that was right on the corner of the building. It followed the architectural shape of a silo attached to the corner of the original barn—not that it went so high—I think it had been only decorative in purpose. But on the second floor level, it had been made into an office and was occupied by Heini—a very small office, at most ten feet in diameter and maybe six-sided. During the fire Heini was very concerned about everything in there. A ladder had been placed up to one of the closed windows, but white steam-like smoke was streaming from the cracks of the window. Heini was even at the top of that ladder when he was prevented by the brothers from attempting to open the window and go in. If one sees steam-like smoke coming out of an enclosed room like that, it is a highly flammable vapor. As soon as it encounters oxygen, it bursts into flame. One sees this in fireplaces—vapor that looks like smoke suddenly turns into flames. Most probably entering would not have been successful and would have been dangerous, possibly to life.

In the office was a metal file (there were no fireproof files in the building) and then books on the shelves. Except for what few things Heini had at home in their apartment, this room contained *all* of the letters that he had received during his lifetime from his father, Eberhard. There were also books inscribed on the flyleaf, underlined, or heavily annotated in the margin by his father. The readings and even some books were replaced with copies from the other hofs. But everything there in Eberhard's own handwriting was simply lost forever, and that hurt our Heini more deeply than any of us can imagine.

The Kurtzes and their two very small girls, Connie and Kathy, were living upstairs at that time. To get out of the building, they were going down the wooden steps with the guest, Mary Stevens. When they started out at the top, there was no accumulation of smoke, but by the time they were at the bottom of the steps, there was so much smoke in the stairway that had they delayed another thirty seconds or a minute, they might not have gotten out—the fire spread that rapidly.

There was a door at the south end of the building that could still be used, since the fire was burning first at the north end. I remember Claud Nelson telling how he went through it to the dining room. People were carrying out chairs and tables, and he went over to the corner and started tugging on the upright piano, but it wouldn't come. Suddenly the whole wall behind the piano burst into flames. That was the wall of the stairwell going upstairs. So he grabbed a tray of salt and pepper shakers and came out with that. Lois Ann was saying, "Get the songbooks, get the songbooks," so people were making sure these came out.

In later years I remember Mark telling how they got out with only the clothes they were wearing—absolutely nothing else— every other item in their apartment burned completely. He said it was a relief—even though they had already surrendered everything and were propertyless—to be suddenly without even the cherished items a family keeps over the years was a relief. He had the feeling that now they could start their vow of poverty quite afresh because everything was gone. While the building was still burning, Jim Warren and Wendell Hinkey were over on one side of the schoolhouse lawn sketching ideas and plans for the new Carriage House, which was to be built on the same spot.

Materially, the main thing saved was the whole Farm House. It was occupied by the youngest children's departments with dwellings upstairs—not a large building. It is located something like twenty or twenty-five feet from the corner of the Carriage House—pretty close if another wood-frame building burns to the ground. The radiated heat was something terrific—Kathy was at home at our apartment in the Primavera House a hundred yards away and it was very hot up there from the radiation—the glass in the windows got hot. The firemen managed to save the Farm House by using hoses in two ways: to direct water at the fire with nozzle adjusted to make a big, flat fan-shaped curtain to cut off the heat, and then behind this curtain of water to play another hose on the Farm House to keep it wet. Thus the firemen managed to prevent the house from catching fire. Meanwhile brothers and sisters had evacuated everything out of that building—out on the grounds and lawns.

Plans for the rebuilding were drawn up quite quickly, using the same old foundations. Underneath the dining room were I beams —I think eighteen inches high—and these huge things had been subjected to so much heat they were sagging several inches. When we rebuilt, we just put blocks of wood on top to even them out so that the floor above would be level. And if you crawl down into the bottom part of that building, you may still see all that to this day.

The first meetings in the new dining room were held on Sunday, March 31—eight weeks after the fire. I remember the floor was covered with tar paper—or something very easy to trip over as you walked across it—so it wasn't as though the room was finished. Nevertheless, that Easter time it was possible to have our very first meetings there. Our first Woodcrest brotherhood room (with three extensions since) began as that newly built dining room. The final move into the new Carriage House took place on June 1, which was four months after the fire.

There was a lot of volunteer help—a group of Old Order Mennonites came all the way from the Philadelphia area and put in several days' work on that building. And quite a few of our brothers came from Forest River to help clean up. (Some were young men from Primavera who had gone to Forest River to help farm for a time.) Jörg Barth, Pete Mathis, Karl Christoph Keiderling, John Arnold, Anna's Dave Maendel and his brothers Josh and Jake, and Lowell LeBlanc all came at various times.

Fire—February

1957 Woodcrest Carriage House

Mennonite carpenters— March

Rebuilt—April

These were followed by Eric Phillips, Gerhard Wiegand, and Renatus Klüver straight from Paraguay, as soon as they could get papers. Not all of the labor went directly into the rebuilding of the Carriage House, but it was nonetheless a real beehive of activity.

During that time, the community—then around 200 people—packed into two of the rooms in the schoolhouse for meals and meetings. The old dining room was simply too small. (Later it became the Kinderschaft room and still later the high school room.) At that time the two schoolrooms on the east side were connected by a narrow hallway and a door to the outside. They helped make an hourglass-shaped dining room, with a gathering of crowded people on each side. In those days we had no idea of using amplifiers during mealtimes and reports. Whoever was reading would stand between the rooms and read in a loud voice, so as to be heard on both sides—people who had just arrived from other hofs and were reporting did the same. Keeping the singing together was interesting under those conditions. I think we sang songs like "Little Sir Echo" quite often.

That spring of 1957 Emmy Arnold made her second visit to Forest River. She was there for nearly three months. But there was no other blessing on our time in Forest River, even though it had its beginning in a genuine longing for a new outpouring of the Spirit, which had fired early Hutterianism. This was because of the way the whole thing was carried out, and that guilt lay mainly on our side. The difficulties grew and their number increased. Most of them had to do with outward things that were simply cultural in nature, but these cannot be the real cause of inner problems; there is always some deeper reason. It led eventually to another division, so that three families remained in Forest River, and the rest of us moved out. The brotherhood decided that we could not continue under these conditions; it was better just to give the place over to the families of Joe Maendel

Senior, Joe Junior, and Alan Baer.

Beginning in April, a search was started for a new community location. Brothers were sent out into the whole area around Woodcrest, to upstate New York, as well as west towards Reading, Pennsylvania, and as far as the Ohio line. There was one place near Connellsville, PA, that was looked at very seriously; it was maybe ten or fifteen miles from what became Oak Lake and then New Meadow Run, but it was not so good and was bypassed. The Summit Hotel, which we pass every time we drive from New Meadow Run to Uniontown, was looked at as another possibility, and it is a jolly good thing we didn't get that! It sat between a main highway and a country club golf course.

Another property we were especially interested in was only half as far from Woodcrest, in the Reading area. Of course in the end, the only thing we found that offered immediate occupation was Gorley's Lake Hotel. We were very grateful for that place where all our brothers and sisters could come relatively soon; it was a gift from God. In the joy of finding this new gift we did not anticipate the struggles that lay ahead to win this place over from the atmosphere of the old hotel nor the lingering effect it would have on our own inner life.

This mountain resort hotel (later the New Meadow Run Bruderhof) consisted of two buildings: the big hotel itself, which was not operated in the wintertime, and a boat house. The boat house was used as a Community Playthings shop; everything else was in the big main house. Unless you were a shop brother, it was possible—but not good—to live out your days indoors and never go outdoors. You didn't need to wear a winter coat, you didn't even need proper shoes, you could use slippers to go to mealtimes and to all the other work departments—school, offices, babyhouse, laundry—all in one building. But that place did give immediate housing for over one hundred people, and what's more, provided everything needed—plus, of course, all kinds of things there was no use for. Some might have gone to a museum, but lots were gotten rid of, such as brass spittoons!

On April 10 a baptism was held in Woodcrest for Dick and Cosette Wareham and Bertha Mills. Bertha was with us for another five years before she was called into eternity. And before Forest River was given up as an "Eastern" community, there was the baptism on April 16 of Aleck and Ruth Dodd and Welton and Kathleen Snavely. That spring a Lord's Supper was held at both communities.

We all think of our brother Dwight Blough, as servant of the Word and as Woodcrest school principal, but at this point he wasn't yet in school. Sometime after the Woodcrest fire Heini had told how suddenly, while the fire was blazing, Dwight had appeared up on the roof, finding ways to save things and to be useful until Heini called him down. Dwight had been in the building work ever since he arrived and was then much involved in the rebuilding of the new Carriage House, which went very rapidly. But in May 1957 he was moved from the building work to be tried out as a school teacher. He left a deep impression on many children. He was very spontaneous and original, with new ideas and love of fun. He did not approach children in a legalistic, cut-and-dried way, but had a heart for them, also when there were difficulties to work through. The Bloughs were baptized in the summer of 1957 in the same group as the Chathams, the Shirkys, and others.

In this year quite different events were often taking place during our preparation for moving a whole community from North Dakota to Pennsylvania. Problems were developing in the business relationship between Woodcrest and Macedonia. A radical change finally brought an inner fire and a time of rebuilding that was not of our doing.

When the assets of Macedonia had been split back in 1954, the Community Playthings business went to Woodcrest. But as

Oak Lake as purchased in 1957

The lake drained for the new meadow—1965

there were still products under development at Macedonia, it was agreed that they would remain as a partner in the Community Playthings enterprise and that their products would be sold with Woodcrest's. However, during the years of this partner arrangement, differences just did arise. For instance, the advertising was done at Woodcrest—the printing of fliers and sending them to our mailing list. Sometimes these fliers had text that was a bit cute in how it was written, and it struck Macedonia as not serious enough, and there were other things . . . At Woodcrest there was a feeling that the quality of Macedonia products wasn't what Community Playthings should be. Some of the wood used was yellow pine, and you just could not finish it like maple.

These problems led to the decision that we had to talk it over, and Ivan Kneeland and Staughton Lynd came to Woodcrest to speak about our business partnership with Macedonia. In the end it was decided that Macedonia would have a separate company and the name would be Macedonia Blocks. They would not use the name Community Playthings anymore, and we would end our partnership. This proposal took effect on the 15th of July, just the day before the title for Gorley's Lake Hotel was transferred.

But our inner relationship was more important than the clarification of our business connection. Earlier on, brothers had said that we can't go on with an unclear relationship; we must have a clear one. This had already had an inner effect on Macedonia before Ivan and Staughton's visit. Macedonia was also not looking at it as just an external, practical rearrangement, and this led to deep-going talks about the basis of living together. These concerns heightened after Ivan and Staughton returned from Woodcrest, so that only a few days later and at Macedonia's request, Heini and Eric Phillips went all the way down for a short visit to search with them further.

Simultaneously, the agreement to purchase the Gorley's Lake

Hotel, signed on June 2, led to work on the move from Forest
River. On the 17th of June the time known as "Park Terrace
time" began. Park Terrace was the name of an abandoned summer
hotel that was a Bruderhof for a while, situated about an hour's
drive from Woodcrest. It provided makeshift housing for those
who were coming from Forest River until they could move into
Gorley's Lake Hotel. It wasn't safe according to state fire laws
and had been condemned to be torn down, but it was still standing
intact when we rented it for one month in the summer of 1957.
It took about six days for everybody to get from Forest River to
Park Terrace, by whatever means of transportation was available.
In early Woodcrest we never bought a car. We just used the
clunkers that people brought with them when they joined the
community, and with some of them it was very uncertain as to
how far and how well they would go to the next place. Quite a
few of us made that long journey—something like 1800 miles—
by Greyhound bus to begin the "Park Terrace time" from June
17 to July 20.

Thinking of the next move to the Gorley's Lake Hotel,
Woodcrest had decided to buy a bus instead of putting so much
money into Greyhound trips; then we would have something
afterwards—our first school bus. Now that was really an old
beast! In order to get the gears shifted, since it did not have a
synchromesh transmission, a man had to learn how or have a
special talent—maybe be born with it, I don't know. I once tried
to drive it, and I never got that thing in gear properly, although
Dick Wareham and others could operate it all right.

There had been real joys during that month at Park Terrace
because it was possible to get together with Woodcrest for
communal events. There had been lovemeals and brotherhood
meetings and then a festival and picnic as a farewell on July 10.
On the 14th of July the first group moved over and into Gorley's
Lake Hotel. The title was transferred three days later and it became

ours. I think that is an old practice of the Bruderhof: to move in before you own a property.

The last group made it on July 20, and that was the establishment of the Oak Lake Bruderhof. One of the very first concerns was to quit saying "the new place," and we didn't want to call it Gorley's Lake, so what should we call it? Somebody remarked that there were lots of trees around and asked what kind. Someone else looked out and said that they were mostly oak trees. Except for the woods, the hotel, and a boathouse, it was all lake. So the name chosen was Oak Lake, which we retained until 1965, when we drained the lake and renamed the Bruderhof New Meadow Run.

On the Macedonia front, Woodcrest was asked if representatives could come down and so more trips took place—not connected with the business anymore but with the question of what makes it possible for people to live together in community. Macedonia Cooperative Community had been started by people who had been in alternative service during World War II, idealists who felt that there must be a new way for people to live together. Macedonia was seeking brotherhood but it was a mixture of all religions or none—and resisting any Christian basis. That had been one of the main issues back in 1954 at the first division. Many things were copied from the Bruderhof, like lovemeals, a daily schedule, and perhaps other things, but the same inner basis was not there. That is not saying that none of the people were Christians—some of the members were certainly Christians, but there were others who counted themselves as agnostics and perhaps something else. Our searching with Macedonia had its good side, and it also had its very difficult side for those who were down there.

In July and August Duffy Black, Mark Kurtz, and Gerhard Wiegand (from Primavera) went in response to Macedonia's request. Finally early in September Gerhard and Duffy asked for

Heini and Annemarie to come down. They did go—to help in
any way they could. Even before the earlier June visits the
membership circle of Macedonia had begun reading together from
the New Testament. (Later whenever our members came down,
we were included.) They had begun reading in the Gospel of
Luke in a search to find the basis for living in community, because
in human community serious problems arise that one does not so
easily find solutions to. Macedonia also had an open door, but
so wide open that almost anybody could come—and stay. And
this presented problems. Some of the Macedonia stories are very
humorous. I never lived there, but at that time some of them
were not at all funny.

A very remarkable event took place in one of the meetings.
On September 14 the Macedonia members met privately—Heini
and Annemarie were asked not to come. When they called our
people in later, they informed them that they had come to a united
decision to dissolve the Macedonia Cooperative Community as
of now: "We want to seek with the brothers; Macedonia is now
a Bruderhof and we are all guests. You are the owners and here
are the keys; please tell us what to do." Just like that! Well, that
was a bombshell. And they were in earnest; they really meant it.
Of course Heini felt that he could only witness to what the
Bruderhof experience was and what he felt, but he could not tell
them what they should do with their own place that they had built
up.

However, Woodcrest and Oak Lake had to find a way to respond
to this serious request. Heini and Annemarie returned to
Woodcrest, and we had meetings to try to decide what to do—
another time when Heini had a deep insight into what was right.
So, from our side, we proposed the possibility of having a
*complete* exchange of families: all those in Macedonia (even
guests) who really meant it should come north to Oak Lake and
Woodcrest to seek a new life together—or they should go

elsewhere. And we would send people down to Macedonia as to a new Bruderhof—to maintain the dairy and everything else. We asked if that was acceptable. They said yes, they agreed.

Those who came to us in 1957 were: Wisers, Burlesons, Melancons, Kathy Brookshire, Geigers, Mommsens, and Kneelands. Staughton and Alice Lynd came for some months. In addition to those who were members by that time, there were a host of Macedonia guests, but that is yet another story.

Again we had the situation of mass travel between two distant places. It started with our sending people to Macedonia in September. The day after the meeting, Mark and Carmen flew down, Carmen for the bookkeeping. Dwight and Norann were among those who were chosen to move there, and they left for Macedonia two days after Heini and Annemarie returned on September 22. Mark and Peggy, Jake Maendel, and quite a number of others also moved down.

About halfway through these southbound trips, those coming up from Macedonia began traveling, sometimes using the same vehicles. Staughton Lynd was the first to arrive in Woodcrest. His wife Alice and their baby came two days later. The Lynds remained at Woodcrest for four to six months. They just could not go along with the Christian basis of the community and never did join us. They left but are still our dear friends.

Burlesons and others came two days after Alice, and Jack Melancon on October 1. The Wisers were on their way when they had to stop in the city of Stanton, Virginia, so that Bill Wiser could be born. On October 14 the Mommsens came, and finally at the end of the line, as soon as Mary could travel, the Wisers came on October 21.

So that was quite something, fitting everything in on both ends— new people, new places, new rooms. It was a scramble all round. Already on October 8 Ivan and Alma Kneeland from Macedonia were taken into the novitiate with others. Earlier, there had been events unrelated to Macedonia, like the arrival of Paul and Esther Mason and Bennie and Esther Bargen, who very soon asked for the novitiate. By the end of October we had a visit from Primavera of Gwynn Evans (one of the responsible servants there).

On November 17 quite a few more of the Macedonia group were taken into the novitiate: Arnold and Dorothy Mommsen, Art and Mary Wiser, George and Vonnie Burleson, and Kathy Brookshire (and with them Bennie and Esther Bargen). They were very serious; they had fought something through at Macedonia during the summer. The earnestness of the seeking was the main thing—it had nothing to do with theology.

Having all these new novices presented something new at the Bruderhof. They were really old-timers at living in community and had had a lot more experience than many of us who were in the brotherhood at that time. So we started to have meetings with them where they could ask any kind of question and it would be gone into with brotherhood members. In this way the seeking could be continued more earnestly. Although in some ways these were like guest meetings, they weren't really with guests but with novices. For want of a better name they were called Special Sessions. At supper there would be an announcement that tonight there will be a Special Session in the dining room. Everybody knew what that was, and all who could come did so.

An incident from the late summer of 1957 will show the unchanging need for flexibility in the various departments of our work. One day Dick Wareham, who was the principal of the Woodcrest School, came down to the shop and called me outside. He asked me to hand over what I was doing—within the next minutes or hour—to someone else, because it had been decided that I should go into the school. Of course at first I thought he was just making a joke, but he wasn't. Macedonia's giving over of the community to the Bruderhof had resulted in our having to staff a new hof with all services—on the spur of the moment. Dwight, who was in the Woodcrest School, and Norann were among those going to Macedonia, and I was to be his replacement.

To be in the school was unthinkable to me, but one must be obedient. So I went up to the school and tried to learn what I could. School had not begun yet; it was just the end of the summer vacation, and I spent a day or two working with the children—I think with the 7th and 8th grades—cleaning up desks and chairs and getting set up for the school year.

But then we had a brotherhood meeting in which we spoke of Macedonia's need for a storekeeper—hopefully someone experienced—and it was decided to send Wilmot Durgin, the Woodcrest storekeeper. To replace him, I was chosen. Staughton Lynd, who was the first to arrive in Woodcrest from Macedonia, would take the school group that I was supposed to have, to make a three-way switch. I had the opportunity then for another year and a half to be the storekeeper in Woodcrest.

The year 1957 ended with a wedding and Christmas. On December 1 we had our very first wedding in Woodcrest, between Duffy Black and Susie Maendel, who unfortunately are not presently with us. As soon as Macedonia became a Bruderhof, decisions were made that more people with years of experience in the Bruderhof should come up from Paraguay, and so it was that Hermann and Liesel Arnold and their family arrived at Macedonia in the middle of December.

Another "first" that December came just after Christmas when a group carolling went to the old Ulster County Jail in uptown Kingston. I was in that group and remember that it had been a special wish of Art Wiser to go to the prisoners and sing. The Woodcrest choir worked on and sang the Christmas choruses of *The Messiah*. We had to buy books to do that, and we were very poor, so it wasn't easy. On the final evening of the year, Mike Brandes and Sharon Melancon were taken into the novitiate at the time of the lighting of the candles on the tree. Before midnight of each

December 31 at the end of a household meeting, any person from
the circle may light one of the candles on an evergreen in the center
and express a concern from the year past or a wish for the new one
coming. And that completes the year 1957.

# 6

# A Year of Gathering

There weren't as many events shaking the whole church in 1958 as in the years following. Perhaps one could regard this year primarily as one of growth and gathering, a year of calm before a storm. But it did begin and end with the loss of three children, all due to accidents: James Paul at Wheathill in January, and Wouter Fros and Rachel Marsden at Primavera in January and August.

Baptism was one sign of inner gathering and growth in number. On the 28th of January Claud and Billie Nelson, Edie Otis, Dick Thomson, and several others were baptized in Woodcrest by Gwynn Evans (who had been in the States since October 26 of the year before to experience the new communities). Straightaway we went into another time of preparation, with the baptism itself about three weeks later on February 16. This included mainly the brothers and sisters who had come to us when the rest of Macedonia joined the Bruderhof. They were Art and Mary Wiser, Arnold and Dorothy Mommsen, George and Vonnie Burleson, Van Geiger, and Kathy Brookshire. In the same preparation was Shirley Kratz (later Brandes). One day later there was the baptism in Oak Lake of Jim Hershberger, Ivan Kneeland, and a few others.

Gwynn returned to Primavera at the end of March, after visiting Oak Lake and Macedonia.

Gathering in the East had certainly been a factor in our decision to return Forest River in North Dakota to the authority of the Western Brothers. It was and is far from our Woodcrest Bruderhof and more isolated from large population centers. The problems in East-West relationships mentioned earlier and the desire for contact with seeking people were other factors in our decision. (Our long guilt for the split between West and East had not yet been recognized in 1958.)

As an additional problem, the practical work there dominated the life too much—perhaps we from the Eastern communities were not flexible enough. It is just a fact in farming—particularly in the large Western farms—that at seeding time and harvest the work simply has to take precedence over everything. During these times of intense pressure, brothers would be out on the tractors almost twenty-four hours a day in shifts. There is a tremendous investment in farm machinery and there are thousands of acres to cover. If the weather is good and the grain is ripe, the risk of financial loss is so tremendous that it just demands that kind of priority. And if the servants of the Word saw the need to have a brotherhood or other important meeting in the evening, it was very difficult, because the farm needed so many brothers. If there was livestock, the church-community life was all the more dictated and run by the farm work.

And that is one reason we have felt so blessed over the years by Community Playthings as an income-earning department— blessed by God. If there is a death in the community or some other special occasion, we can just say, "Well, tomorrow may be Tuesday, but we will make it like a Sunday." On the farm you cannot do that; you cannot just any time come to a united and gathered pause.

Almost all of these same considerations about Forest River

also played into the final decision in the spring of '58 to move
our Bruderhof in Macedonia, Georgia, and gather in the Northeast.
Part of the income at Macedonia was from the dairy farm, and
cows must be milked twice a day no matter what else is going
on. Isolation too was a very important factor at the time. There
was no telephone at Macedonia. It was so far out in the woodland
that no telephone line had ever been laid. To pay to have it done
would have been prohibitive. So if the servant of the Word in
Macedonia wanted to phone with Heini in Woodcrest, he had to
drive to Clarkesville—a seven-mile drive by car on back roads—
and make the call from a phone booth. And worse, if Heini
wanted to call Macedonia, he would call the taxi company in
Clarkesville and a taxi would go from Clarkesville to inform our
brothers. Then they had to drive a car all the way to town in
order to use the phone. Now compared with Primavera, that was
pretty good, but still it imposed a hindrance on the closeness of
our relationship. With modern technology, the kind of phone
contact we have today even across the Atlantic is amazing. And
between our communities in the States today, the normal thing
is to have joint communal mealtimes and meetings over the phone,
virtually every day.

When various efforts to sell Macedonia didn't materialize, it
was agreed to have auctions. There were two auctions, and there
were quite a few stories about the first one on May 2, 1958. I
remember hearing how amazed people were that an old moth-eaten
horse collar, hanging in the barn and unused for many years,
touched a beautifully high price. Or an old jeep was sold for
more than they had paid for it. I don't think it all went that way,
but in the South, a farm auction of this kind was a big social
event, involving catering and feeding all the people; it was like
a big fair. Lots of people went just for the entertainment. That
auction was for all the movable property. The land auction came
later in June, auctioned in various parcels, but finally sold in one
piece.

Arrangements had been made also to search for a new site for a Bruderhof. We had several prospects in line—one very nice property called Hillcrest in the Rochester area in upstate New York. Brothers made many trips there trying to get that place. The owner wanted to sell it, but she had an impossible lawyer. On July 3 the negotiations just plain collapsed because of the intransigence of the lady's lawyer. We never bought it, and I think that has been a blessing. The property we did buy is only an hour and three-quarters drive from Woodcrest, whereas this place was a good four hours. It was also in the section of New York known as the snowbelt, with much greater snowfall than Woodcrest.

It wasn't until a month after the Macedonia land was auctioned off that what was to be Evergreen (later called Deer Spring) was finally investigated for purchase. On the 10th of July brothers went to a property called Castle Kennels, where a certain Stuart Olson was raising dogs. Eventually we bought this property. It was called Castle Kennels because it was built like a Serbian castle. If you want to know more about that, there is a book in the library there about the inventor Michael Pupin who built it—quite a fascinating story, but also a very capitalistic one.

I don't know if it is true, but I heard that when brothers and sisters first moved into Castle Kennels and were trying to think what to name it, one of the brothers (thinking of the Bulstrode property that became our next English Bruderhof) suggested "Dogstrode." Another story about naming the new Bruderhof was that Wilmot Durgin made a trip to New York City to buy some chinaware. It was a light green tint and if you turned it over, there was an imprint of a couple of pine trees and the word "Evergreen." There are certainly many beautiful evergreen trees there, and the name Evergreen was manifestly appropriate.

The move of Macedonia to the north and our occupation of Evergreen continued true to Bruderhof form. On July 22, 1958, we had signed only the initial contract with the previous owner and three days later the first group moved in—Mark Kurtz and the Greenwood family with Rachel Maendel. Jake Maendel and Wilmot Durgin arrived the same day with a big semitrailer load of furniture and belongings. That was on the 25th of July, and it wasn't until a month later that the final deal was made and the property became ours. I don't know what the owner thought, but somehow we were able to give him guarantees that he would get his money. He hadn't moved so very far away—if you took a certain shortcut on the way to Woodcrest, you always drove past the front of his new place.

Once again we had a series of trips. Dwight drove the bus up from Macedonia with Sarah and Dorothy Maendel and quite a few children along with the Tremblay family—all arrived on the last day of July. The next day the rest of the Kurtzes with Norann arrived, and so it went. By August 2 we were able to have the new arrivals over to a joint lovemeal in Woodcrest to celebrate the newest Bruderhof in the North. And by the 10th of August all of the moves were completed; it had taken three weeks.

To get enough proper housing ready for everyone was a scramble that continued for some months. We did not yet know the local contractors or where to get materials and credit. (In the early years in the States this was a problem for each new Bruderhof.) The single girls lived in a balcony-like hayloft of what had been a barn and was later called the Lodge. It had a hastily-built railing along one side of it, and was hung with bedspreads, sheets, or things like that for privacy. The rest of the area was a drop-off down to a lower floor where the laundry was set up. It remained that way for quite a while, until we were able to build in a floor where the present medical and dental facilities are—below the offices and above the laundry.

A little over a month after coming into the Norfolk area, Evergreen held its first open house for the people of the neighborhood—as an introduction to ourselves and to our life together. We had heard they were mostly well-to-do people and were provincial in their outlook, cautious of outsiders and strangers. So we hoped for mutual acquaintance and a good relationship as soon as possible.

In the middle of that December 1958 the Bloughs needed to have a time in Woodcrest—a wonderful six months for them. So I was sent to take over the school in Evergreen—another mistake! But this time it did last until Dwight came back, and both Kathy and I were in the school. Part of the scramble to set up the hof had been to convert the main floor of one building for use as a school. The entire second story was almost finished for housing—for apartments—when the fire marshall came. He wouldn't approve it and said there could be absolutely no housing above the school. He even insisted on the brothers kicking holes in the Sheetrock and closing off all inside access, including the removal of all stairs. In Connecticut the fire marshall is part of the state police system—a uniformed inspector with a gun on his hip—and he made very nasty threats about it all.

Meanwhile, the upper school had been meeting in the top of the north tower of the building we called The Lodge, in one big room with a few desks squeezed in and a fire in the fireplace. I was introduced to the school there, as the main school building wasn't ready. The 5th through 7th grades (my group) were in the only room with a fireplace. That December was bitterly cold with very strong winds. We wondered if we were going to survive. And there was something wrong with the chimney. Instead of taking the smoke up, the wind blew it into the room—we had a mighty wretched time trying to hold school. Later the wind changed and it wasn't quite so cold. Kathy was in the other wing with the younger children, 1st and 2d. The school was very small; I think in the 5th through 7th grade there were seven children in three grades.

The extreme cold that first winter, without insulation and heating, was very depressing, especially in the first weeks. I got an encouraging letter from Heini written on December 29, 1958, and he expressed what I've heard from him a number of times since:

> I am not surprised it is hard. There is no reason to feel ashamed if we have to fight and if we sometimes feel weak in this fight, since we cannot do it with our strength. There is no harm if we feel weak, as long as we stand together in expectation. We still are in a fight, but the joy is greater than the fight.

In all our basic education at our American Bruderhofs, a wrong direction had come into our community life. Heini had fought against this direction with all his might, as soon as he became aware of it—the establishment of something called a "clearing room" for children. When there was a problem with the children, like mockery or naughty language or something similar, all of the children would be put in a schoolroom and would have to be quiet, with their heads down. One at a time they could come up and tell what they knew or had done. It was not a good approach— it was a terrible approach. It came, not from the Bruderhof, but from members who joined from outside. As soon as Heini was aware of it, he fought it tooth and nail. Unfortunately we didn't listen, and so this wrong approach too often continued. But that certainly was the stand that he took.

About church discipline Heini expressed the same concern very strongly—that church discipline *must* be carried out in love. If there is rancor or bitterness or annoyance involved in church discipline, it is a sin. When anyone is sent away from the community, it should be simply "a time of consideration," as it was called in those days. It was to be a time for getting your bearings, a time of finding your way back, with whatever inner help the community could give—hopefully lots of it. On that too we failed, in part because the weight of it all was just too much for the communities to carry, particularly in '61 and '62, as will be told later.

To come back to January 1958, Hardy Arnold and his Martha, then known as Sekunda, returned to Paraguay to work on their immigration. Until the end of the previous year they were in the United States only on a visitor's visa and so had to leave again. In March they returned as immigrants with their daughters Edith and Heidi, joined that summer by their son Franklin.

On February 21, 1958, Tom and Florrie Potts with Miriam and Margaret went to England by ship—Tony was in school but did go over later. In those days we rarely flew; it was before jet planes had come into use, and if there was no hurry, journeys across the Atlantic were made by ship. Today it is almost impossible to get passage by ship and it is forbiddingly expensive.

This move of the Potts family was specifically for Tom to continue helping with the income-earning departments in England. In 1957 he had gone over alone for a shorter journey to consider what business enterprise (other than farming) might be set up for the support of Wheathill and possibly for a second Bruderhof (which in 1958 turned out to be Bulstrode). There was a skit about the main suggestion of baking good bread—with dialogue about Bromdon Brown Bread Beautifully Baked by Bearded Brothers! Of course Wheathill had developed Bromdon Products (metal farm gates) as an income-earning department. At that time it was felt that Community Playthings would not be successful in England as an industry. But after the Bulstrode Bruderhof was founded and the Pottses had returned to Woodcrest in 1960, Community Playthings was started in England and has done well.

The wedding journey in 1958 of one early Woodcrest couple was unique: Dick and Collette Thomson were to travel by boat

Evergreen
was purchased
and . . .

the Dwight Blough family arrived
from Macedonia in August 1958 . . .

Evergreen
became
Deer Spring
in 1975

Bulstrode Bruderhof, England

to one of our Primavera hofs after they were married in June, taking a big consignment of crates and barrels. They had to put up with quite a bit of humor—how boring it would be sitting out on the deck surrounded by barrels, the long time it would take, and so on. The program at the lovemeal on the evening before the wedding at Woodcrest was entitled "A Jungle Jamboree"; it was altogether original. The music represented different animals they would see in Paraguay. One piece was supposed to sound like an armadillo toddling through the jungle, and the person playing the piano climbed up on it and did something to the strings to produce a series of thumping tones. The first sisters from the West to go to Primavera were Dorothy Maendel (now Kaiser) and Barbara Maendel (her distant cousin), who left on December 6, 1958.

In the fall of '58 there was an event that everyone then in Woodcrest will remember. It was a Sunday, and there was a household meeting in the Carriage House dining room. All of a sudden it was reported that there was a fire in one of the buildings. Another '57 fire? The alarm was given with such urgency that the meeting broke up and everybody rose and went out. The stream of people were directed south towards the Hillside and Orchard Houses, but as there was no fire in them, they went on—past the quarry where one could see the smoke rising from the woods into the sky. And what was it? Some older school girls had built a log cabin, using old and dead trees, burlap, and tar paper. It was known as Pinecrest. They had built a little fireplace in there with an improperly engineered chimney, and that morning during the household meeting Pinecrest burned down. It was a dandy fire—I can tell you it really blazed high and hot! In the same general area another cabin was erected—it was called Hickory. So we had our excitement that day.

On the 3rd of November we had a visit from a guest by the name of Eleanor Roosevelt, *the* Eleanor, the widow of Franklin

D. Roosevelt. Since I was storekeeper at that time, I remember that the menu was lamb stew—people said we should have had something better than lamb stew for the former First Lady. And she spoke to us. She was very well known for her concern for social causes, and we asked her to speak on some such subject.

From the beginning of Woodcrest, parents or relatives had lived with us until their death, as had Pop and Mom Kurtz. Hazel Brownson's Aunt Maud, who also belonged to the very earliest years, had moved out to Oak Lake with Hazel. She died on December 13, 1958, and was buried there.

In 1959 too there were other less shaking events—and problems. One problem involved a family whose father or grandfather became quite famous in America because he was one of those unlucky individuals that got caught in Senator Joseph McCarthy's communist-hunting net. He had lived for years in China, and he did not regard the government of Chiang Kai-shek as a sound and viable one for all of China—which it certainly was not in 1952. He was therefore labeled a communist and bombarded with questions, trying to prove him a communist. His son and wife had come to the Bruderhof because the son had known Sibyl and wanted to seek with us. They moved to Evergreen in July 1959 with their six children, including twin babies. In January of '60 the wife became ill with pneumonia and was to be hospitalized for several weeks and then was to have a one-to-three-month convalescence. Now, she did not want the community life; she had no feeling for it. She was there only because of her husband's interest. It was a very difficult situation to cope with for a small hof of less than a hundred people, especially to care for their family too with our few single sisters.

Related to our growth in 1959 there were membership requests, baptisms, and happenings in our children's community. Edna Maendel became a novice. Others took the step with her but are no longer with us, like Sid Emerman and Phil Maglin. And

Woodcrest received some interesting guests. Milton and Sandy Zimmerman came for a three-week visit on May 2, and it meant so much to them that they returned—by the 5th of July they had asked for the novitiate. In May Jack and Sharon Melancon were baptized, and in June Glenn and Marlys Swinger arrived in Woodcrest for a one-year visit and stayed. (That's how we came too, for a one-year visit.)

On the first Saturday in September sixty of us from Evergreen went over to Woodcrest in their school bus and spent the whole day in a circus they had prepared. From it we have a couple of very good pictures of Bertha Mills and others who have since died. (I had made a set of slides.)

One last incident in the year was a lot of fun. Woodcrest in those years didn't have any suitable Christmas trees on their land. But Evergreen was just loaded with all kinds of very beautiful ones. So Wilmot Durgin and Hermann Arnold and I dressed ourselves up in Santa Claus suits. We got the Santa Claus suits and all three of us into the cab of our truck—loaded to the gills with Christmas trees—and drove over to Woodcrest with them. We had a lot of fun on the way, seeing how people reacted to three Santa Clauses sitting in the front of a truckload of trees, especially at the Kingston-Rhinecliff Bridge with the toll taker. And we were able to wish everyone a merry Christmas 1959.

Early in 1960, Woodcrest perceived that our Oak Lake people were getting rather low in spirits. So a group consisting of George and Vonnie Burleson, Thelma Chatham, Sibyl Sender, Edie Otis, and Jack and Sharon Melancon drove out there unannounced. Before going on the hof, they changed into outlandish costumes. Then what did they do but burst in on a mealtime! Now that same day, a man at nearby Chalk Hill had gone berserk. From some high building he had started sniping at drivers of cars as they passed. All this had been on the radio and people were scared, but of course the travelers knew nothing of it when they appeared suddenly at a mealtime. However, they were very soon recognized and people realized they were just cheering up the community. They had a program of songs and what all else — all nonsense.

Nonsense went very much with our life in those days — not that it doesn't now, but it was very characteristic then. The recurring inner struggle, the illnesses, and the various problems on our small hofs in trying to absorb people into the church — people like us, square pegs for round holes — all this was a strain on the services. Sometimes the servants or the witness brothers were called into situations that would just make your heart weep and you didn't know how to carry it. Just then these brothers might start poking fun at each other — suddenly in innocent ways doing little things like pouring water down the neck. These practical jokes occasionally went on late into the night. The residents of the hof probably thought they were daft. But it may well have done some good, since at one period in our history some people unfortunately had had an image of servants of the Word and witness brothers as so awesome and exalted that they would never crack a smile. When the high jinks started on those trips, it certainly destroyed that image.

One memorable incident of no historical importance took place on an icy day in March of 1960. We sent our truck from Evergreen loaded with Community Playthings over to Woodcrest — at least the destination was Woodcrest. There were two main ways to travel: one was especially winding and the other had a long hill and a hairpin turn. The driver decided to avoid the hairpin turn. On the very winding road one of the hills was like glass, black ice. Our driver lost control, and the truck went off the road and over on its side, stopped by a tree from falling into a ravine. The damage to the truck was limited — we could keep on using it after that, although it had some ugly dents in it. But about a mile back along the road another truck was loaded with cases of hardware, mostly knives, destined for a Sears, Roebuck and Company depot.

That truck couldn't make it up the hill and started slipping back. The driver tried to stop and couldn't. The truck ran backwards off the road, across a meadow, and into a little brook.

There was snow everywhere. The back of the truck was covered with canvas with many ropes crisscrossing it and holding it down. When the truck came to a stop against the opposite bank of this brook, the force of the weight inside the truck—it was overloaded—burst the ropes. Out shot cases and cases and cases of pocket knives of all sorts and also knife blanks for hunting knives. Later in the day the same wrecker that pulled our truck back on the road pulled that truck up too, and the news of this accident got all over the nearby town of Millerton. The driver and whoever was with him managed to shove and push and get many of their cartons back into the truck. Then people flocked out there to fill their pockets and get themselves as many of these knives as they could. Everything lost was covered by insurance. When the truck and all these people had left, there were still many, many of these knives—under water.

That was when our brothers came along and said, "Isn't that a pity!" They went down there on this creek—in ice and snow conditions, mind you—reaching into water above their elbows. They got buckets and buckets of knives of three basic types: Scout knives, little gold-colored ladies' knives on a chain, and Barlow knives—I'm sure there are some from that batch still in use. In those days it was common for sisters to sort some laundry or do their mending in brotherhood meetings. Later on when we were dealing with very serious subjects, we decided it didn't fit to have mending and all that going on, with every sister behind a big sewing bag or basket of wash or whatever. So we *all* stopped.

But before that decision and after this knife incident, what we had in the middle of the circle was usually two or three buckets of kerosene about half full of knives. We would go over, reach down into the smelly stuff, pull out a few knives, and with sandpaper and rags polish away until we had gotten enough rust off them to be OK for use. The whole place would smell; nearly everyone was cleaning knives. I think the knives were also called "Hilarion" knives. It was just after Hilarion Braun had come up from Paraguay to the States, and he must have written quite a letter back about it—but he had nothing to do with the accident.

In three coming chapters I want to give some picture of what the church went through in the years 1959, '60, '61, and '62—all very decisive and important years for the Bruderhof. It will be difficult to say the right amount about some of these events, but the important developments in this time of crisis began in 1958 and belong to that picture: Hans Zumpe, the main servant of the Word in England, was reported to be discouraged and not himself. There had been some correspondence about it, and Heini became concerned to do what he could to support the circle and the services over there. So on August 16 Heini and Annemarie with Emmy Arnold took a ship to England. Of all the journeys that Heini made from Woodcrest, this was one of the longest—a full two months. During Heini and Annemarie's absence, Hardy came over from Oak Lake with his family and took the responsibility for the Woodcrest Bruderhof.

On November 22, 1958, in response to a request from Europe, we sent the Hinkeys, Wendell and Pep with their nearly three-months-old Larry, to our Wheathill and Sinntal communities. This journey also proved important in what followed. Wendell had some architectural ability and background. In addition to helping at Wheathill to design a new kitchen building with accommodation above, he was sent to visit the Sinntal Bruderhof, to help get a financial base there and to evaluate suggestions for the future location of the Bruderhof in Germany.

That brings us then to the year 1959, a time referred to as the turning point in our recent Bruderhof history. Before launching into that story, a background is needed, going back to 1935 and before.

# 7
# *Two Atmospheres In Conflict*

Until the late 1960s the new American brotherhoods had not been told about the crises in the twenty years of our history after Eberhard's death in 1935. Later chapters will make apparent *how* little was known in the States about the sin and struggle of those two decades. However, for the reader's perspective on the events that followed, it is important to know here that for old and new members of the Bruderhof, the past was always assumed to be forgiven and forgotten. Only the disunity that culminated in the shaking events of 1959-61 showed clearly how much unforgiveness remained. These three years (to be covered later) revealed an urgent need for redemption from the sin and struggle of those twenty years.

In the short span of this book I have made no attempt to cover the years 1937 to 1954, between the conclusion of Emmy Arnold's *Torches Together* and the beginning of *Torches Rekindled*. (I could not of course give any personal account of those important decades at the Cotswold and Wheathill and Primavera Bruderhofs.) However, as essential background for understanding the more recent Bruderhof struggle for renewal, the next four chapters will of necessity refer to the darker and more painful side of those earlier decades, 1935-54. Therefore, I want to repeat at this point that God's protecting hand was over the Bruderhofs in those years and that this was evident in the life and witness of many brothers, sisters, and children in both Europe and South America. I want in no way to minimize or cast doubt upon the positive fruits of God's working in that time.

Before going ahead then with the report about 1959, it is necessary first to give some perspective on the struggles or crises of those earlier years. The sins in the period following the death of Eberhard Arnold in 1935 are not to be seen as the result of the wrongs of individuals only, but also as a result of the "struggle of the atmospheres" as Eberhard termed the conflict between the Spirit of God and the spirit of Satan.

In this conflict the sins of rebellion and all the terribly sinful directions reported in the Old Testament are not unique to those people. They are characteristic of the human race, and that means every one of us. The inclination toward sin, and the seeds of every type of it, are inborn in us human beings. It is what theologians call "original sin," and we inherit it from Adam. So in telling about persons or events, it is a mistake—what's more a serious mistake—to think of that person, "How terrible that he would do such a thing." Every one of us is capable of it, but we are under a spiritual protection from God, so that *we have no idea* what it would be like for us were we not under God's hand, protected by his good spirits, who obey his will at all times.

If one reads the engagement letters of Eberhard and Emmy Arnold or their writings in *Seeking for the Kingdom of God* and *Torches Together*, it is very clear that our communal life is not founded upon a social ideal of brotherly community. It is founded upon love to Jesus. Brotherly community is a result of love to Jesus—an inevitable result of love to Jesus if it is truly love to him. Eberhard made this very clear. In one period of our history it was said that in his later years he repudiated his earlier love to

Jesus and his personal references to him, but Emmy Arnold and Heini and Hardy have very clearly told us this is *not* true. Hans-Hermann and Emy-Margret have also testified that Eberhard Arnold did not repudiate the love to Jesus; what he did repudiate was false piety.

In 1920 this love to Jesus was the foundation for the beginning of living in community at Sannerz, and it was the foundation of what Eberhard represented until the day of his death on November 22, 1935. But he was indeed very chaste (chary), as we also choose to be chaste—reserved, reluctant to over-use religious words and religious terminology—because we want to be genuine. There is no other reason for it; love to God and love to Jesus are the very rock and foundation of our life together. The brotherhood is not the foundation and not the center; the services are not the center of our life; but Jesus is.

When Eberhard made his journey to America in 1930 and 1931 and joined with the Hutterian Brethren, this was a demonstration of what he deeply felt—that he did not want to be a leader of a movement. He wanted to be a humble follower of Jesus, wanting to join this already existing movement that he knew to be part of a continuous movement from the time of Pentecost onward. Unfortunately, however, during the weeks immediately preceding Eberhard's death, something had happened in the life of the brotherhood at the Rhön Bruderhof that was very distressing to him. The love had grown cold, and the fight for God's kingdom had gone out of the members there. This was so serious that on the 7th of November the brotherhood agreed to dissolve itself as a united circle and to seek repentance together, mostly in silent meetings.

Five days later Eberhard went to Darmstadt to have an operation on his leg; he had fractured it two years earlier and it would not heal. The most horrible outcome that could have been feared happened; he died after two operations, and he died in agony.

His physical agony could not compare with his agony of heart because of the love grown cold in his beloved brotherhood at the Rhön Bruderhof. He had had an inner feeling, an inkling, that he might not survive the operation. If one reads his last two letters—one of them written to Hans Zumpe (the only remaining servant of the Word) and the other one to his wife, Emmy Arnold—one can see in their language his feeling that he might not survive. They were like a last request:

> I hold firmly to the inward and outward uniting of *genuine old Hutterianism* with the *attitude of faith* of the two Blumhardts and with the life-attitude of the true *Youth Movement* as a real and wonderful providence for your future; whereas I regard a merging of Hutterianism with modern pietism as a misfortune. The Baptist Church ought to be sufficient warning to us.

Eberhard and Emmy Arnold believed that it is where Jesus proves that he is alive that a struggle breaks out afresh between the Spirit of God and the spirit of Satan—*two atmospheres in conflict*. In this attitude of faith as regards the struggle between two spirits, this struggle for the kingdom of God, two prophetic men—Johann Christoph Blumhardt and his son Christoph Friedrich*—had a decisive influence on the life of Eberhard and Emmy.

Soon after Eberhard's death—already in the month of December—even though his direction was very clear in his last two letters, Hans Zumpe took quite the opposite way in a number of instances. The change in direction was 180 degrees and continued into January 1936. During these months Hardy, Heini,

---

*Johann Christoph (1805-80) and Christoph Friedrich (1842-1919) were pastors in Southwest Germany (Württemberg). For influence of Blumhardts on Eberhard Arnold, see Emmy Arnold's *Torches Together*, 2d ed., Plough Publishing House, Rifton, N.Y., 1971, pp. 171-179.

and Hans-Hermann were all in Zurich, Switzerland, working or
studying in their trainings. Because of the Nazi regime and because
of the military service in Germany, Eberhard had very strictly
forbidden his sons to enter Germany. They would have been
immediately imprisoned. So they could not be there at the time
of Eberhard's death; only Emmy Arnold and Moni, her sister,
were present at that moment—the other family members were
in Zurich or at the Alm (the Bruderhof established in Liechtenstein
in 1934 as a refuge from military service for our young men and
a refuge from Nazi teachers for our children).

Later, during the early part of 1936, Emmy and her younger
daughter Monika came to the Alm. Emmy could then visit Hardy
(who was married) and Heini and Hans-Hermann. These four
were aware of the changes made, one after the other, quite contrary
to the direction Eberhard had pointed out. They got excited about
this, they protested, they weren't listened to, and they got more
excited. Heini in telling of it has always blamed himself for
getting excited—it was not right. But the points on which he and
they got excited were definitely right, because they were a reversal
of the fundamental direction of love to Jesus.

The result was an encounter that took place in the brotherhood—a
struggle called the "Zurich *Handel*."* Its conclusion was that these
four family members were placed under varying degrees of church
discipline—Heini was excluded from the brotherhood. They were
told that they were being emotional and legalistic in insisting on
following their father's direction. Hans Zumpe's terrible statement
is still remembered: "The dead hand no longer rules."

Just in this crisis time the government in Liechtenstein had told
us they could no longer guarantee that the Nazis would not come
and take our young brothers for military service. Fortunately our
English members had already been sent to England from both the

---

*In this context, a clash between opposing directions.

Rhön and the Alm to look for a property for a Bruderhof. They located a Cotswold farm as a likely place, and in March 1936 the first people moved in. Heini had scarcely been reunited with the brotherhood after the Zurich clash when he and Annemarie were married, also in March. Their flight to England was achieved, practically speaking, by the fact that they were going on their wedding trip. Otherwise they would not have been given the right documents to enter England. Other brothers of military age made it there by various and even miraculous ways.

Now this direction, contrary to Eberhard Arnold's, continued and grew in the community. When brothers from the Western Hutterites, David Hofer Vetter and Michael Waldner Vetter, arrived at the Cotswold Bruderhof in February 1937, their coming was a decisive event. From the Cotswold they also visited the Rhön Bruderhof, and we are sure the brothers' presence as Canadians and foreigners had a staying effect upon the hand of the Nazis when the Rhön Bruderhof was dissolved. Our people were not sent to concentration camp; they were able to leave Germany and go to England.

Another very important aspect to the presence of these two brothers was the effect their visit had on our whole inner life and direction. Heini had not had any kind of service yet. There had been only one confirmed servant of the Word for all three communities. David Vetter and Michael Vetter said this was an impossible situation. Just two days before leaving England and returning to North America, their last church action was to confirm Hardy Arnold and Georg Barth in the service. They had to press this through because there were objections, but their insistence on it and actual doing of it was of extreme importance. After they left for America, there was continued correspondence in 1938 between Georg Barth and Hardy Arnold and the Brothers in the Western United States, also with the Elder Joseph Kleinsasser Vetter, the father of the late Elder Joseph Kleinsasser Vetter

Eberhard at the Rhön Bruderhof

The Alm Bruderhof . . . Heini and Annemarie were
married there in March 1936

The visit of David Vetter and Michael Vetter in 1937 was decisive for our Bruderhof future

Fritz Kleiner at the Cotswold Bruderhof, a very hardworking brother, a proletarian in background

whom we knew. The dictatorial actions of Hans Zumpe, the only servant of the Word at the time of their visit, became clear through this correspondence, and he was asked to lay down his service for quite a length of time. The Brothers even wrote and recommended that his service never be restored. Unfortunately the letter (which we have now located) got lost from sight and memory until the late 1960s. And so the recommendation in this letter of July 1938, written from Milltown Colony, Benard, Manitoba, was not carried out. Extracts in English translation follow:

> To Georg Barth and Hardy Arnold
>     The grace of God, the love of Jesus Christ, and the community of the Holy Spirit be with you and us all. Amen.

> You beloved and worthy brothers:
>     We received your letter of June 16 in due course and learned and understood from it the sad affair with Hans Zumpe. It is very sad to hear this, especially when it concerns a servant of the Word who has been trusted and for some time should have been a leader and adviser of the community.
>     We can well imagine how hard it must have been for you to experience such a thing, especially from a person in authority. But we also have to thank God for giving you the strength to put this foulness and evil out of the church and to punish it seriously. It is God's will that evil be done away with, as Christ the Lord teaches in the Gospel: "If your right eye, your hand, or your foot leads you astray, cut it out and throw it away, lest the whole body be spoiled." This does not mean natural limbs but members in the house of God.
>     God cannot and does not want to be with a people who do not expel evil. One example is that of the people of Israel in the story of Achan's theft, when God said to them through

Joshua: Unless you destroy every single thing among you that is forbidden under the ban, I will be with you no longer. You have forbidden things among you, Israel. Paul says: Drive out the wicked person from among you.

It is a grace from God and a blessing for a people when they have zealous members who fight against evil. And it is also a proof that God has not abandoned this people, but his Spirit is still at work among them.

After giving eight specific instances (with names) of the misuse of his service, the letter continues:

Hans has also shown himself to be an unwise and undiscerning leader in that he did not even know that only those can partake of the Meal of Remembrance of Christ's suffering who have been accepted into the church through baptism. That is easily understood from the writings of Paul to the Corinthians. In Israel no uncircumcised man was allowed to eat of the paschal lamb. Circumcision was the sign of the covenant of the Israelites. Likewise, baptism in the New Testament is the sign of the covenant of the children of God. Only a person who has been accepted into the community of the faithful through baptism may partake with them of the Lord's Supper. In the writings of our forefathers it is also very clearly stated that anyone who has not yet accepted the covenant of Christian baptism, and is therefore not yet a part of the body of the church, cannot hold the Lord's Supper with the faithful. It says clearly that one should not pass the bread and the wine to them.

Hans showed with this unwise action that he did not understand the deepest meaning and basis of the Lord's Supper according to the teaching of Paul. And if he did understand it, he acted very irresponsibly and proved himself to be an unworthy servant of the church.

If he acted so irresponsibly in this important matter, how could he lead the people on the right way in other important matters. That cannot be expected. Without a doubt this is why things have gone so far with him. No church should have such an unwise leader lest wrong ways and evil enter into the church and no separation from them can take place. Since the above situation shows that he has been an unworthy and unwise leader, he should not be reaccepted into the community without serious repentance. And after he has been reaccepted, he cannot carry the service of the Word anymore because he misused his service so very much and led the church in such a wrong way. In this whole matter he has proved himself to be totally unwise.

It is deplorable that things have gone so far with him. May God have mercy on him and help him to find true recognition and repentance, so that he may not fall into total blindness and ruin.

May the almighty God and loving heavenly Father give you understanding and wisdom and the leading of his Spirit, so that you may act with justice and fairness and take God's Word alone as your guide. May you diligently follow the example of the men of old, those who have gone before us as a cloud of witnesses, thus following them on the way to blessedness.

Signed: Joseph Kleinsasser and David Hofer

In 1938 the Alm Bruderhof was closed and all finally came together at the Cotswold in March. In June of that year Heini was appointed to the service of the Word for the first time—quite a young man. He was born December 23, 1913, and that made him nearly twenty-five. He was confirmed in the service the following year.

Then came the war with Germany and either internment for our German members or emigration for all of us. We chose the latter. In 1940 Paraguay was the only country that would take us in. There the immigration of the Mennonites previously had opened the door for us. It was an amazing, one could even say miraculous, departure from England: the movement in wartime of all those ships, with more than six groups—one with 158 people on board, another with 83, another with 60—altogether about 350 people. They traveled from the Cotswold Bruderhof in England to Paraguay in South America, through submarine-infested waters, zigzagging all over the ocean, under blackout at night—and all made it safely. Among the 350 were 155 children, and in the first year in Paraguay 5 died from tropical sickness.

In 1941 in Paraguay, Heini had a flare-up of an old illness—he had been treated for it in England—an ailment that became extremely serious down there. It continued to affect him the rest of his life, but it became deathly serious in August of that year. He was put under sedation for relief from pain, which was very necessary. We were fortunate in having doctors in the community and they did their best, but they did not have the right medicines for treating this illness. In wartime, of course, medicines were extremely hard to come by. Over a period of two months it got worse and worse; Heini became very seriously ill, showing signs that the doctors identified clearly as those of a dying man. One day they gave him only six hours to live. At that time Heini was the only active servant of the Word; for one reason or another, the others had been temporarily removed. Since he was the only confirmed servant, he was extremely concerned by this prediction of the doctor, by his own experience of weakness, and by his frightening symptoms.

In a series of meetings—all who were there remember them very clearly—Heini gave a strong call to repentance. Remarkably enough, we have notes of what he said from his bed, taken when the community was gathered around the hut in the night. His message was as if he spoke for the future too. He based most of what he had to say on the Gospel of John, which he loved so deeply; it was a very clear cry for love and for repentance. On October 3, 1941, he said:

> What I have to say to you is this: the fight against Satan comes first. It comes every time Christ enters into our midst. Then comes repentance, and then the future kingdom. The coming of Christ! If we love Christ and his cause, we will have the interest of his kingdom at heart. For it was to bring the kingdom on this earth that Christ came to this earth and suffered. The Church has the very great task of mission for this kingdom of God, which may come very soon. But woe to us if we think we will get to heaven because we live at the Bruderhof. I don't believe that. If we do believe it, we don't love Christ enough.
>
> If we read the New Testament with this in mind—not only the agreeable parts—we will recognize what is God's will and what Christ truly wants. Then we will see that God's will is that he alone rule and that all hate and all war cease. In fact, the very last, the ultimate thing, is the conquest of death. It was Blumhardt who made me realize this; he says, "Many people read the Bible for the sake of their own gratification. But the will of God, the will of Christ, has no meaning for them."

In one of Eberhard Arnold's last letters before he died in 1935, and specifically in the letter to Hans Zumpe, he advised Hans to work closely together with Heini and Hardy and Georg, even though at that time Heini had never yet been in the service of the Word. Now because Heini was told (and thought) that this was his deathbed, and because his father had wished it in his last letters, he believed that if the services of Hans Zumpe and these two brothers could be restored, then God's blessing would be on this church action and things would again be in the right order. And so on October 3, 1941, in a meeting from his bed—a very touching and moving meeting—Heini confirmed Georg and Hardy and Hans Zumpe back into the service of the Word.

Heini did survive the illness, but because of the type of medication he was given—and our brother Milton Zimmerman, himself an M.D., has said the doctors had no other medicine to give—the side effects became increasingly serious. There came a time when he had very serious hallucinations and was not himself. It got so desperate that finally he was taken from Primavera to a hospital in Asuncion, a journey that was not taken lightly. Primitive roads, where there were any, were absolutely horrendous! And if you went by air, the takeoffs from and landings on rough camp land were extremely dangerous—avoiding termite hills, telegraph wires, and cattle. Heini was in Asuncion for a couple of months in the hospital, where they had the right kind of medicines and treatment, and then was able to return home.

Now the Asuncion doctor had made no stipulation to Heini about his work. But Hans Zumpe, only just reinstalled to the service by Heini, said to him and to the community that "Heini should have a rest from all spiritual work because he was not recovered and had lost so much weight." And with that Heini was effectively removed from the service of the Word! And the inner life of the community suffered—I am speaking of the brotherly relationship that should have obtained, the love between brothers and sisters. And this continued on into 1942.

The love to Christ was becoming so noticeably lost that on one occasion in July there was a meeting of the responsible brothers, the witness brothers, in the woods near the community, and Fritz Kleiner was one of them. (He died some years later in Primavera, a very hardworking brother, a proletarian in background.) Fritz stood up and voiced a very strong protest against the direction in which things were going. It was in 1944 during those same difficult years that he wrote the song that has come to mean so much to us, "Ever again a longing rises." It was put to music in 1948 by

Winifred Dyroff. In 1958 Gladys Mason translated it into English, and it was in the Wheathill songbook. After the collapse that finally came in 1961, these words took on fresh meaning for us all. Verses 1, 4, and 6 follow:

> Ever again a longing rises,
> Again we look t'ward a time
> When into darkness, gloom, and trouble,
> Eternity's bright light will shine.
>
> Again the old traditions bind us—
> Man as he was, with time-worn ways—
> And yet a path is now made ready,
> Leading to everlasting day.
>
> Again the first new love is living,
> The first belief, steadfast and true.
> O man, awake, and give thy powers
> To Jesus Christ, thy Lord, anew!

If one reads the song in the context of the time, one can see what a deep longing there was for something new to break in from God. The communal form of the first church was there, and the harsh physical conditions ensured the poverty it avowed. But these do not guarantee dependence upon God if everything is based on human strength without the love to Jesus.

After this meeting in the woods there came a human judgment, and Fritz, Heini, Hardy, Emmy Arnold, and Hans Meier were excluded from the brotherhood and household, placed in a very serious exclusion. And that judgment continued the break in Heini's service for a long, long time. This decision might have been seriously questioned by the newer English members (who had become novices or been baptized in the final days of the

Cotswold Bruderhof and had been allowed by the British Home Office to go along to Paraguay). They might have asked, "What is this? We don't understand it." But they were "excused" from the meetings dealing with this serious struggle. They were told: "You would not understand it. It has roots going back before you joined." And so their view of Bruderhof history was seriously—for some finally—curtailed.

In 1942, just in these critical years, the Wheathill Bruderhof was first begun in England. There were only three brotherhood members there at the beginning—our Stanley Fletcher and Charles and Hella Headland. They had stayed behind for the sale of the Cotswold after the emigration to Paraguay. As told by the early Wheathill members, it was a time of a wonderful outpouring of the Spirit of God in a spirit of love and enthusiasm. Later on the Hindleys were sent there, and then others—the Hindleys particularly to get the farm going. In 1943 the Arnold Masons and the Pauls were also sent from Primavera to England. Through a falling away from the love to Christ and to the brothers, the early love in Primavera and in England was lost.

Although the ones excluded in 1942 had been accepted back by 1944, the inner situation was again getting so difficult that Heini and Hardy were beginning to meet, although it was forbidden them. They were both in the transport department, driving wagons, but they lived in different communities. They would meet halfway and speak a few words before going on. The inner condition of the community was pretty impossible.

It must be very shocking to those of you who have never heard this reported before to hear that impossible conditions prevailed in a life based on love to Jesus and love to the brothers. But *if you take away the love to Jesus*, the love to the brothers grows cold, and this was what had happened. A bureaucratic approach to community life had gained control, a humanistic approach centered not on God but on the brotherhood, not on the united church but on "the will of the people," and not on the leadership of Jesus but on that of Hans Zumpe. For the brotherhood is not the center, the services are not, but Jesus is.

In the year 1944 there was another crisis, and this time a much larger group was excluded. (I think it was sixteen brothers and sisters.) Heini, Hardy, and Fritz were sent away from the community—separated from their families. And Heini was away the longest—nearly two years. When they left, they had to shave off their beards, were not permitted to wear the Hutterian clothing, and each had to fend for himself with G25 (guaranies—in 1944 roughly a Paraguayan worker's wage for a day). Eventually Heini got himself a job at a leper colony in the southern part of Paraguay, managing the farm there.

Speaking about this in later years, Heini said what a blessing the time was to him inwardly, because it brought him so low—and to be brought low is to be brought near to the kingdom. But it was a time of anguish and torment, quite apart from his longing for the family. He was told that he had to give up his ideas or not return. He was told that his love to Jesus had no place in our community life—also that his concentration on the Gospel of John was simply emotionalism and piety. Well, he did hold to his love to Jesus yet was finally allowed to live in the household; all but one of those excluded with him had long since returned. (As of now, one is still away.)

First Heini went to Loma Hoby with Annemarie and the family. Just over a year later they lost a child and experienced great love towards them from the community through this second loss— another had died at the Cotswold Bruderhof. During 1946 a third community had been built up at Primavera—Ibaté. After Fritz Kleiner was called into eternity in December 1947, Heini and Annemarie moved with their family to Ibaté.

A very important visit to Primavera in 1950 was made by Samuel Kleinsasser Vetter of Sturgeon Creek in Canada and John

Wipf Vetter of Spink Colony in South Dakota. This was the second such visit from our Western Hutterian brothers since Eberhard Arnold's America journey in 1930-31. These two brothers spent about two months in Primavera, visiting us out of love and bringing with them a consignment of practical aid—clothing and all sorts of other things. In the latter years older members have told about that time with great sorrow, because those two brothers were not treated with the respect and love due to them.

These brothers sensed that there was something missing in the community, as their brothers had sensed during the first Cotswold visit in 1937. So in 1950 they asked that we take on certain "points" that are traditional amongst the Western colonies. (I have mentioned these traditions before in connection with Forest River.) The brothers had a series of these points from their rules of church order. The next day our brothers brought an equal number of points and said, "We'll accept yours if you will accept ours." Now this was a very disrespectful response, and not in a spirit of seeking unity. I remember Fred Goodwin in particular, before he died, speaking with great sorrow about our treatment of the two brothers.

When these two days of serious confrontations took place, Heini and Will Marchant had already left Primavera on their way to the United States. They had been sent to raise money and were gone for about ten months, during which they met the Potts and Rhoads families. In 1952-53 Heini made another trip to the States—this time with Annemarie—when they got to know the Clements and others. As our history turned out later, one can feel that on these journeys the seeds of Woodcrest's beginning were laid.

When Heini had moved to Ibaté, his service—first as a school teacher, then as a witness brother, and finally on the mission journey to the States—meant so much that he was reappointed to the service of the Word on September 26, 1951, ten years after he had been removed. Two years later in 1953 he was reconfirmed in that service. It is important to know that in the years after the death of Eberhard (1935) until the year 1962, there was in our Eastern communities no Elder, nobody who had been formally appointed or confirmed in that kind of leadership. For a short time in 1940-41 Heini, as the only confirmed servant, would have amounted to that. But for the nearly two decades that Hans Zumpe assumed control, there was no named Elder, and because of that there was something lacking in the church order, which in 1962 was finally restored.

I cannot tell here the whole story of Wheathill, but tragedy was also there—a series of crises, one after the other, as a result of this same deeply damaged church order. Brothers who were sent to Wheathill from Primavera to straighten things out were themselves straightened out later by somebody else coming up with a change of direction, but none came with the fundamental basis and clear foundation of love to Jesus. The beginning at Woodcrest, however, was a time when God made it possible for this love to Jesus to be rekindled, despite the problems in Forest River. In doing the service at Woodcrest, Heini, with Annemarie, was free to hold to his father's direction, and he was also protected in that. (One of the main reasons Heini was sent to North America was that people did respond when he went around begging for money for the hospital. It was said by Hans Zumpe about him, "One does not kill the goose that lays the golden egg": for Heini to be in Woodcrest would be a source of help for Primavera and Europe.)

Well, that gives a bit of background. I have not always mentioned names. I didn't because I wanted to reassert what I said at the beginning: On this earth there is always a spiritual struggle going on; *the two atmospheres are always in conflict*. It is essentially the atmosphere that matters, not individuals, even where it has been necessary to use names to avoid confusion. There is a spirit in this world that wants to destroy the brotherly life based on love to Jesus, and that spirit wants to destroy it right now, right here among us. Every one of us has the responsibility to seek that love through which we may live the first commandment "to love God" and the second commandment "to love the brothers." Then the brotherly life can be lived, and this is what we seek together. I wanted to give this background before getting into 1959 and the following years.

# 8
# A Turning Point

The year 1959 begins a period that is very difficult to report, a period when a great many human failures and failings were revealed. The purpose of reporting this period (as I have said before) is not to point at individuals. The spirit that we want to oppose in this world is active in every one of us, and we cannot divorce ourselves from it and from the sins of others by saying, "Oh, I could never do such a terrible thing." Jesus certainly said, "I have come to undo the works of the devil," but we cannot even participate in that unless we give ourselves completely into Christ's power. Just at this most central point of surrender to Jesus, a fundamental departure from him had been taken by the Bruderhof. It was taken with the same deviant thinking as in all human social movements, and that kind of thinking is always a delusion: that through one's own idealism or even one's own beliefs, one can effect any basic change that solves the problems of mankind. Any such change can happen only through discipleship and dependence upon God and his power.

I have mentioned earlier that 1959 was a turning point in our recent Bruderhof history. This crucial year began with a struggle for Miriam Way,* a young novice sister who had come to us in Woodcrest two years earlier. As Miriam grew closer and closer into the life of the church, resistance began to build in her that was not in accord with her own will but even opposed to it, quite unlike the experience of any other novice in our recent history. It became evident in time that here was a case of possession—not a case of mental illness or schizophrenia, but a case of possession. As Heini said later, taking up this fight against darkness in February 1959 represented a fundamental turning point in our history. As in the struggle for Lotte Henze in our early Sannerz time (1925)—and on a larger scale in Johnann Christoph Blumhardt's Möttlingen struggle for Gottliebin (1842-43)—it definitely represented a turning point for Woodcrest and for our Bruderhofs in the States. Even though the battle for this one person did not seem to end in a full redemption for her personally, it began a breakthrough in our Bruderhof struggle for renewal in a return to Christ as Center.

We hadn't known that her parents, particularly her mother, had been active in dealings with the occult. In the middle of May, in an effort to find some answer to the inner struggle for Miriam, Annemarie flew home with her. Their house was a place noted for strange, unexplainable happenings. She needed to confront that spirit in her home and to free herself from its power, to say publicly she would have nothing more to do with it.

I wish I could say that was the end of it all, but it was not. Later she had to be hospitalized for her own protection, and as with Lotte Henze, we never did come through to a full freeing. She had a deep respect for Heini and Annemarie and they kept in contact over the years. But if we think of what happened in 1959-1961, we have to conclude that the fight for Miriam Way

---

*A pseudonym.

was decisive for the whole Bruderhof movement, and it began with this girl at Woodcrest who suffered from demon possession.

Early in 1959 another visit was scheduled to Primavera, and Gwynn Evans came to us in Woodcrest en route to Paraguay. (Gwynn, as servant, with his wife Buddug had moved to England in November 1958.) He was to have picked up a witness brother or servant from the States to go along with him. Gwynn arrived in Woodcrest on the 10th of February, just ten days after this struggle with the spirit in Miriam Way had become more serious. Three days after Gwynn arrived, Wendell and Pep Hinkey with their baby also arrived back home in Woodcrest from Europe. One of Wendell's tasks had been to go to the Sinntal Bruderhof to help get a financial base going there. I think the Bruderhof *Werkstätten* (Community Playthings in Germany) was already under way, and Wendell taught silk-screening and how to get the best hardwood (beech in Europe) and the right wood-working machinery.

From the very beginning one big problem with the Sinntal Bruderhof was that it was either wholly or partially a gift, without being a place we would otherwise have considered for a new Bruderhof; it was on a very busy road, with no land to speak of. The whole area surrounding the Bruderhof had the atmosphere of the spa there, Bad Bruckenau. Beautiful green meadows or lawns were neatly clipped and sloping down to the Sinn River that passed through. If you looked out from the buildings at any time during the day, you would see people walking along carrying a glass of mineral water. They would take twenty or thirty steps, stop and take a sip, then another twenty or thirty steps and another sip. This sort of thing was going on much of the day. For a growing Bruderhof, it was altogether not an ideal situation.

Still another property called Schondratal had been located for the task in Europe. From what I remember, it was an unfinished, very costly new building deep in a valley somewhere and would not have made a good Bruderhof either. The responsible servant and perhaps one or two others were very keen on it, and many who were not keen were possibly not courageous enough to speak out. But when Wendell Hinkey came to Sinntal, he went to Schondratal and was outspoken in his opposition. And from that moment on he was treated shabbily, in ways that should never occur on any Bruderhof. It affected him so much that when he returned to Woodcrest on the 13th of February, Heini immediately noticed that something was wrong—he looked like a crushed man. Since other servants were already there—I think Balz also— to talk about the upcoming visit to Primavera, they listened together to Wendell and Pep's full report. It was so hair-raising that Heini felt something must be done.

The servants all concluded that Heini should go to Europe to Sinntal to face this disunity openly. Gwynn should go along and support him, because Gwynn also found the report impossible to countenance. It was quite a daring thing to do, our communities not being really united; Heini was in no way recognized as an elder or as *the* Elder or anything like it. And Gwynn had been sent by three brotherhoods on a journey, but here he turns around and returns to Europe! Heini asked the Woodcrest brotherhood if in trust we would let him go to put a question to a brother in Europe. He did not want to tell us the question because it might be unjustified. In trust we sent Heini with Gwynn. They flew on the 19th, and the Kurtz family moved to Woodcrest because of the Miriam Way situation. That could not be left unattended.

During the month Heini was in Europe, there were many meetings—first in Germany and then in Bulstrode—very, very difficult meetings. They were difficult because the Bulstrode brotherhood—first the witness brothers and then the brotherhood—had to understand this whole situation. Can what Wendell and Pep reported really be true? If it is true, what should be done? It was a long and difficult time. The final conclusion was that

Hans Zumpe was overburdened in the service. (Heini had gone to support him in August 1958 because he had been depressed and needed encouragement.) It was clear that the only answer lay in his having a rest from the service of the Word, and the brotherhoods in Europe decided this.

Just before Heini's return home on March 15, Gwynn took Heini aside and stressed the importance of his being careful that the "Arnold influence" did not become too strong in the United States, since Hans Zumpe was no longer in the service to counterbalance that influence. This warning was full of the unforgiveness and hatred that became revealed fully only in 1961. From the beginning of Woodcrest, when so many new people had joined, Heini had been free to live actively for the love to Christ and his unity, as represented by his father. Heini had assumed the past was forgiven and forgotten. On his return to the States he shared his pain only with Mark and Balz. The rest of us heard of Gwynn's warning only a year later.

A few weeks later (April 21) the Zumpe family moved to the States—not to Woodcrest, because Woodcrest was still in the thick of the difficult struggle for Miriam Way. And it was out of the question for the Zumpes to have gone to Oak Lake, for Balz Trümpi and Duffy Black were visiting in Primavera and Uruguay—from the 2d of April until the 21st of June. Since the Kurtzes were back in Evergreen, the Zumpes went there.

Some things that Balz and Duffy experienced in South America were reasons for concern. One was about the young people, particularly the young men in whom there was a strong spirit of macho, of manliness based on ability to ride horses, go hunting, do physical feats, and so on. Another concern was about cruelty. One of the stories I remember them telling was that a gang of boys had managed to get a monkey down out of a tree and with sticks had beaten it to death. That was a profound shock to everybody. What a contrast to the picture of the younger Primavera children playing their *Reigen* (circle games).

Gwynn Evan's arrival at Woodcrest . . .

Buddug with Ibaté kindergarten

Children's *Reigen* . . . Primavera

The young men loved hunting birds and agouti and other animals, as well as ranching with horse and lasso—roughing it out in the bush with a knife in the belt. Because this attitude was growing among the young men and because the Bruderhof was not keen about this direction, it was hard for a young man to choose to stay in the community. (I mention this as a part of the concern that came in 1960 for the future—a concern to become more united in our Bruderhof communities and through this to help one another more.)

In July quite a few went out to Oak Lake for the report of Balz and Duffy: Heini and witness brothers from Woodcrest and Evergreen, Mark and Peggy, Dick Domer, Paul Pappas, and Bob Clement. So the report was made, but during the time of reporting, the situation of the community at Oak Lake became revealed; it was not as it ought to be in Christian life. When the underlying causes of what was wrong were revealed, a crisis developed. So a few days later more help was sent out, more brothers and two sisters. Into that situation came another blow. The Moodys were living there at that time and they had a stillborn little baby on July 18, 1959.

It was a time of inner struggle and inner distress, trying to find the way in many things, for instance in brotherhood meetings: someone in the brotherhood would try to clarify things by citing an incident of wrong done, only to have someone across the circle say, "No, that's not quite how it was. It was like this," and he would retell the incident. Then another would no sooner correct him than he would be corrected by someone else. And this correcting would go back and forth until everybody was confused and nobody knew what was what. The situation was very difficult and led to the same conclusion as in Europe: the feeling that it was also just too much for the servant and the housemother, Balz and Monika Trümpi. They should withdraw and have a rest, and the whole hof should relax a bit and make a pause for inner refreshment.

As people took in what had happened and what the situation was, they became freer to raise questions they had had all along. Things that should have been fought through years before were brought up. That shouldn't happen on this way of unity; everything should be cleared immediately. All had to recognize their common failure in letting things go and grow to a point where a breakdown was unavoidable. People in Oak Lake were fearful that at the end of the period of withdrawal the servant and housemother would come back, and they didn't want to face that possibility. Woodcrest was in the middle of all this, going back and forth to talk with those involved to try to get everything clear. Some were fearful and others were angry, and all I can say again is that it was a mess!

There could not be a resumption of the situation that had prevailed before. So it was decided on all of the places that that family should not return to Oak Lake, and during their time of withdrawal from the community, they moved to the vicinity of another Bruderhof. At this point a mistake was made—quite a costly mistake. Since we wanted to give the parents a chance to be by themselves for inner quiet and needed rest, we asked the Bloughs to take care of the children at the Bruderhof while the parents lived nearby.

The Bloughs had come to the Bruderhof with no children, but by this time they had two, and shortly after that they took on this very difficult task. In spite of the fact that Dwight and Norann did a wonderful, loving job of caring for them, it was an unhappy situation. We saw it afterwards as a real mistake to take on the care of the children without their parents. It was not understood and only caused more problems. It could have all turned out differently.

So there was again a shifting of families—a number moved to Oak Lake and the Moodys moved back to Woodcrest. The Kurtzes went from Evergreen to Oak Lake, where Mark did the service of the Word, and the Mommsens and Pappases moved there too. That left me, a witness brother, as the only one at Evergreen with any service, so Duffy and Susie Black came to us. But the Bloughs had come in June of 1959 and to my immense relief had taken over the school again.

In the late summer there was a baptism preparation in Woodcrest, with a group consisting of Paul Mason, Anneli Arnold (now Maria Maendel), Emma Maendel, Dan Maendel, Johann Christoph Arnold, and David Maendel. The group withdrew to a farm house on the way to the Minnewaska State Park. It was a difficult time for Heini and Annemarie. The struggle for Miriam Way continued, as did the repercussions from the crisis in Oak Lake. Mark Kurtz, the servant at Oak Lake, phoned Heini constantly. So for most of that preparation time Heini was not even present. He traveled back and forth between the farm house and Woodcrest making phone calls. James and Harriet Alexander held the group meetings when Heini was not there. But finally on September 7, 1959, there was the baptism of Paul Mason, Anneli Arnold, David Maendel, Johann Christoph Arnold, Katie Maendel, and Sibyl Sender. (Sibyl and her husband Ramon had been in the previous baptism preparation. They had been separated but had hoped for reconciliation in coming to the Bruderhof. Unfortunately, this did not happen.) Heini took this baptism with Gwynn Evans, who had come to Woodcrest for talks with Trümpis and Zumpes. The following day Christoph Arnold, Dave Maendel, and Katie Maendel started their studies at Orange County Community College in Middletown, New York.

Beginning in October 1959 there was still another period of struggle to find again the right basis in our community life. During the years following World War II, many had come to the Bruderhof out of movements of social concern, some reacting strongly to churches and churchiness and false piety. We wanted therefore to be all the more careful with the use of the holiest words and to be chaste with religious expressions, as I stated previously. It cheapens the deepest things to be talking constantly about the Lord this and the Lord that as though we were speaking about grass and bushes and common objects. But then one thing must always be clear: that we are Spirit-led, and that means led by the Holy Spirit of God and none other.

Of course these same social movements had ideas more human in their base than Christian. So in 1959 and 1960 we also struggled over their human moralisms and equalitarian concerns—even with some in the brotherhood, because these questions were raised seriously. Certainly these equality concerns came the strongest whenever anyone in the services took to himself his responsibility and the trust shown him and got proud about it—or even became abusive towards others and mistreated them. The questions came, "Does the answer maybe lie in not having any services? How would it be if we didn't name anybody, but everybody has equal responsibility and nobody is appointed to have special responsibility or leadership?"

Some of us had the reaction to this from the beginning, "No, no, you can't do that, that is unscriptural; in the New Testament it simply is not that way and it won't work that way." And coming with these questions—mostly buried or hidden but occasionally very direct—were quite personal attacks on individuals in the service of the Word, and particularly against Heini.

Others asked, "Doesn't that inflate pride to have a servant of the Word, to have witness brothers, housemothers, and different appointed services like that? Shouldn't everybody be equal and do pretty much the same kind of work?" Some years later this was referred to as a desire to have everybody be a little gray Easter bunny. This is one of those things that looks good on the outside but has a devilish divisiveness underneath. In case after case of this sort, there was underneath a desire for power. Heini and Annemarie fought that spirit in every way they could. But

since many of the questions were directed against Heini because
he was a servant of the Word, he was often knocked out of action,
and others had to try to speak up for him.

Those of us who knew Heini over the years know that during
his whole lifetime he had a very genuine, and thorough-going
social consciousness, a concern and love for the poor, and a
willingness to give up everything for their sake. He was concerned
about our standard of living, that it doesn't get too high, that we
are grateful and do not waste food or have a despising attitude
toward it. But he also represented generosity and love and that
the main thing is unity. If the effect of any of these social concerns
is to break up the unity, they are devilish (as are also concerns
about equality). And we experienced again and again that someone
would come along with the question: "Are we doing enough for
the poor?" Objectively it could be a valid concern. But when it
came with a needle of accusation in it and when one fought it
through, underneath would often be a very proud person who
wanted power and who wanted to be listened to, and that would
bring division. Believe me, these things were hard to discern
because so often they looked so good on the surface.

Another very human tendency that Heini tried to fight was that
of coming under law, also in little things. Once when he came
back from a trip he said, "Every time I go on a journey and return
to Woodcrest, I find that some rules have been made." This surely
did not mean that everyone should do as he liked. The crucial
thing is the spirit of unity, that we agree to behave in certain
ways and do certain things because we are all in innermost
agreement—not because there is a rule. A hard battle was waged
against rules that kill.

In the first years we were very poor. After the fire we lost the
whole housemother room and everything in it, all of the food
stores, all the records for Community Playthings—who the
customers were, who had things coming to them, who had paid

and who hadn't paid—all that was destroyed in the fire. And we really felt it. The money just did not come in early enough for us to see how the hof was going to be supported in the coming days. But somehow it always did come in, and we were always carried through. In between it was even possible sometimes for Woodcrest to send large gifts of money to Primavera or to Wheathill. So there were occasions when suddenly an unforeseen sum of money would come in, for instance from an inheritance or something like that. And I was astounded when, in the midst of being poor and not having enough, Heini would say, "Let's celebrate this donation and everybody have ice cream for supper!" Ice cream was something we scarcely tasted then. Someone was sent down to New Paltz to the Dairy Queen and would bring home enough to feed the whole community—a loving, generous impulse that we know was also in Eberhard. At such moments one is thankful for what God gives, and things are not measured in a stingy way, penny by penny.

When Heini had returned from Europe early in 1959, he had told about one occasion on his journey. He said that before things became clear, he felt there was a very hostile atmosphere in the Bulstrode brotherhood towards him. And he said how glad he had been to have his return ticket in his pocket. Now legalistically speaking, on a longer trip you should take your ticket to the steward to hold. One of the supposedly church-order questions that was put was: "Didn't Heini do wrong in keeping his ticket in his pocket?" Maybe it was out of the usual order, but the whole situation was not in order. It was a situation of hostility and crisis, in which (according to one of Heini's word pictures) we are like a flock of sheep. If you have a big flock of sheep in a field and there is one gate and the sheep get into a panic, instead of going in order through the gate they get to jumping on each other, dashing into each other, and hurting one another. And that is how we act, we human beings.

Then the question of having services hinges on the matter of
trust, which is the foundation of a Christian life together. Look
at the whole range of trust betweeen two extremes. If my aim is
to be perfectly safe, then I take the attitude: "Well, I am not
going to trust anybody, I am just going to look out for myself,
have my own money, my own everything. I won't trust anybody,
and I am going to look out for number one!" And if a person
goes all the way in that direction, he is eventually either
imprisoned or he is hospitalized for mental illness, because we
are not created for isolation; we are created for fellowship. That
is the one extreme.

The other extreme is Christian community, being "of one heart
and one soul," as it says in the New Testament. And you cannot
be of one heart and one soul without trusting. And if all of us
entrust ourselves completely to the Church—also if we entrust
ourselves to the Elder and he entrusts himself to us—then we
open ourselves and make ourselves totally vulnerable. Any of us
can be deeply hurt if the trust is betrayed. And so it is a choice.
Are we going to take that risk of being hurt, with no guarantee
that we won't be, because we are all human beings? Or do we
move back along the scale and find some other in-between place
where we will say, "Well, yes, I will trust this much, but that
much I won't trust." But since we have chosen and do choose a
total war against all works of the devil—all separation—we seek
to be of one heart and one soul, united with the Church. Therefore
we open ourselves to one another, and we make ourselves
vulnerable.

Now the bad times in our history usually, or often, involve
betrayal of that trust—not always on purpose, sometimes it was
not meant like that, but there have also been times when it was
something deliberate. Thus some of the questions that were put
to Heini at this time in the fall of 1959 were really pretty nasty.
In one case a witness brother in Evergreen hid his ambition behind

his questions of equality (these are mostly a screen for wanting "to be more equal than anyone else," as was said earlier). Mark flew from Oak Lake to Hartford for talks that he and I had with this brother, then talks with Heini—back and forth—and it led to this brother's exclusion.

Right in the middle of that situation and just as it was beginning to get very serious, Hans and Anne Wiehler's first baby Dirk died. We turned from everything and gave our attention to this terrific loss—this young couple married exactly a year on that day! And when we had done all we could and had had the last meeting with little Dirk, there we were in the very difficult situation of someone having raised questions towards Heini that were absolutely way off. They were based on a humanistic idea of equality that had no basis in Scripture and no basis in history for ever having worked. Tragically, we had to turn our attention back to this attack again. So the fight was, you see, first in Europe, then at Oak Lake, and then at Evergreen.

At one point this same kind of question was raised still again: should services be named? It had been raised so often that Heini finally said: "All right, tonight we will have a brotherhood meeting; we will call in one of our members who is outside trying to find the way back to the brotherhood; and we will have a talk with him. But I will not be present, I won't even be in the room." The witness brothers were not to speak, and it was agreed that the meeting be taken by brothers and sisters who had no special service. I don't know what the person to whom they were talking thought about that meeting, but it was a meeting that was a turning point for Woodcrest. After it was over, the brothers and sisters really found their voices and said, "We'll never, never do a thing like that again." One sister said it was like a body without a head. All said, "We are never going to fall into that direction again. It is unbiblical, it has nothing to do with the New Testament, or with Jesus' way."

But even that wasn't the end of it all. The question was then raised by three or four brothers in Woodcrest as to whether all of these strenuous struggles weren't wearing Heini out, and in a way you could see they were: he had very little energy and looked poorly. It was asked whether he shouldn't have a rest. But the way it was put was that he should have a total rest from the service. Someone even suggested that it should be for three months. And our doctor Milton's name was brought in, although nothing of the direction it turned into came from him. So the action was taken—this was towards the end of October—that Heini and Annemarie went to Kingston and were in some sort of lodgings there. And to their amazement they found that they were no longer in regular daily contact; they were as if cut off. And they couldn't find out anything. They would phone up the hof and say, "How are things?" and would get the answer, "You are supposed to be resting."

As for myself on another hof: I would phone up the responsible brothers in Woodcrest and ask for advice on something and get no answer from them, and I didn't feel free to phone Heini in Kingston—although I think I did it once or twice anyway. Heini was so longing for contact with brothers that he was glad just to hear my voice, and yet we'd been told we shouldn't contact him.

Finally, one of those same brothers at Woodcrest just came right out and said that it is all hypocrisy—you, me, all of us—all I want is power and all you want is power. He spoke in a way that had nothing to do with Christ or the Church, or with belief in Christ and the power of God. He just made wild statements like that about others and himself. And all of us said, "Well, you can speak for yourself," which he was; he was openly stating his position. But like that one couldn't begin to come together in unity. And this brother also had to take a time for consideration. So it was difficult, very difficult—this whole year of 1959. Such a time had still not really hit the communities in Europe or in

Paraguay, except to the extent that the main servant in Europe had lost his service.

Although Heini and Annemarie were back home again, the equality question was not completely settled; it was still being struggled through in the brotherhoods. Heini's leading was very clear in one direction, but he was very strong in his refusal to force people; he waited for people to come to clarity themselves. He was very patient with anyone who approached questions idealistically instead of, let me say, from the Gospels. He would explain, but then he would wait; he would not use pressure. It was because he truly loved people; he didn't want to push or force anybody. I am sorry to say that this was very often taken advantage of.

From the same "equalitarian" spirit another situation developed late in 1959 that had serious repercussions the following year. It all began with the proposed travel of Emmy Arnold from England to the United States. Emmy was back in England at the time; she had first come to the States via England from Paraguay in 1956. She had gone back to England in 1958 because her visitor's visa expired. Although everything had been tried to extend the visa, it had been refused—the only hope left was immigration.

As a matter of fact, on her first round-trip across the Atlantic (1956-58) Hardy Arnold had been working very hard with United States Senator Langer from North Dakota, who tried to put through a personal bill on her behalf—senators can do that for individuals or friends. This personal bill on behalf of Emmy Arnold would have set aside the legal requirements for her immigration and would have allowed her to immigrate into the United States. She was born in 1884 in Latvia, a part of Russia at the time. Therefore, by the immigration laws then current in the United States, she was Russian-born. The Russian immigration quota was so low it was hopeless to wait for the regular channels. But if Heini and Annemarie were American citizens, that would make all the difference, and this is how we finally got around it. They became American citizens and suddenly she was eligible. Early in 1960 she could finally come into the States as an immigrant.

There had been grumbling in Primavera about this travel money (something like $250 at that time): "It might not look like very much money in the States, but down here that is a lot of money," etc. A letter was written to the communities in the States suggesting that it was an unfair use of money to send Emmy to America again, as there were other grandmothers in Primavera, and so on. (Her children Heini and Annemarie and Hardy and Sekunda were in the States.) And there were other questions that indicated lingerings of feeling against the Arnolds as a family, based on something in past years. At that time we had no idea what this was. And so Mark Kurtz from Oak Lake was corresponding with certain brothers in Primavera about these questions. And the questions that came in these letters from Mark were taken positively and seriously down there, so that a whole Bruderhof would break off having prayer in the Gemeindestunde (meeting for worship) until certain questions were cleared up, also because they involved the services there.

Over the years, from 1935 onward, after Eberhard was called into eternity and particularly in the Primavera years, the original fire and love for Jesus had grown cold. The remark had been made, maybe often, that the three brothers, Heini, Hardy, and Hans-Hermann should be separated and not be together on one continent, and now a journey was begrudged Eberhard's widow to emigrate from England to the States, despite their exclusion and forgiveness in the '40s. The deep root of this spirit was revealed to be an opposition to the witness to Jesus that Eberhard had been called to establish.

# 9
# *The Storm Breaks*

The storm that broke in 1960 was related to the correspondence begun the year before between Oak Lake and Primavera about Emmy Arnold's travel money. I quote from a letter written by Art Wiser, who was in Oak Lake at the time and knew the correspondence firsthand. First Art's letter gives some background for this crucial year in our history.

> Until the year 1960 our experience of the *Gemeinde* (church) was entirely in keeping with what is described in the Acts of the Apostles:

Here Art is focusing on the direction and guidance that he experienced and that we experienced in the same way in our first years in Woodcrest. Just here he's not speaking about the problems.

> We human beings were visited again and again by the Spirit of Jesus. His Spirit moved so powerfully that again and again we saw clearly that we human beings are the obstacle, even the opponents of His will, as Eberhard Arnold put it. We

experienced here at Woodcrest in 1958-59 Jesus' victory over demonic powers in the struggle for Miriam Way. In every baptism each of us felt again our original conviction and redemption. We felt again the power of Jesus' call with his judgment and forgiveness.

After one baptism at Oak Lake in 1959, Mark and I, deeply moved, each wrote to the other hofs sharing the experience, mentioning how one of those baptized, a seventeen or eighteen-year-old girl, had wept openly, confessing the mocking attitude she had had. (However, we learned much later that in Primavera there were mocking remarks about our letters. In the Thursday meeting of the servants of the Word, one of the servants had said, "Heini is too emotional." Heini? He did not see these letters till the Woodcrest brotherhood got its copy as the other hofs got theirs, after they had been mailed. And what is too emotional if Jesus' own call to repentance is taken seriously? From childhood I had known the shortest verse in the Bible: Jesus wept.)

About the Bruderhof past we had heard nothing except things that made us long to give our own lives more completely: experiences, particularly in Sannerz and the Rhön, that were alive for us. Emmy (Eberhard's widow) especially brought these to life for us. We heard about the heavy sacrifices in the early years in Primavera, about the lives of children that were taken because of tropical diseases. Philip Britts and Fritz Kleiner (both had died in the late '40s) were alive for us. Their songs and songs from the Sannerz and Rhön times were ones we sang and sang.

Then Art goes on with the story of the Oak Lake/Primavera correspondence:

In the fall of 1959 a letter from Bud Mercer in Primavera to

Mark raised a question about a proposed trip of Emmy between England and the States. Mark wrote back to ask if there wasn't a lack of love in the question and asked how it had come up. In this exchange of correspondence, letters came to the States on behalf of all three brotherhoods in Primavera, saying that there had been a lovelessness and that in this being brought to light, they felt a new call to love. The Oak Lake brotherhood accepted this with joy, feeling ourselves completely united again. There was, however, an uneasiness in the Oak Lake brotherhood about one letter from one brother, and Mark wrote again to him for the brotherhood.

In a final letter to Primavera everything was closed and put under forgiveness, except for this last small question to the one brother.

The servant of the Word in Wheathill had supported all the rest of Mark's letters to Bud and the Thursday meeting (of Primavera servants, stewards, and work distributors). But now, without warning to Oak Lake, Gwynn and the European brotherhoods sent cables to Primavera and to Oak Lake protesting Mark's last letter.

In a letter following their cable, the Bruderhofs in Europe called into question the whole basis of the new direction in America. (On the 30th of March, ten days before this cable was sent, Emmy had returned to Woodcrest from Europe with Burgel Zumpe.)

Now we in the States were facing the question of what to do about the draft, the Selective Service draft for young men. All of our brothers were conscientious objectors, but until this moment none had been required to do their alternative service. We wanted to visit General Hershey, the Director of Selective Service, to appeal to him and get advice from him so that our young men could do their alternative service on one of our own hofs, but of course as stipulated in the law as to work and the distance from home. (Over the next years there were five cordial meetings with General Hershey, and our request was eventually granted.) But nobody knew what it would be like to go to Washington for this first meeting to talk with General Hershey and make our proposal. We knew that during World War II Tom Potts had been involved in Civilian Public Service camps and that he would have an acquaintance with the situation and would be a real help. (Much later than we wished, he did come to some of the meetings.) So a request for Tom Potts to come over for this had been conveyed to Wheathill and Bulstrode. However, on April 9, 1960, a cable was received in Woodcrest from England:

Feel unable send Tom. Sorry. Writing. Bulstrode.

The very same day another cable came from England to Oak Lake:

Have cabled Primavera that we disagree your further questioning 29 March. Letter following. Greetings. Bulstrode-Wheathill Joint Brotherhoods.

That was a bombshell! What to do? Heini could see right away the danger of cleavage right down the middle, one of the most dangerous times in our history. With different telephone calls back and forth between Oak Lake and Woodcrest and Evergreen — at that time we had no direct lines — we decided that those carrying the main service on the three hofs should meet immediately, that same day, at Reading, Pennsylvania. Heini and Doug from Woodcrest, Mark from Oak Lake, and Paul Pappas and I from Evergreen drove to Reading, and checked in at the YMCA.

Even in a time of difficulty like that when we were trying to think what to do next, Heini's humor was just delightful. When we were checking in at the "Y," we knew that ministers get a discount, and Heini really enjoyed teasing Paul Pappas about being a minister, just the one who so objected to my seminary approach. The expressions on Paul's face were priceless. That evening we thought and thought and thought, "What shall we do?" Here we were suddenly presented with a situation that could mean a real split of the Bruderhof into separate and opposing parties. Up there in the bare rooms of that YMCA, we composed cable after cable and threw them away without sending them.

On April 11, when we were all back in Woodcrest again, we phoned Wheathill and asked for the wording of the cable that they had sent to Paraguay on April 9, so we would know it more exactly. They had sent the following cable:

> Find your letters March 9 to 16 acceptable. Disagree Mark's further questioning 29 March. Letter follows. We communicating States. Warm Easter greetings. Bulstrode-Wheathill Joint Brotherhoods.

On the same day we received a cable from Primavera. It was of crucial importance how Primavera would take Europe's cable, because it was over the correspondence that had been going on between Primavera and the States. When *this* cable came in, it was an enormous relief and joy to Heini. He was standing between Paul Pappas and me as the cable came over the telephone while one of the brothers wrote it down on a piece of paper on Heini's desk. We were reading over Heini's shoulder when suddenly he grabbed Paul and me by our necks and suspended himself between us like a swing. He swung his legs back and forth for pure joy and relief—to know that there was not a split coming in at this point—even though it was still a serious situation. This was the cable from Primavera to Oak Lake and Woodcrest:

Brotherhood joyfully united. Received cable Wheathill-Bulstrode
April 9, which shocked us. Suggest Primavera, England, North
America meeting. You suggest place. Inform England this mes-
sage. Loving greetings. Primavera.

So we did that. We passed the word on to England suggesting
that the meeting should take place in Oak Lake, since the issue
had to do with letters and correspondence with the brotherhood
there. It was quite a conference: Mark and the witness brothers
in Oak Lake; Heini and Doug from Woodcrest; Paul Pappas and
I from Evergreen; Gwynn Evans, Rudi Hildel, and Tom Potts
from England; Georg and Moni and Leslie Barron from Primavera;
Hans-Hermann Arnold from El Arado*; and Peter Rutherford from
Sinntal in Germany. Although Moni at first stayed in Woodcrest
to be with Emmy (since they hadn't seen each other for a long
time), she came out later with Emmy and Annemarie. All came
together for this conference in Oak Lake to determine what was
right. It took some time to get everyone together. By the 1st of
May all had arrived.

The first meeting took place on May 2. Georg was asked as a
neutral party to open the meeting. We sat together in a circle in
Mark's office (the office that was later Dwight's as well as other
servants' over the years). One has to say there was real tension
in the air. Georg said—I'll never forget it—"We're all brothers,
but we are not united. To start, let us each one tell only what he
has done wrong, not what anyone else has done wrong." And
that was the note on which the meeting and the conference began.
That first meeting lasted for three hours. The meetings were not
all easy, but we really tried to seek the truth and the answer to
the rift between the English brotherhoods and the American
brotherhoods—that attitude was the starting point.

---

*Small Bruderhof settlement near Montevideo, Uruguay.

Any history is difficult to follow if everything is new, and if you don't know the people and their names. It is hard to know what the issues are when they are told in cable form. But the picture will be clarified as the story is told, some of it by another portion of Art Wiser's letter that I have already quoted. He writes of this conference, called because of the threatened division:

> This was a serious hour, and something quite different from anything we younger members of the American brotherhoods had experienced. In the brotherhood meetings the English servant of the Word was asked by Gerd Wegner if he had had any feelings against Heini that lay behind the attack on Mark's letter to Hans Meier.

Wasn't there some deeper cause that had to do with feelings against the Arnold family or against Heini and his brothers?

> He at first denied this, but he was confronted with his last warning to Heini just before Heini flew back to the States in 1959.

Art now refers to what I have told in the previous chapter of Gwynn's parting warning to Heini about "Arnold influence" (since Hans Zumpe had lost his service), which Heini had shared only with Mark and Balz:

> Then, after the cable and letter attacking Mark's letter came, Mark and Heini felt it should be shared with the witness brothers. That was the first time I heard the phrase, "Arnold influence," or that there was any feeling against Heini in the sense of the influence or direction that he represented.

The meetings progressed slowly but did come to some tentative conclusions, so that it was possible, two days after the meetings began, for a cable to be sent to all the Bruderhofs on the other continents: "All together in Oak Lake seeking truth; all grateful for talks. Warm greetings." And then the cable to each Bruderhof was signed by the brothers who came from there. Now, continuing from Art's letter:

> These meetings ended with Gwynn, Tom, and Rudi asking for forgiveness and a chance for a new beginning, and saying that Mark's call to love and a repentant heart spoke especially to them. Georg, Paul, Mark, and Heini accompanied Gwynn, Tom, Rudi, and Peter Rutherford to England. In the Bulstrode brotherhood Hardy asked the English servant if he had not lied to the Wheathill and Bulstrode brotherhoods in his handling of the letters and cables. Then another brother stood up and said he knew that the brother had lied, and only then did he admit it. There was deep distress in all three European brotherhoods. The suggestion was made from Europe and accepted in Primavera and El Arado, that one of the Primavera communities and El Arado be moved to Europe to strengthen the brotherhoods and services there (because at that point there were no more servants of the Word left in Europe at all). These moves took place late in the summer of 1960. It was an extremely difficult time, but we in the States felt that we had been led through, and that through this struggle, we were bound even more together in a unity among all our communities.

Meanwhile, in June (1960) something very, very serious became revealed about Hans Zumpe, the main servant of the Word of Europe, who had lost his service previously and was still with us in the States. It came out that he had been living in adultery for years, and it was impossible to come to church discipline and forgiveness because his attitude was not one of repentance but even one of resistance. Then too he was not legally allowed to work to support himself outside the Bruderhof, and the time allowed him to stay in America on a visitor's visa was running out. So we decided he should return to Germany, and he did. In the following years there were many attempts to reach out to him by letter, by phone, and by visits. He was asked to seek repentance in order to find reconciliation, but he never did, and his life was tragically ended in 1973 in a plane crash.

Of all who had gone over to Europe in May 1960, Heini was the first to return. He came back on June 26, bringing with him to Woodcrest Bette Zumpe (now Bohlken). At the end of June Hans-Hermann flew to El Arado with Alan Stevenson and Leslie to present the suggestions to the brotherhood there, to get the wheels moving for the closing down of El Arado and one Primavera community, and to arrange a charter jet flight to Europe for all these people. In the meantime more help had been sent to Europe: Wen Hinkey, Gerd Wegner, Jack Melancon (who had been baptized very little over a year), and Mark's wife, Peggy. Then Hans-Hermann came back from El Arado and moved to England with Fran and Pearl Hall, both brothers in the service of the Word. All that was in the hope of strengthening the communities in England and Germany.

On July 30 there was a cable sent round the places in North and South America as follows: "Joyfully united brotherhood— stand with Bertha and all in faith Christ's victory. Bulstrode." After her stroke, Bertha Mills was in very, very serious condition.

So with the decision to close El Arado in Uruguay in this critical hour, it was decided that the Loma Hoby Bruderhof would also be closed down, and the hospital with it. Most of the services of the hospital for the neighborhood had become redundant because of the presence of a better hospital in the nearby Mennonite colony. And El Arado had not yet become an established Bruderhof. Those two hofs were closed, and 176 people from South America went to Europe. Unfortunately this group had not experienced the struggle and the victory in England, and to some extent it made the going in Europe difficult all over again. Georg was then the servant of the Word at Wheathill; Hans-Hermann Arnold, who came from El Arado, was the servant at Bulstrode; and Jörg Barth, who came from Primavera as an appointed servant, was the servant at Sinntal. And Leslie Barron, a witness brother, went to support Hans-Hermann at Bulstrode.

This move from South America to Europe was quite an adventure. Many had grown up in Paraguay and had never even seen a big airplane—then to walk on board the chartered Boeing 707 full of brothers, sisters, and children dressed in a hodgepodge of odd-looking clothing! We did not have a Hutterian *Tracht* at the time. One hundred and seventy-six people flew to Europe on the 24th of August. Three days later, as if to defy all the heavy seas of 1960, we had the wedding of Mike and Shirley Brandes at Woodcrest.

Now the Bruderhof at Evergreen had never fully found its feet as a functioning community—one could perhaps say similar to El Arado. Earlier that summer while so many were in England, there had been a struggle—as there had been pretty continuously—to find the way as a brotherhood and as individual brothers and sisters to a life of love to Jesus, without self-seeking, self-will, and pettiness. As an Evergreen witness brother, Paul Pappas came home early from England to help.

Then quite suddenly on August 8, 1960, on an all-day trip of the Woodcrest preschool groups, Wen and Pep's little son Peter died. It was a great shock—he was five years old, a jolly, active, robust boy. His kindergarten group was on a field trip to the Bronx Zoo in New York City, and he got separated from the others. Not knowing where else to go, he had gone back to the car, climbed inside, and was found unconscious on the back seat with a terribly high temperature. Though rushed to the hospital there in the Bronx, he did not pull through. At first it was thought to be heat prostration, but the final diagnosis was viral encephalitis. (Of course the father, who was in England, had been told

The hospital at Loma Hoby . . .

Charter flight arrives, Europe—1960

immediately, and he and the brothers who were there had flown
back home again.)

Only one day before the burial, there came an attack on the
church in Evergreen, which I introduce with a few more words
from Art's letter:

> A child, Peter Hinkey, died while his father was in England,
> helping to face the problems there. On the next day when Wen
> returned to this loss, there was a meeting in Evergreen, where
> they were thinking in silence of Peter Hinkey and his parents.
> After Merrill, who had the responsibility there, had suggested
> the song, "All poor men and humble," a certain brother walked
> out of the meeting, saying out loud, "I can't stand this hypocrisy."

What was this accusation of hypocrisy referring to, and what
was behind this totally unexpected outburst? Well, there was a
stunned silence, and everybody who was in the room just
scattered. They went out in all directions for a walk to try to get
their bearings. The following day most of us were to go over to
Woodcrest for the funeral. Yet we were in the midst of this very,
very serious situation, because this outburst had occurred in a
meeting thinking of the little boy and his parents.

The burial was on the 10th. Immediately following—on the
11th and 12th—Heini, Doug, and Mark were coming over to
Evergreen during the day and having to go back again in the
evening because it seemed that Bertha Mills would also pass into
eternity at any moment—her situation was that serious. Heini
and Alan Stevenson were going back and forth again on the 13th
(the day our daughter Joyanna was born). That same day there
was a brotherhood meeting in the evening. The brother who had
said it was all hypocrisy had told us (for his wife and family),
"We're leaving. We don't want any more talks or to clear anything

up, we're just leaving. Please make it possible for us to leave."
And they did leave, a pretty bitter pill for all of us in that time
of sorrow and crisis. The very next day came the news of Moni
Barth's stroke in Sinntal—another blow.

Maybe we now have some feeling of how these events piled
up, one on top of the other. Really, it felt as if a hand beyond
human minds and human hearts was reaching in and shaking up
the church—here and there and everywhere—in an effort to
totally destroy and break apart what had been given and established
by God.

And as we have seen, the inner situation at Evergreen was
extremely difficult in this whole summer of 1960. Brothers had
had to make many journeys to Europe and between the hofs here,
and there wasn't a week in which there wasn't some real blow
draining the brotherhood's strength. Heini would turn this way
and he would turn that way, and brothers very young in the
community had to be used to do very sensitive tasks. They were
sent here and sent there. We might talk about looking forward
to when things would be "normal," knowing that there was no
such thing. During that summer we didn't have the strength to
go on, but we didn't know it, and so we kept struggling in the
Evergreen brotherhood. Heini made many trips over to help us
out, to think what to do: how to reshuffle those in the service of
the Word between the three hofs, which had already been done
time and again.

Meetings continued, trying to find a way out. What can we
do? The family who requested to leave, had left; others were
tottering and shaking in their faith, not even sure if they could
continue on this way. As a functioning brotherhood, Evergreen
broke down completely. Kathy and I were invited to Woodcrest
with our two-week-old baby, because we had lost our bearings
too. They made the high school cabin room ready for us and
called us over. We experienced in a very real way what it means

to be carried in the arms of the church when we needed that kind of support.

From there we went back to Evergreen for a series of meetings, trying to figure out how to reshuffle between all communities those few who were still left in the service after the struggles. One family was moved here and another there, and then again another family and another, and so on. How were we to rearrange the composition of our hofs so that this Bruderhof could find its bearing and go forward as it should?

Then in early September, after we had wrestled with the question of how to shuffle these services and having no answer, there came one of those meetings where Heini suddenly came out with something that nobody else would have dreamt of. He said, "Maybe it's crazy, but why don't we close down Evergreen?" And that was the suggestion, that we would staff the place with only two caretaker families. After everyone got over the first stunning effects, it looked as if that was really the answer. We closed down the hof, staffing it with two families at a time for the whole following school year. In their care were also the few high schoolers who kept attending high school in Winsted until the future was more sure. The place was simply maintained, something like a Bruderhof House. The caretaker families were to be changed every couple of months, and the whole Evergreen household would move to either Oak Lake or Woodcrest.

During the first half of September, therefore, we again had a series of moves, and people were getting established after switches to make room on the other two hofs. (A year later this "maybe it's crazy" suggestion led to the one possibility for the immigration of all those who came up from Primavera. They could occupy that empty hof, with housing and a shop all ready to go.) The Blough and Mow families both moved to Woodcrest between September 5 and 10. Dwight went pretty directly into the school to begin a very wonderful period of years of work with the children.

On September 11 Mark's father, Pop Kurtz, died. Mom and Pop Kurtz had been in Woodcrest since its beginning. Again there was a death in the midst of changes. Yet with this series of moves, one felt that the hofs in the States were stabilizing and finding their feet. And we hoped it was happening in Europe with the large group that had gone over on the plane from South America. In November Heini made a short trip to England to visit and see how things were.

That Christmas 1960 we attempted a choral work with solos—the first time for us in America—*The Christmas Story* by Heinrich Schütz. Dwight's approach to the solos was so unaffected, so much from his heart, that it was always a special occasion to hear his clear tenor voice. The many long recitatives are not very melodic, but they tie the whole thing together in one story. The Meiers (Hans and Margrit), who were visiting us from Primavera, were able to take part. We worked hard and it was wonderful—so much so that in the contact with Westtown and Pendle Hill, we asked them if they would like us to come down and do a concert. And they said yes they would. So in early January 1961, the whole choir from Woodcrest (grade 6 up) went to Philadelphia and out to the Media Friends Meeting House to sing *The Christmas Story*. After a sumptuous supper at Pendle Hill, we drove home in all our cars and vans on terrible winter roads. Out we jumped by the vanload to push the heavy cars strewn ahead of us—haphazard and helpless on those icy hills before the turnpike. What laughter, what fun together as we pushed all those stranded vehicles. Unforgettable! It was a wonderful ending for the year.

# 10
# *Aftermath*

I would like to begin this next serious account by quoting again from the letter of Art Wiser that I used earlier. He writes about the time after the leading servant of the Word had to leave the Bruderhof because of the serious sin revealed in his life, and about things relating to it that lead us right into the shaking year of 1961:

> After the enormity of Hans Zumpe's sin was revealed in June 1960, Emmy Arnold came very hesitantly to Heini in Woodcrest and asked him if it would be right for her to have her Darmstadt diary, in which she herself had written down Eberhard's last words in the few days before he died.

This is Emmy's personal diary, not only with Eberhard's last words in the hospital, but with all the experiences she had with her husband during his last days.

> That diary had been taken from her by Hans Zumpe when she had been excluded sixteen or eighteen years before, and it was not returned to her when she was back in the brotherhood.

Hans Zumpe had said, "The diary is not good for her." Heini shared this with Doug and me and asked if one of us would write to Primavera to ask for it. Her diary was found and returned. I learned later that Emmy's letters and some of Eberhard's manuscripts were taken from her by Hans Zumpe at the same time. Emmy was so forgiving, so trusting and loyal to the brotherly life, that she had never even shared this pain, feeling that the past should not be brought up.

Then early in the new year Heini raised the question whether Bud Mercer (who at that time was the only servant of the Word in Primavera) was overburdened and had too much to carry, as this seemed to come out in his letters. Heini asked Georg, the servant in Wheathill, if he had that same feeling, and Georg said that he did and that he thought a visit from the States would be a real support to Bud. In this sense we decided to send someone from Oak Lake with Heini on a visit to Primavera. It was decided at Woodcrest that Doug Moody would go with Heini, and at Oak Lake that I [that is Art Wiser] should also go.

Mary and I came to Woodcrest for a few days before the three of us left for Primavera. During that time we spent a precious hour with Emmy. She had in her hand her Darmstadt diary, which had recently arrived from Primavera, and she shared with us very touchingly some of Eberhard's last words.

Doug and Ruby also spent time with Emmy, and for the first time Doug caught the fact that the Rhön Bruderhof was in a deep inner turmoil at the time of Eberhard's death. Later Doug said to Heini and me that he was quite sure that he had heard here at Woodcrest when he was first a guest that the community only found its feet after Eberhard's death because the community had been too dependent on Eberhard. Doug thought a certain brother had said this, but he was not sure. Heini said that he could ask that brother, since we would be seeing him in Primavera. This was all we knew about the painful history of the early forties.

And so it was that on January 28, 1961, Heini and Art and Doug flew to Paraguay, arriving in Asuncion two days later on the 30th. Art continues:

> On the long flight down in the plane Doug and I asked Heini to tell us more about the early '40s. We just could not understand how it could have happened that someone would take from his own mother-in-law, the widow of our beloved brother Eberhard, her only diary and record of his last days. But Heini would tell us nothing. He wanted us to experience Primavera ourselves as it now was, with no prior feelings.
>
> I can only testify to my own excitement and joyful anticipation of meeting brothers and sisters I had never known before, who had stood with us in Oak Lake in very difficult hours the preceding year—I refer to the cables and correspondence of 1960. I went with gratitude and joy and assumed that Doug felt the same. In Asuncion we were warmly received by Bud Mercer, Will Marchant, Karl Keiderling (who had all flown there from Primavera), and by Johnny Robinson and the Asuncion household.
>
> In my first letter from Asuncion I wrote to Mark and Mary at Oak Lake:

> An amazing thing is that at Isla last Friday night, the 27th, the Primavera brotherhood independently reached the decision to ask the communities in the States for help. The first word that Primavera received of the coming of three of us was through our cable that arrived two days late and while they were still in a meeting. Bud says there was an audible response from the brotherhood that was joy, gratitude, amazement. Someone asked, "Did you already cable, and they respond so soon?" And Bud said to us later, "You see, we are not that far apart." He meant that when our hearts are close, we are in touch with each other in a way that overcomes distance. Coming from the

airport, Bud was so moved that he almost wept as he told Heini of the Isla meeting and expressed his joy at our arrival.

Later he came into our room and got Heini and Doug into such a bear hug they almost fell over. Johnny is also just as warm as he could be. He is also a great big man. And Heini is absolutely right when he says you could draw a picture of Johnny by drawing a heart and then putting arms and legs on. At the airport after we had first greeted each other and had felt the joy and warmth from them all, Johnny said of the three flying down, almost exulting in it, "Maybe we have broken the bank account, eh?" And then with a wink, "We can chalk it up to investment."

On the 31st of January the three of us arrived in Primavera in a small plane and again we were warmly received. It was only a joy to be among brothers and sisters. That night we were welcomed in a household meeting at Isla, joint with the Ibaté household. We were asked to report and we just opened our hearts, reporting about Woodcrest and Oak Lake and our gratitude for Primavera's support in 1960.

We have already heard about the struggle over the years from 1935 onward, how a direction contrary to Eberhard Arnold's was brought into the communities, and how Heini and Annemarie and Emmy and a number of others kept in their hearts and also fought for a restoration of the vision and love to Jesus that Eberhard had represented and had been given by God. The journey to Primavera was with the particular concern to reach out to and support the brothers there. At that time there was only one confirmed servant of the Word in Primavera. He had written and asked for a visit, and so our going was a brotherly response.

Heini knew what he might face down there, but he did not convey it to anybody else. Heini did not tell negative stories. Those who went from the States—Art and Doug and the other

Americans later—had all been accustomed to look toward Primavera as the mother church, as the place where the Spirit was strong, the place that founded Woodcrest. We looked in that direction with trust and with love, and that is what came from Heini. We did not know that there were deep-going inner problems. Then in Primavera Doug and Art were hit in the face by things in the atmosphere that they had not imagined. Art continues:

> All this led to a further talk with one particular witness brother, and there Doug brought out what he remembered hearing in the early days in Woodcrest when he was a guest. The statement was in the direction that the community only found its feet after Eberhard's death, because the community had been too dependent on Eberhard. Bud said he had heard something similar at Woodcrest. When we went into it with the brother in question, he said he certainly had felt that, whether Doug had heard it from him or not. And then his face became contorted and he said that Eberhard Arnold had been crammed down his throat and that the main fight of his life had been against Eberhard Arnold and against Hutterianism.

That crass statement opened up the whole chain of events that revealed the spirit that had crept into the community life. It opened up a spiritual battle. It was not against people, but to our great sorrow it involved people.

> It was this confession of this brother and his enmity to Eberhard Arnold, and nothing that any of us did or said, that brought up the question of the past—the early '40s. These were serious and painful days. On Sunday, February 5, Wolfgang and Lisbeth's baby was born without breath; the baby was named Dolores and was buried the next day, February 6. It was a time of grief.

February 7 was the first opportunity in a joint brotherhood meeting to report. I wrote home in one of my letters:

> Our report centered mainly on the attack on Eberhard Arnold. The reactions were so startled, incredulous, that there was almost danger of bedlam. And we made a five-minute pause. From some there was enormous indignation; a few remained like statues.
>
> We sat down again, and this same witness brother came in and made a short statement. He said he had betrayed the Church and lived a lie. He said he had felt and represented that the communities had been too dependent on Eberhard Arnold, that only after his death had the communities begun to find their feet. After a short silence, there were questions to the brother from four or five, and then we asked him to leave the meeting. He had expressed that he wanted to repent and find his way back, and he himself asked for a separation. But this confession and the meeting with him led many to ask for talks. They were mainly confessions, including how Emmy's exclusion took place. These talks were a real burden and pain for Doug and me.

One example of unforgiveness was told to us later by Georg. In 1942 after the three Arnold brothers had been in exclusion *and were united again*, Hans Zumpe had taken on the main service of the Word in Primavera and had said to Georg repeatedly, "See to it that these three brothers never again live in the same community." We were also told that there was a certain cupboard in the Primavera archives that was kept locked. In this cupboard were kept all of the notes and papers that were used later for the book, *Torches Together*, Emmy Arnold's collected writings about the beginning and early years. This cupboard was referred to by Hans as the "poison cabinet."

During the first days of Heini and Art and Doug's visit and while they were trying to cope with incredible and staggering

things, Hans and Margrit Meier returned from the States.
Primavera asked if more help could not be sent down. They
requested that Annemarie, with a witness brother, come to stand
by and support Heini, and that was decided by the brotherhoods
in the States. Then very shortly before they were to depart,
Annemarie had chest pains that indicated heart trouble. Now this
was before the days of jet flight—it took several days to get to
Primavera—and the doctor was not willing to let Annemarie fly
and undergo the stress of such a journey. Annemarie said, "There
is nothing wrong with me; I'm going!" But she was not allowed
to go.

So Gerd Wegner and I went down on February 22, 1961. We
arrived two days later in Asuncion and were met there by Heini,
Art, and Doug. I will never forget what a look of sadness was
on Heini's face, a look of deep-going grief for the Church and
concern for his Annemarie. We went back to Primavera together.
Art reports the following about the time just before we arrived:

> Irmgard Keiderling came one night and said to Heini,
> "Perhaps you do not remember it, but just before his death
> Eberhard had a terrible vision from which he woke with a great
> cry." He had seen a vision of candles representing the Church,
> and he was filled with great joy. Suddenly a hand appeared
> and Eberhard was petrified because he thought the hand would
> extinguish the candles. But no, the hand began to move the
> candles, putting them in each other's places. Where clarity
> should have been was put love, where compassion should have
> been was put clarity, and so on. The picture of the Church was
> thus so distorted and misshapen that Eberhard cried out and
> awoke. He spoke then to the brotherhood and told them about
> the vision and what a terrible danger he saw in it, and he
> pleaded, "Let it not happen!"
>
> Heini not only had not forgotten the vision but had shared

it with us only two or three days before. He said that this was
just what it feels like here now. Everything is twisted; in the
wrong place there is understanding and loving concern, and in
the wrong place there is sharpness.

As I look back today, I have to say that at the time we were
there this distortion was not absent. We were in the same "conflict
of two atmospheres," and it was very hard to find and discern
the right way; it was very, very difficult. The first brotherhood
meeting that Gerd Wegner and I were able to attend was a stormy
one in Ibaté on the Saturday that we arrived in Primavera, February
25. The meetings were joint meetings of all the brotherhood
members from both hofs, Isla Margarita and Ibaté. Here we
experienced again the bedlam that Art wrote of. Something would
be said, and it so agitated others that there would be outcries
from all over the circle; it became impossible to talk or to listen.
And then there would be a pause and Heini would give a cautioning
word before beginning again, "We cannot go on unless we listen
to one another." Then the pattern would be repeated—outcries
and protest followed by another pause. This involved a gathering
of about 150 people.

The brotherhood met again the following morning, Sunday the
26th, and again it was a stormy session, which was then stopped
for a pause in order to become quiet, to listen to the inner voice.
How shall we go on in this impossible situation? Heini asked for
suggestions, and when the circle of 150 gathered again, the
proposal came out of that circle, "Heini, why don't you with
other brothers from the States make a list; you decide who should
be in the brotherhood." Heini right away responded, "No, no,
we cannot possibly do that. We will help in it, but this is something
that must come out of your own circle."

It was suggested that we get together with those who had been
standing very close in the fight to find something new. Together

we would go over the whole list of everybody and make a
suggestion, so that there would be some place to start. It was
said, "Like this it is impossible; we must have a united circle
even if there are only two or three in it; there must be a united
brotherhood, and from a united brotherhood the circle can grow."

And so we got together with Karl Keiderling, Bud Mercer,
and Christoph Boller—there might have been others—but I
believe at least those 3 were there. We went over the list and
read out some names to the entire brotherhood, to everybody,
and 21 of those names were unanimously agreed to by everyone,
with no questions. So there we had it, a group of 21, agreed to
unanimously by all 150 people. Then about 15 more were named
who could be in the new brotherhood after a small question was
cleared up. If that was all right, their names would be added.
And within a day that also was accomplished. Each day more
were added to the growing brotherhood. Within a couple of weeks
it was a circle of 67.

The first six weeks, including the three weeks since Gerd and
I had arrived, were totally exhausting, and the main burdens of
them were on Heini. He had the added problem that we brothers
who were with him were sometimes being too sharp or too soft
or too undiscerning, bringing about more problems rather than
helping to solve them. He carried all this in great love. It was
through these things that the past was opened up. Before that,
Heini did not and would not speak of sins of the past. He left
them alone, but others then brought them up to be free of the
burden of their unforgiven guilt.

It should also be said that in Primavera at that time we felt a
strong support from quite a few. Most of those who had
experienced Sannerz and the Rhön with Eberhard had a memory
of and a longing for a restoration of that Christ-centered life of
love which was lived in Germany. I think particularly of Alfred
and Gretel, Karl and Irmgard, Ria Kiefer, Anni Mathis, Margrit

Meier, and a number of others. Bud and Doris stood very closely together with us. In the younger generation—Christoph and Maidi, Pete and Susanna, Jakob and Juli, Allister and Judy, Jerry and Jane, Seppel—there were many who had a longing in their hearts for something new, something they had never known. The older ones longed for what they had known decades before.

In the evenings after a late meeting we would get together with Heini—something that we will never forget—to end the day together being a bit *gemütlich* (pleasantly relaxed). At those times Heini would open up for us the past, with wonderful stories about his father and his aunt (Else or "Tata," Emmy's sister). Different things there would also remind him of Fritz Kleiner or Adolf Braun, and we would hear about them. It was often very hot, and we would sit sweating and having a drink together, and Heini would tell these stories. It is unforgettable. Later when he left, we went with him on the overnight boat down the river to Asuncion. Then on an evening or two in Asuncion, he took us for a walk through the town and showed us around and used his Spanish. We would go to a little cafe and have coffee together and hear more stories. Those were wonderful times. Heini delighted in taking the brothers out like that and showing them a bit of Paraguay.

Very soon after Gerd and I had arrived, Heini began to feel he should return to the States. Annemarie's health was concerning him very much and his health was concerning us. It was extremely hot down there and he needed to get back to the States. We did not want him to break down under the strain. So on the 8th of March, an extremely hot day, we from the States and maybe eight or ten of the responsible Primavera brothers met at the port in Rosario in a little shed. In this meeting, afterward referred to as the "Rosario Meeting," there came a suggested direction of giving up Primavera entirely and moving all brothers and sisters to the northern hemisphere, either to Europe or to the United

States. I don't think it is possible even now to fathom the magnitude of that suggestion and direction. How could we ever manage that? Immigration into the United States was so very difficult. Later on this direction was decided in all brotherhoods, although it looked utterly impossible. Somehow doors were opened because it was the given thing, the right thing.

At that time the only communication between Primavera and Asuncion—and then by cable to the States—was over the radio. And whatever you broadcast over the radio, you broadcast to everybody in the whole country who might be interested in listening. If it was in Spanish, nearly everyone could understand; if it was in German, there were many Mennonites and Germans who also could understand and would love to listen and learn as much as they could. Sometimes Stan and Hela (if one was in Asuncion and one in Primavera) would speak in French, assuming that very few people knew French. Anyway, we had to develop a code, and so the term "Rosario direction" was the code name we used in referring to this agreement. A few days later it was agreed to by the joint brotherhood in Primavera.

We went by boat down to Asuncion that night, and on the 10th of March Heini left for the U.S.A. Heini wrote the following in 1972 about how he felt at that time:

> I am held particularly responsible for so many having been sent away in Primavera in 1961. In fact, I was not present for most of the brotherhood decisions. I was in the U.S.A. to meet Georg and Hans-Hermann from England and discuss with them the situation of Primavera. I had flown to Buenos Aires with the slow planes of those days.

You had to go a thousand miles south to Buenos Aires in order to get to the States from Primavera.

I had to stay many hours to get a connection to the U.S. In those hours in Buenos Aires I was in deep distress, especially because Johnny Robinson had been sent away; I had been present at this decision. I had also a special concern for the Cocksedge family because Edmund had met me with trust in Primavera and because Edmund, together with Karl Keiderling, was responsible for Ibaté. I knew there were questions to Edmund and Amy. If I had had enough money, I would have flown back to Primavera, particularly because of Johnny Robinson and Edmund Cocksedge.

When I met with Georg and Hans-Hermann in Woodcrest, a cable arrived from Primavera telling of the many families that were being sent away. I know that Georg came to me and expressed his uneasiness about this, and we shared this uneasiness. I asked Georg to come with me to Primavera, which he turned down because Moni wasn't well. And so I flew back with Mark and Peggy to Primavera.

This concern about people being sent away grew out of the terrible anguish of the hour. It is never a question of people—we do not, and may not, point a finger here and there; it is always a question of the struggle for the life and heart of the Church. And the real question is always that of "two atmospheres in conflict"; every one of us has to decide whether he is on the side of Jesus and of love and compassion that give clarity to discern and find the way, or whether he is on the side of power, efficiency, gifts, or anything else that misleads us into a crisis situation.

I have quoted Heini's letter of November 1972 describing his own feeling at that time: if he had had the money, he would have turned back from Buenos Aires and gone back to Paraguay. He was worried that injustice might be done to people who had been asked to take a time of consideration away from the community. From this time on Heini's health was in danger.

Those of us from the States who remained in Paraguay were Art Wiser, Doug Moody, Gerd Wegner, and I. We were there over Easter and were scheduled to leave Asuncion on April 10 to return to the U.S.A. We were expecting Mark and Peggy to come down on April 7 as a replacement. We had gone to Asuncion on our way to the States and were at the airport to meet them. When the plane pulled up on the tarmac, Mark and Peggy appeared at the door of the plane and came down the steps. We were all lined up at a fence, no more than fifty yards away from where the plane stopped, waving like mad. Peggy went right down the line shaking our hands one after another. Things were rather loose in Asuncion—they had not been through passport control or to customs yet, and here they were shaking hands with us who were on the other side of the barrier. But Mark behaved strangely; he backed off to one side and was focusing a camera at us. We didn't know that he was waiting for our reaction to the next thing that happened. Suddenly Heini appeared in the doorway of the plane at the top of the ramp; he was totally unexpected. It had been kept a complete secret, and Mark wanted to get a picture of the reaction of all of us, and he did a good job! That picture is a very striking photograph. (Well, Heini's letter had ended, "And so I flew back with Mark and Peggy to Primavera.")

As soon as we all got to Asuncion House, Heini had to go straight to bed; his health was that poor. In spite of this, they wanted to repeat the surprise when he arrived in Primavera, and so they had him hidden in the back of the truck that came on to the hof, crouched down in a box, in the tropical heat of Paraguay. Everybody was greeting Mark and Peggy when suddenly the box opened up, and like a jack-in-the-box Heini jumped up. But, mind you, he was still not well.

While Heini was there, two brothers mistakenly signed a document with the mayor of the nearby Mennonite colony of Friesland, agreeing to the sale of Primavera under conditions that

61 surprise arrivals . . . Heini's at Asuncion Airport and

at Primavera

were totally unacceptable. As a result, a good part of Heini's trip was used up in trying unsuccessfully to deal with the mess. He had to return to the States after only two weeks, and the alarming results were only straightened out on Heini's return to the States when he went with some brothers to the Mennonite Central Committee headquarters at Akron, Pennsylvania. And so Heini was unable to give adequate attention to his concern for those who were being sent away, perhaps unjustly—for instance the Robinsons and Cocksedges.

Shortly after all this he became ill again. This time the sickness was more serious. He was completely run down and inwardly exhausted, and to top it off he had a severe nosebleed that wouldn't stop. By June 4 he had to be hospitalized, and we feared for his life. The only way the specialist could stop it was by something called "packing" (his nose was packed with gauze or cotton and stretched to the size of a golf ball). It was excruciatingly painful. He was a number of days in Vassar Hospital.

We maintained twenty-four hour watches with him, and it is heartrending to remember. He was in the most awful pain and misery; he could only sleep for ten or fifteen minutes and then would wake again from the pain. One would go in there and sit by his bed, and maybe he would be dozing under his oxygen tent when you came in. Then he would open his eyes and see you sitting there, again a different person on watch. Immediately he would start apologizing for having been asleep. And then if he would drop off again, he would also apologize. He was only concerned about the person who was there, to reach out to him and to be loving. (We should never have subjected Heini to all this well-meant love.)

It was a great loss for us all that he was absent. His judgment and help were very badly needed in England and in Germany, where it was still a crisis situation that needed clear inner direction—direction from the Spirit, which unfortunately we young brothers just did not have enough of. Heini's absence, including recuperation, lasted close to eight weeks; on July 6 for the first time in two months he came to a brotherhood meeting again. And these two months were a time of the most crucial crisis and pain in trying to straighten things out after the collapse in our communities in South America and in Europe.

Just as Heini was on his way to the hospital, an important letter was written by Gwynn Evans from Wheathill on June 3:

Dear Heini,

Two or three days ago I was given your letter to Georg of May 17 to read. This letter together with Doug's and Art's letters to Georg and Art's letter of February 23 from Primavera, which I read last week, have given me very much to think about. There have also been a number of talks with one and the other here in Wheathill since my arrival here about incidents which, though not directly bearing upon those things that come out in the letters from the States and Primavera, have helped me a great deal to get a clearer picture of how things have been going with me since the earliest years of my Bruderhof life; and I feel I have to write to you about this because so much of it directly affects my relationship to you and what I now feel to have been so very wrong in my attitude towards you over very many years.

I am deeply grieved that what I have to write will be a great pain to you, for it will show you how very unfaithful and disloyal I have been to the great love and trust you have shown me. I would do much to be able to avoid giving you this pain, but if things are ever to get clear again, I do not see how it can be avoided, much as it shames me to write it.

It is very clear from your letter and Doug's and Art's that you feel very indignant with me, particularly as the result of what has come out through Alan's revelations. I want to say

right at the outset that I feel that this indignation is in every
way just and right, and though I long for it, I do not feel that
I have any justification whatsoever even to ask for your
forgiveness after coming to see the way in which I have treated
you as well as other members of your family — but particularly
you — and have returned your love and trust with such treachery
and underhandedness. I am left dumbfounded when I ask what
has happened to the warmth of affection and trust which we
once had for one another and when I begin to realize all that
I have done to destroy it. I cannot even conceive how it can
all be put right and a new trust found. And yet without it what
does life hold?

The news of Alan's revelations came as a very big shock
and surprise to me. Though early on in this crisis I realized
that much in my attitude stemmed from the early years in
Primavera, I had completely forgotten the things that Alan
reported. Even now, apart from what Alan has said about my
having been the leader of an anti-Arnold nationalistic clique of
young Englishmen and that I spoke in a hateful way about the
Arnolds in the hall in Isla Margarita and in walks to and from
Loma Hoby before and after Brotherhood meetings, I do not
recall details of things I said nor have I any recollection of
meetings in the hall. But I know that my mood and spirit at
that time were such that I must have given expression to much
that was destructive and treacherous. It is also clear to me that
my influence, both then and since, was much greater than I
realized. In fact I consciously sought to avoid gathering people
to me in the early years both because I knew that the clique
spirit was contrary to the spirit of the Church and because I
was aware that in this lay a special danger for me because of
my background. And yet it is now quite clear that I fell into
the very thing I believed myself to have abhorred.

You will remember, Heini, that in the Cotswold, on the ship, and in Primavera from the time of our arrival up to Advent of 1941 I was fully with you and responded with a full heart to all that you were seeking to bring into being in the community, also with your repeated call to repentance, and I believe that at that time I was prepared to go to all lengths in response to the vision I believed we had been given through the life in the community. Buddug says—and I think she is right—that I had never in my life responded with such emotional warmth to any man as I had to you—though my impression is that it was not primarily to you but to the vision of a life that you particularly were helping us to see. Life at that time offered the promise of a hope that I had not known before and have not known since. Then a proud judging spirit entered in and I meddled in with things that I certainly did not understand and—as I know now—grievously misinterpreted your need at a critical period of your illness, and I dealt with you with great lovelessness and insensitivity. I became suspicious and mistrustful. I became ashamed of my own emotional responses and resolved never to let myself go again as I had done during those early months in Primavera. I became hard and unyielding and suspicious of the emotional responses of others, and it was while I was in this state that Hans Zumpe and I "found one another," as I described it later. From then on I became mercilessly relentless in my quest for and insistence upon clarity and gained a reputation for sharpness, for which I was commended but also feared. I do not think that it would be too much to say that particularly in the period of the crises and the periods that led up to them and followed them, this attitude of mine bordered on fanaticism. It makes me shudder now to think of the hard things I allowed myself to say and to do in this mood—let alone the dreadful perversion of the gospel message and the harm done to people's souls through this. (Ultimately I came to revolt against this too and turned to a permissive humanism, but I will write about this later.)

What concerns me now is the hard-hearted attitude I adopted towards you, Hardy, Hans-Hermann, and Mama; for it was particularly a revolt against what you had represented—which I had come to distrust so—and my own emotional response to it was this hard unyielding attitude of mine. Consequently when the first crisis broke out in 1942 shortly after my baptism, my bitterness knew no bounds and found expression in the things I said not only to the group Alan mentions but in my relations with many. You may remember a talk you tried to have with me in the Isla Margarita schoolwood at this time, when I was taking *Hort* [supervised play]. You were obviously wanting to explain to me how you saw things in relation to the struggle that was just upon us. But I was already so prejudiced that it was soon obvious to you that I was not prepared to listen. I had had a talk with Hans Z. shortly before and came to feel that you, together with Hardy, Fritz, Hans-Hermann, and Mama, were seeking to undermine his position. Clearly I was partisan in spirit and I was concerned to find fault with everything that would help to establish our case. I felt that Hans Zumpe and Georg—but particularly Hans—were being done a grave injustice and that you and the community in Loma Hoby, under the leadership of Hardy, Hans Meier, and Fritz, were seeking to bring division in the church. Some of the things Hans Z. said to me—though I cannot remember them specifically—fostered this impression strongly, but also the things I said to him must have had the same effect on him. I, at any rate, had no ears for the things you were seeking to represent, and I rejected them with scorn and derision. In the meetings in Loma Hoby during that first crisis I can see now that a terrific battle of spirits was taking place—which I failed to appreciate—and it led to a rejection of the gospel. The gospel had no place in my approach to the crisis, for it became for me a struggle of one faction against another. And how blind I was to what was really taking place in me came to expression in a remark I made to Georg shortly after the exclusions following this crisis. I expressed my gratitude that no spirit of resentment or revenge had come to expression in the carrying out of the exclusions.

That the suspicions to which I gave free range at this time had not left me even after the periods of exclusion were at an end is shown by something I said to Georg when he visited Asuncion in September 1944, when Buddug and I were responsible for Bruderhofhaus. I had just been reinstated as house father after having been in some difficulties, and shortly before Georg left to return to Primavera, he confided to me that he was disturbed by the talks that were going on night after night between Hardy and Fritz in the Kleiners' arbor. "I only wish I knew what they were talking about," he said. "It can't be good." It was obvious that he felt things were building up for another crisis, and I said to him: "If there is another crisis, Georg, I ask to be called back to Primavera." In fact I was called back to Primavera immediately after Georg's return without knowing why at the time. On arrival at Primavera I was told—I think by Hermann Arnold—that the worst crisis that we had ever experienced had broken out, though I was told it was not a real crisis because it only affected a small clique but the church had remained firm. By the time I had arrived in Primavera the issues seemed to be clear, and for the most part it only remained to determine what should be the consequences. I remember how shocked I was by the severity of the proposals and especially by the document that was first agreed upon in the Brotherhood and then, I think, read to the sixteen of you and called the "*Handel*."*

---

*In this context, a solemn action of the brotherhood.

But I suppressed all sympathetic considerations and gave myself fully to the direction that was decided upon. Actually I have to say—though it shames me to say it, especially in view of the harshness of the action that was taken—that I concerned myself little, if at all, with the real issues that were at stake or what it was that you were trying to represent. I only know that I had for a long time previous to this set myself firmly against the direction that seemed to be emanating from Hardy, represented by the words *Barmherzigkeit* [compassion] and *Gnade* [grace]. I knew both by the things Hardy did and said in my hearing that he was resistant to the direction taken by Hans and Georg, and I interpreted this as being an undermining of the Church and felt that the crisis brought it all to a peak. Consequently I allowed myself to be convinced that the severity of the action taken was fully justified by the seriousness of the threat to the unity of the Church. But your question as to whether it did concern a loving Church is well founded. From what I have just reported it is clear that there was no open, trusting relationship between us; we allowed suspicions to lurk and waited only for the strategic moment to strike, without seeking to resolve what differences existed in a spirit of frank, direct brotherliness. When I think about it now, it is only with great abhorrence and deep grief. What was there here of the love of which Jesus spoke and of the unity by which he said his disciples were to be recognized? And worst of all, it was all believed and said to be in the name of Christ and his Church. I am at a complete loss to know what to say about all this and the evil active part I played in it.

I did not know what economic provision had been made for you for your settlement in Asuncion and did not take the trouble to enquire. What I do remember—and here again I shudder to think of my callousness—was my visit to you in the name of the Brotherhood at the house where you were living in Villa

Morra to require you to take off your beards because of the
bad effect your presence in the town was supposed to be having
on the name of the community. I know that in that meeting
with the three of you living there I just steeled myself against
any feelings of sympathy or compassion that could have arisen
in me on seeing the poverty-stricken conditions in which you
were living. Just on that account, I am certain, I became harder
and more unyielding so as to counter supposed tendencies to
weakness in myself. I just do not know, Heini, how it has been
possible for you to treat me with such love and kindness in the
years since, after the hardness with which I treated you then.

Later a neighbor of yours at Villa Morra called at the shop
at *Bruderhofhaus* and pleaded that we do something to ease
your situation out there. She was a Catholic and said that she
understood the necessity for discipline in a religious community
such as ours but felt that your condition was far too hard. I did
nothing about it but remained rigidly by the instructions I had
been given that we were to have nothing to do with you unless
one or the other were to come to the house saying he had been
without food for a couple of days. On one occasion when Hans
was in the house in Asuncion, your landlady came and spoke
with him, pleading that he should do something to help you in
your desperate inner need. He reported the talk to me, but I
did not lift a finger to urge him to do something about it, and
as far as my recollection goes, nothing was done—though just
before I went off to Argentina in 1945, he and I did have a
talk with you in Parque Caballero.

It was in 1952 that I saw you again for the first time after
your return to Primavera, when Buddug and I returned from
England to Paraguay. At that time and for the following time
I thought that the past was past and that our old relationship
had been restored, but I now have to recognize with great grief
that lurking within me unrecognized was the same unforgiving,

suspicious spirit that had found such bitter expression in the
early years in Primavera. How, indeed, could it have been
otherwise when the spirit in which I had acted so terribly against
you in 1941 to 1944 had gone unrecognized for what it was
and unrepented for—just smeared over? From your side, Heini,
I know and believe that everything had been forgiven me that
had destroyed our relationship; on my side, though, it had just
been smeared over and I only tricked myself and you into
believing that the past was really past. That this was how it
was with me has come to expression in so many ways—in the
references to emotionalism in the States when I returned to
Paraguay in 1958, similar references to Hans Z. and probably
many others, in the rejection of the very loving invitation to
immigrate with Buddug to the States, in that wicked talk with
Hans Z. in Sinntal in February 1959, in my attitude to your
handling of Miriam Way in her great need, in my gossiping,
indirect remarks to Balz in February 1959, in the remark I
made to you in Bulstrode before your departure for Sinntal.
These are only instances—and there must be many others—of
a mood that must have been constant in me over many years,
but particularly strong in more recent years and culminated in
such disastrous consequences for the whole Church at Easter
1960 and in the arrogant, self-assured, self-exalted way in which
I came to the States, defiant and contemptuous of the Church
on all our places and dealt with the Brotherhoods in the States,
particularly Oak Lake, in such an unbelievably shameful way.

What does it mean, Heini, to say that I am sorry for all this?
All I can say is that a deep abhorrence and shame possesses
me when I think of all these dreadful things that I have done—
how I have treated brothers and sisters as I would not dare to
treat strangers or even friends in the world—how I have so
grievously misused what I allowed myself to assume was the
authority of the Church to do those things that were the very

antithesis of Christ's teaching and of the true spirit of the Church. But however deeply grieved I feel over what I have done, I have to stand before the fact that all my sorrow is powerless to put right what has been so deeply wronged: that I have quelled and destroyed life and that I have crushed or misled the spirits of many and that I have betrayed the vision that was once given me, distorting it into a caricature of the truth, and that I have spurned and held in contempt the spirit of the Church. I know there is absolutely nothing I can offer in correction of all this, and yet I know, too, that unless there is healing, life no longer holds meaning for me.

I can only say, Heini, that it is my deepest longing that this healing may be given for all the wrong I have done—also for the grievous injury I have done you—and I want to hold myself open to face up to anything that may still be lurking in me, cost what it may, that threatens to hinder it.

In this letter I have confined myself mainly to how my wrong relationship to you has affected my relation to the Church and my conduct within it. I know this letter is very inadequate even though it deals with such a heavy weight of guilt, and there are many other aspects of this guilt I still have to face up to, but it is my longing that I may be given the insight and the courage to face it in the spirit that will enable all things to become new. You and others will certainly have questions to put to me and I want to face up to these in the same spirit.

Your Gwynn

As I have said, it was eight weeks after his illness began before Heini was able even to appear at a brotherhood meeting, let alone face the results of this year's overwhelming collapse. Had he been there to respond, the light that Gwynn's letter threw on this most difficult time in our history might have reached and helped many others who were also away.

Fortunately Heini did gradually get better and begin to carry any difficulty with us from a motel near New Paltz, where he and Annemarie and Doug and Ruby were for a time. Phone calls from Europe would come to Woodcrest, and brothers would go out to share them with Heini. At Woodcrest during this time of rest we had some unpeace between brothers working in the shop, where I had a responsibility. I laid the problem before Heini and asked for help. Then he invited all the responsible brothers to come and have tea and talk it over. At last he did come back home to Woodcrest and carried everything completely with us. Under all conditions Heini had great love and wisdom from the Spirit. We are thankful to God for the life of this brother, our Elder, who at that time was not yet named Elder but who certainly carried the whole Church on his heart.

During the time in Paraguay when George Burleson, Kathy, and I were there, we experienced two deaths, six days apart. On July 31 Elsbeth Friedrich, who was in her eighties, died suddenly and unexpectedly, and then Jens Mogensen, an elderly German brother.

In August we had a little excitement in Primavera over something we had heard about earlier in the year. A religious group that came from Russia, known as Molokans, had colonies or communities in Canada, and at that time also in California. The California people were interested in Primavera. They were looking for a place to settle outside the zone of nuclear danger, for some wilderness refuge. So for some weeks we had something tangible to work for, and our concentration outwardly was on sprucing up the hofs, getting in the crops and hoeing the weeds, and getting the place to look more like a going concern to impress the Molokans' representatives when they would come down to look at it. But on August 17 we got news that they were no longer interested. So that fell through and brought a real deflation of spirits for everyone.

People wondered, "Will we ever get out of here? What is the use of putting in all this work?" Then Heini was particularly firm and encouraging in his advice to us, which came by cable, that we should on no account cease the work. The worst thing you can do, even if there isn't a visible purpose at the end of it, is to abandon things and sit around and have nothing to do. Keep the farm going! In our inner situation, this advice was a very great help. It was a miracle that between October 1961 and February 1962 we all were able to move to the northern hemisphere.

In September Mark, Wen, and Pep came down to Paraguay to join Howard and Marion, who had flown the day before bringing with them an immigration lawyer from the Philadelphia area by the name of Fil Masino. Fil was to work on the immigration of those meant to come to the U.S.A. Until then all immigration into the States had been done on an individual basis; each individual person or family who came to America had to be sponsored by somebody in the States who could prove that he would support them for a year without their becoming public charges. And here we wanted to bring in a really big group, a hundred or more including children, and that was unprecedented. That was why we had to bring a lawyer all the way down to talk with the American Consul in Asuncion. We also had to work on it from the Washington end to try to get permission.

Here it became clear what a leading from God we had had a year before—unknown to us all—when we moved all of the families to Woodcrest and New Meadow Run and closed down Evergreen. (During the intervening year there had been only two caretaker families there, changed off in relays, caring for a few highschoolers.) Now we could go to the Consul and say, "We have a complete community: houses, land, workshop, machinery, everything ready to go, and we have many unfilled orders. We have work for them all; they will not become public charges."

We had figures to back that up: Community Playthings was growing at a rate that called us to get those machines into operation in Evergreen. And here—with God's leading the year before— was a whole community all set up and empty, with room for everybody.

That opened the door, and on October 22 the first group of thirty arrived from Paraguay. Group after group came after that until the end of January, the last group arriving on January 29. In the meantime those who had remained in Paraguay were able to close the deal for the sale of Primavera. (Finally it had gone through to the neighboring Mennonite colony of Friesland—this time under acceptable conditions.) The receipt of money from the sale covered travel and many other expenses and helped us send as much as we could to our people who were away.

If one looks back through all the events of the years 1959, '60, and '61, it is just incredible—the struggle was constant! Could *this* have really happened only two days after *that*, and three days later something else, and then a week later something else? Heini turned to others constantly, but he and Annemarie were the ones to whom we *all* turned for carrying and for strength. And that year of 1961, when we were trying to sell Primavera and to arrange the immigration of all the people to Europe and America, we were without funds. Somehow God carried us through that whole year, and in the end everything worked out.

In that year there was a steady relay of different brothers and sisters until October, when the first quotas opened up and the Primavera move began. And at the same time brothers and sisters were going over to Europe to Bulstrode, Wheathill, and Sinntal. All these were young brothers like myself with very few years in the brotherhood—some as short as two years or even eighteen months and barely appointed to the witness brother service— having to take on the responsibility of a whole Bruderhof, the direction of which was unclear. Heini has been accused very much because of those years, and I do want to say that where wrong things were done, they were done by others of us. Heini fought for love to everyone, but there was just too much going on on three continents all at once for him to have had all the oversight.

My diary account of 1961 alone is a record of so many comings and goings that I couldn't tell of them all. It would be too long and too confusing. I thought I would summarize our 1961 journeys in a more statistical way: Heini spent only nine weeks in two trips to Primavera; Art Wiser was nearly eleven weeks in Primavera, his wife Mary with him for another eight weeks in Europe; Doug Moody was nearly eleven weeks in Primavera, with Ruby in Europe over four; Gerd Wegner was nearly seven weeks in Primavera, with Gertrud in Europe for eleven; I was away in Paraguay a total of eighteen weeks on two trips, Kathy with me for eleven of them; and Mark Kurtz, one of three servants of the Word at the time, was nine weeks on two trips to Primavera and two weeks in England, Peggy with him for seven of those weeks in Primavera. (Howard and Marion Johnson went down especially in connection with the sale and the winding up of Primavera.) These eleven brothers and sisters, plus fourteen others (witness brothers, with and without their wives), made a total of twenty round trips to Paraguay and twelve to England—all in support of the service of the Word. This involved twenty-five different people, away for an average time of thirteen weeks each. These trips were all made in relays, usually no more than two couples at a time. This summary does not include the many other kinds of journeys of 1961.

Our American communities were not so strong inwardly that they could afford all this; it just was that way, it had to be, there was no other solution. And the remainder of 1961 continued like that—one journey here and a journey there, and then these people would become exhausted and come back and have to be replaced by somebody else. And so it went and so it went and so it went.

In England and in Germany a pattern emerged similar to that in Paraguay, except that Heini was not able to participate in it at all, and thus more injustice was probably done. The pattern was similar in that the brotherhood dissolved itself and a small group was formed, from which a new brotherhood would grow. And the hofs moved together. Those who were in the brotherhood or close to the brotherhood moved to Bulstrode from Wheathill and Sinntal. Those not so close stayed in or moved to Wheathill or were away elsewhere. Sinntal was closed down and eventually sold. The decision to sell Wheathill was finalized in October. (We had done the same in Paraguay—those close to the brotherhood were in Isla Margarita, and the others in Ibaté.) In a practical way this was the only workable solution, but inwardly it was not good. Words cannot express the upheaval and pain of that time!

# 11
# *Love Can Raise*
# *the Broken Stone*

"We would be building . . . waiting till Love can raise the
broken stone"                                        Purd Deitz

In 1961 the whole house was severely shaken. And since that
time God's salvaging and reclaiming has been constantly at work,
since very valuable material was used in the parts to be rebuilt.
Much reclamation still remains to be done. During the last twenty
years of his life, Heini constantly had on his heart the many
brothers and sisters who were away and a longing for the healing
of the rift in the Hutterian Church. And above all, he yearned
that Love might raise these broken stones.

November 22, 1963, was the 28th anniversary of the death of
our Eberhard Arnold, and a lovemeal had been planned for that
evening. During the course of the day we learned of the
assassination of President John F. Kennedy, an event that stunned
the United States and the world.

For us on the same day there came the first important visit

187

from the Western Brothers since the break in Forest River in 1955. At that time we of the East were under the Hutterian Church discipline of exclusion (the ban); contacts that were purely social were not supposed to take place. The visitors included Samuel Waldner Vetter of Springfield and Fritz Waldner Vetter of Poplar Point. On this visit a very special love for the brothers in the East was kindled in the heart of Fritz Vetter, which bore fruit later in January 1964, when Heini, Dwight Blough, and Art Wiser made a trip to the West.

Our unity with the Hutterian Brethren that God had given to Eberhard Arnold after a difficult, year-long journey in 1930-31, had been broken in 1955 by a spirit of arrogance. There had been much sin then on our part, not on Heini's part but mainly on the part of some who had been in Primavera. This journey to Manitoba in 1964 came out of Heini's great longing for reconciliation and took place ten years before God gave the full reuniting. Art reported on it verbally in 1982, eight years after Dwight Blough was killed in a plane accident and just two months after Heini's death on July 23. Art relied heavily on Dwight's very full diary account of 1964:

> It is good to know something of the earlier background, because one thing that quickened Heini's longing and may have given him hope was a visit to Woodcrest in late 1963 by Fritz Waldner Vetter of Poplar Point and Samuel Waldner Vetter of Springfield. (A few months later Fritz Vetter was at the January 1964 preachers' meeting.) Their first stop was at Oak Lake.
>
> There were only a few among us at Oak Lake who had met any Hutterian brothers, and then only during the difficult time at Forest River. To meet these down-to-earth, straightforward brothers was the beginning of a change in our hearts. First they disapproved of a great many outer differences; when they went on to Woodcrest, of less; and by the time they came to Evergreen, they were very warm and friendly. This showed up

in the part Fritz Vetter played the next year when our brothers traveled to Manitoba.

Dwight writes in his diary that on Sunday, January 5, 1964, the brotherhood decided that Heini should call John R. Hofer Vetter and offer to go to Manitoba. John R. Vetter was the older brother and servant of the Word who had come with our John Maendel and Edna Baer on the very first visit from the West to Woodcrest in March 1955. That visit had meant a greal deal to John R. Vetter, and Heini felt he was our best friend among the Hutterites. He was the first servant at Bloomfield. Heini wanted the advice of one of the Hutterites and felt he could speak to John R. Vetter in confidence and ask about making a visit. After two phone calls with him, the brotherhood decided that a trip to Manitoba should be made soon and that Heini, Dwight, and Art should go.

The first flight openings were for the next day—late on Monday—and we arranged to meet in Toronto. In the meantime Heini had also called Georg Barth in Bulstrode; he responded favorably and added a hope that peace would come from the visit. In Toronto we stayed in a little motel near the airport. (Dwight writes that it cost only $12.50 each.) The next morning we flew from Toronto to Winnipeg and arrived there one hour late because of ground fog. We rented a car, signed in at the "Y," and then Heini called the Elder, Peter Hofer Vetter, at James Valley.

In 1955 at the time of the Forest River crisis, Peter Vetter had been the Elder, and he was the one of whom Heini particularly wanted to ask forgiveness. At a crucial point in that year, Heini (who himself had represented respect and deliberation) had taken a letter to the elders, shown it to Peter Hofer Vetter, and asked for permission to read it. Peter Vetter had read it and given Heini permission. One of the brothers had stood up and said, "Sit here, Heini Vetter. Take my place," while he sat on a heater. They loved Heini. But unfortunately

others from among us had then forced their way into the room—
they didn't trust the way Heini might handle the situation. And
that had brought the meeting to a stormy and unhappy end.
Heini would not dwell on such past details about others. He
had shared them with us earlier, but out there he took everything
on himself.

So then in 1964 Heini phoned Peter Hofer Vetter, who asked,
"Where are you?" and Heini said, "In Winnipeg." Peter Vetter
said, "If you have come this far, we can't refuse you a hearing.
Call Jörg Wipf Vetter in Lakeside and do what he tells you."
We heard that Jörg Vetter was in Winnipeg with John R. Hofer
Vetter. We went to the Mennonite Book Store, which was
located in a definite area where Hutterites in town tended to
gather to do their shopping and selling. We could see trucks
with names of colonies on them and young brothers unloading
grain in the wheat elevators. We did not find either one of them
and had to give it up. So we phoned Jörg Vetter, who was a
bit cool on the phone but said we should come out to his home
in the morning.

The next morning Jörg Vetter met us at the door of his
servant's office at home. He frowned but told us to come in.
The weather was cold, around 20 to 30 degrees below zero.
He pointed at me (Dwight and I were by then appointed or
confirmed servants of the Word) and said, "Do you let that
man stand before his congregation without a beard?" The next
morning I didn't shave and have not shaved since. Then he
asked us to sit down; it was close to breakfast time. Because
of the split in 1955, by their church orders we couldn't eat
together. Jörg Vetter pulled out part of his desk and had his
food brought to him there, and about two feet away was a little
table that was brought in for Heini and Dwight and me. Jörg
Vetter said grace before the meal, and we respectfully put our
hands on our laps, lowered our eyes, and really felt with him.
But after he was through, he said, "Don't you know how to

pray? You should have your arms on the table and your hands up."

There were so many things Dwight and I simply didn't know, and I think even Heini was taken aback at how important these things were. I don't think I would have been selected to go along if, for instance, we had realized how important the beard was. After giving us a pretty stiff lecture, Jörg Vetter went to the phone and called Peter Hofer Vetter. He spoke in *Hutterisch*, but Heini could follow a little of what he said: "I believe they mean it well. I see it in Heini's eyes." That touched us very much.

Then we went to James Valley to see Peter Vetter. Heini drove with Jörg Vetter at his request, and Dwight and I followed in the car we had rented. In that short drive Jörg Vetter extracted from Heini the promise not to wear a wristwatch; so Heini never did, the rest of his life. (In 1974 after the reuniting, Heini asked to be freed of this traditional point. Jörg Vetter was very loving—and he especially loved Heini—but he was unrelenting on that particular rule of their church order. He said, "You should never have had a wristwatch to begin with.")

Peter Vetter was asleep when we arrived, so we were entertained at the home of the steward Josua Hofer Vetter, who treated us very courteously. He offered us a little meal, and Heini noticed (Dwight and I didn't know enough to notice it) that their unbaptized daughter sat and ate with us, while the rest of the family just waited; they ate later.

When Peter Vetter awoke, we were taken into his room. He was very warm. Heini said he had come to ask the Hutterites for forgiveness, particularly Peter Vetter. Peter Vetter said, "You are forgiven," and embraced Heini. (That became an important question ten years later in 1974.) And then he was very childlike; he was by then an old man. He showed Dwight and me his normal school diploma, his good grades—and they *were* good—and talked in a very friendly way. On very short notice he arranged for a meeting of preachers at Milltown for the next day. Heini, Dwight, and I went back for the night to the "Y."

The next day while the preachers were gathering at Milltown, we were invited into Dave Waldner's home. Over all the years, through thick and thin, Dave (one of the five carpenters who had built for Woodcrest in 1955) had remained loyal and faithful to what he had experienced, and he had had a lot of "thick" going. (He showed this loyalty again in July 1982, when he came so quickly to stand by the Arnold family, arriving the day after Heini's death.) While we waited to be called into the preachers' meeting, Dave was with us. We sat there together like four guilty fellows, Dave completely identifying himself with us in that situation.

Then we were called into the meeting in the new dining room at Milltown before seventeen preachers. (Just this became a crucial point in 1974: not only was Heini forgiven personally by Peter Hofer Vetter in his bedroom, but the next day he was also forgiven by these seventeen representatives. That made the issue clear.)

Heini stood up and asked the brethren if it would be all right to speak in English (since Dwight and I didn't understand German), and the brothers allowed that. But as the meeting went on, it lapsed into German. Heini took on himself all the guilt for what had happened in 1955 and begged for forgiveness from his heart. Dwight and I each spoke. Neither of us had been in the brotherhood or even in the community at the time of the Forest River crisis, and therefore we were free to say all we knew of Heini's longing for a peaceful settlement—even back in 1955. Heini had been trusted through that whole crisis. The brothers said his main guilt had been that in 1955 he hadn't stood up to the other brothers from Paraguay who had come to Forest River.

Jörg Vetter was very kind. He asked if we would feel all right about leaving while they talked. We went into the children's dining room with Mike Waldner Jr. and sat there for about forty-five minutes. We heard quite loud talking from the meeting.

When we were called back in, Jörg Vetter again talked very kindly, and Peter Vetter admonished him for being so soft on us. Then he asked all in the meeting who had been in Forest River and in the struggle there to speak. Joseph Kleinsasser Vetter spoke pretty sharply, but that helped to clear the air and to bring the meeting to a united close. As we all know, he became a very special friend. Then they gave their verdict, which was that they forgave Heini; and Heini was so responsive in his heart, so happy, that he just burst out with, "Can we shake hands and eat together?" (Later he said he wished he had restrained himself; if he hadn't asked, it would have just happened.) They had to answer according to their church order and said, "No, this is not the forgiveness of your Bruderhof. It is personal forgiveness for you, Heini Vetter."

They asked us to go also to New Rosedale and ask Andreas Vetter (the responsible servant of Forest River in 1955) for forgiveness. He was blind, and we assumed that it was because of his health that neither he nor his son Andrew had come to Milltown. Heini very readily agreed to that. In New Rosedale Darius Maendel, who had also been one of the five carpenters at Woodcrest, invited Dwight and me, and Andrew invited Heini. We didn't realize that he then took Heini straight to Andreas Vetter. Heini later told us that the conversation was quite deep but did not really lead to peace. Later Andreas Vetter spoke to his son Pete Hofer about it, "I have forgiven everything." (He was not physically able to come to the reuniting ten years later on January 7, 1974, but said about it afterward, "I feel completely with the meeting.")

When we went on to Bloomfield, John R. Hofer Vetter met us with embraces and sat down with us immediately and persuaded us to spend the night there. Quite early after our arrival, John R. Vetter asked Dwight how old he was. Dwight said, "Almost thirty," and Heini got the biggest kick out of that. (For the rest of the year, whenever Heini was with Dwight, he would bring that up and say, "They might just have been smart enough to realize that if you were almost thirty, you were only twenty-nine!") That night when we were upstairs in John R. Vetter's home, Heini came in his pajamas and said, "You know, when you grow a beard, you have a big problem. Every night when you go to bed, you have to decide whether you are going to put your beard on top of the blanket or the blanket on top of your beard." That was a wonderful time together, difficult as parts of the journey were.

The next morning John R. Vetter came up before breakfast with a tiny glass of brandy. One of their customs is to have a little sip, as they call it, before breakfast. It was against Heini's medical rules, but he said that out of love he could not refuse that little drink. John R. Vetter sat there at the foot of Heini's bed, and we felt a terrific love coming from that brother.

Then we left for Winnipeg. Heini had asked if we could visit some colonies, and Peter Hofer Vetter had said, "Yes, but keep in touch with us." We were only able to visit Rosedale and Bloomfield and to stop at Lakeside to say good-bye to Jörg Vetter before we left. Then we went to the airport to arrange our flight for the next day. I have no idea how Fritz Vetter could have found out where we were, but he turned up and insisted on taking us to supper in a little cafe in Winnipeg. He was very warm.

Just before we left, while we were at the airport signing in early for the plane, Heini made a phone call to each of the preachers who had come to the meeting, to thank them for coming and to thank them for their forgiveness. John R. Vetter asked on the phone, "Did Fritz Vetter find you last night at the airport?" Heini said, "Yes," and John R. said, "Did he take you to supper?" Heini said, "Yes," and John R. was satisfied.

Only four weeks after the brothers came home, John R. Vetter was killed in a tragic accident just down the road from Milltown. He was on his way to a servant's meeting when his pickup was struck by a fast train. This event was a very deep and shocking hurt. We don't understand its deeper meaning; it felt like a real setback. Heini loved this brother dearly and straightaway sent Art to the burial. This tragedy hit Heini deeply and made things more difficult for him in his longing to restore what his father had been led to, which had been rejected in the Forest River time.

The next afternoon when we were at the airport to take the plane, Fritz Vetter came again with a letter he had written himself—laboriously because it was written in English—in which he made proposals that he felt would bring peace. One proposal was that all baptized members who had originally been from the West and had left Forest River should return there to be excluded, leaving it open for them to come back to us. Another was that Heini and all of our people from the East who had been at Forest River should be excluded for a short time. This letter had so clearly been written out of love that all we could say was, "Fritz Vetter, we will carry your letter back to our brotherhood, and we will consider it seriously."

Only a little more than two weeks after our return home, Dwight and Heini and Annemarie were on their way to Bulstrode in England, with the intention of visiting members outside. In those short two weeks before the journey, Heini went through a deeply painful time, after which he came to the brotherhood with the request that he be excluded. He felt that to send the

Hutterite brothers and sisters back to Forest River was out of the question, and also that it was out of the question to exclude all the brothers and sisters who were at that time baptized members. But he felt that if he were to be excluded, that would meet the biggest request of the Hutterites. Fritz Vetter, who had written that letter, must have been in touch with Peter Hofer Vetter about it.

Here I will quote from Dwight's diary, written at home in Woodcrest:

> On Wednesday, January 15, 1964, I talked with Dick Domer about Heini's request to the brotherhood. We felt extremely torn but felt we should consider it seriously. The next day, the servants arrived from Oak Lake and Evergreen, and we met in the afternoon to consider Heini's request for exclusion.

I remember vividly our meetings and how depressed we all were. We felt very torn about Heini's request. We couldn't bring ourselves with a good conscience to exclude him; it was Heini who had led us in this search for repentance. We then met in the evening in a wider circle to consider Heini's question again. We expressed very strongly that it would be against our Order and against our consciences to exclude him, that it would be a much stronger witness to love and unity to turn down his request, and that Heini should go to Europe to visit former members as one sent by the brotherhood. Heini had said that if he were in exclusion, he knew that there were several in Europe out of the brotherhood who would take him in; whereas he was certain that if he went as a servant or an elder—or even as a brotherhood member—the door would be shut to him. Dwight wrote at the time:

> Perhaps there are people who can never be reached because

we did not accept Heini's request, and my heart is simply torn by the sacrifice he wants to take on himself and on his family. I hope we have not hurt him.

Now that is Dwight's heart. I have to say that I didn't realize how we had missed Heini's heart. I don't know if we should have decided differently, but I feel we missed his heart, I missed it. If we had followed Heini into the depth of anguish he experienced in his longing and concern for those no longer in the community, if we had been willing to suffer as Heini suffered, doors might have been opened. We were not really of one heart and one soul, and I at least, was not deep enough to share the anguish and to be that much of one heart with our brother and Elder. It is still a very real torment for me. But Dwight was truly of one heart with him at that point. And I'm so grateful there was one brother who could feel Heini's heart and support him as Dwight did in that hour.

When Heini realized that we weren't able to bring ourselves to propose exclusion to the brotherhood, he simply accepted it and said, "All right. It would have been very difficult for Georg in Bulstrode to understand if you here excluded me. Let's start thinking about the best way to answer the Brothers with love and respect, and let's arrange a trip now by Dwight, Annemarie, and me to visit as many outside as possible."

That evening the whole brotherhood from Evergreen came to Woodcrest. Heini reported the two main points of Fritz Vetter's letter. One was that those baptized Hutterites from Forest River who had joined us would all have to return to be excluded. The second point concerned Heini's exclusion. Each baptized member from the West was asked to write to the elders and to Andreas Vetter, asking for forgiveness and for permission to stay with us. Each one agreed to write and did so. About Heini, we decided a letter should be sent, signed by all the servants here in the States except Heini, telling them why we could not bring ourselves to exclude him. Heini would also write again to Andreas Vetter asking for forgiveness.

Then the question of the trip to England was raised, and Heini made the suggestion that he and Annemarie and Dwight go to visit as many as possible of those who had not yet been visited. That was soon agreed. We also agreed that Dick and Lois Ann should go to Manitoba and visit Hutterite colonies, which we now had permission to do. It was Jake Kleinsasser Vetter (Jake Vetter), later the Elder, a young minister then, who was their guide and who accompanied them on most of that trip from one colony to another.

When I think today in 1982 of how we met in Woodcrest's new dining room on January 7, 1974, to come to prayer to support Heini and the brothers who were at Sturgeon Creek asking for forgiveness, I realize how very far behind Heini's lead we had been in 1964. How gently and with what amazing patience he held firm to the leading he felt; yet he never pressed any of us, not a single individual. He would rather wait a year for a decision on some question of clothing or costume.

I would like to emphasize what Art said about our unreadiness. Heini was ready, and Dwight was, and there may have been others, but we as a community—and I speak for myself—were not ready. I remember that ten years later in Manitoba in 1974 we had with us an excerpt from a letter Hans-Hermann had written to his mother in March 1937 during the visit of two Western brothers to the Cotswold. The community was vibrating over certain Hutterian "points" (of their traditional rules of order) and whether they would be required. Hans-Hermann had written that he believed if we as a community were deeply in Jesus, if when we went to our mealtimes we were more concerned in our hearts to feed our souls and spirits than our bodies—if Jesus was really the center of our life together—the Brothers would not require *any* points. (Hans-Hermann's belief became fact in 1974, as we shall see in my account: "re points" there were "NO demands.")

I think this is true of the Brothers through all the years, including 1964—they were responding to something they felt lacking in us, and we perceived it as rigidity in them. I would even say God prevented the attempt at reuniting in 1964 because it might have been a disaster. We went through some real struggles in our brotherhoods in 1964 in seeking God's truth and unity. We were then still far off, and I put myself completely under that appraisal. It is amazing that we were brought together.

# 12
# Of One Mind

"That we from our hearts love one another,
of one mind in peace remain together."
Martin Luther

To continue the story of the relationship between East and West, I want to move ahead ten years to the time of reuniting with the Hutterian Brethren in 1974. Until 1973 there seemed to be no possibility of mending our relationship with the brothers in the West, broken in 1955 through sin and wrongdoing on our part. None of us had an inkling of the depth of longing and of prayer in Heini's heart (for eighteen years) that West and East be "of one mind in peace." In 1973 God stepped in more decisively, and we were able to listen more. What happened becomes most vivid through what was reported at the time. I quote first from two servants of the Word:

*Don Alexander*: Heini had a burning longing in his heart for reconciliation with the Brothers and for the reestablishment of the bond that had been made in 1930 by his father, our Word leader Eberhard Arnold. Those of us privileged to be at the reuniting in 1974 certainly felt that the 1964 journey was all-important to this event ten years later. Yet God had been at work in the intervening years, also in our own circle, helping clear the path and preparing us for this gift that he gave on January 7, 1974, at Sturgeon Creek, Manitoba.

All this applied in a special way to the 1964 journey, but also to the year 1972 and our whole experience with Heini's brother Hans-Hermann Arnold: those of us in our brotherhood and household circles will never forget that Advent time with Hans-Hermann. We were seeking an answer to our questions concerning the head covering and simplicity of dress. Heini led us to consider these questions deeply in the light of what is said in the New Testament. For me it was a revelation to feel that the modesty and simplicity of our dress should be an expression of our relationship to God and the Church Above. This seeking also led us together. It was a wonderful time, with Hans-Hermann, Heini, Hardy, and Emy-Margret telling about their father and the early years of our Bruderhof life.

In our brotherhood circle in the Easter time of 1973, we again considered the question of dress and the meaning of the head covering. We turned again to the New Testament and felt together to adopt a head covering for Gemeindestundes, brotherhood meetings, and celebrations of the Lord's Supper, out of respect for what the apostle Paul writes concerning this. God was leading us to a renewed relationship with our brothers in the West, although we were not aware of it at the time.

Then while Heini was in Darvell early in 1973—before the idea of any brothers from the West visiting had even dawned upon anyone—he wrote to the brotherhoods on March 8:

> I do not claim to know, but I have the presentiment that something is happening in eternity, where the fight of the atmospheres takes place. I do not dare to say more than that.

I believe that for the communities in England and in America
the train switches will now be set right. It is my deepest prayer
that they not be set by anyone who has a special service, nor
by the brotherhood, but by Christ himself.

Dwight had come to Darvell with Heini, and they returned
together in March. I still remember the phone call Dwight made
from Woodcrest to Darvell after their return. He told about the
lovemeal welcoming them back, and I could almost think we
were present. The doors opened, and there stood two brothers
from the West, Jacob Kleinsasser Vetter (Jake Vetter) from
Crystal Spring and Jacob Hofer Vetter from Elm River,
completely unexpected. They simply walked into the middle
of the lovemeal on a surprise visit. Heini and Dwight each said
that as soon as they saw those two brothers, they felt it was
an important and historic moment.

*Glenn Swinger*: We had no idea that a Hutterian brother would
be within a thousand miles. They hadn't come straight to the
dining room. They had first stopped at the Primavera House
and met Sibyl and Jeanette, who were the children's watches
over supper. Sibyl told us later that when she found out who
they were, she spoke right out, "You will be very happy to
hear that we've all quit smoking," but she noticed it didn't
seem to impress them too much. The brothers had been
somewhat fearful of coming, but they found Sibyl and Jeanette
very friendly, and that encouraged them. They had been in
Ottawa on business, and at a certain point in their travels had
simply felt led to turn in our direction and come to Woodcrest.
We later heard from Jake Vetter that on the way home they
said to each other, "We have to go to work for a reuniting."
And they really did.

In May 1973 at a joint conference in Woodcrest with all three brotherhoods, we read "The Darmstadt Report," the report by Emmy of the last days of our Eberhard. It contained his hope that each one in the circle could answer the question, "Why do I love Christ?" Heini brought this same question to us at that conference.

Then there was a two-week interval, during which our beloved brother Fred Goodwin was very suddenly called into eternity. The brotherhoods gathered again for a second conference to fight through inner concerns and to consider the possibility of a meeting with the Brothers. Four days after the brotherhoods returned home, came the next important visit toward the reuniting: three Dariusleut ministers arrived in Woodcrest on June 6, 1973. They came especially to see Heini. After they left, he wrote a short report.

*Heini*: In the early afternoon of Wednesday, June 6, Annemarie came to me and said she saw three men with black hats and suspenders and one man in ordinary clothes walking toward the dining room. Since no one had told me that Hutterites had arrived, I thought they might be Jewish rabbis or Amish people. In about fifteen minutes my son Christoph came to tell me that there were three Dariusleut preachers from Alberta, Canada in the lounge with a Mennonite sociologist, John Hostetler. We invited them home for tea.

I waited for them at the door of our living room. First came the oldest man with white hair and a white beard, Peter Tschetter Vetter. He stretched out his hands to me, and I embraced and kissed him. We all went in and sat down. When he saw my mother, Peter Vetter jubilated; he would never have believed he would lay his eyes on "Emma Basel." He was very warm. At this teatime there were, besides Annemarie and myself and our children, Merrill, John and Sarah Maendel, and later Hardy and Doug. I think I never experienced Hutterites so warm and loving as these three brothers were. (I heard later that several sisters had greeted them by saying, "I am a Hutterian sister," and that Peter Vetter had replied, *"Sehr gut, sehr gut,"* "Very good, very good.")

Peter Tschetter Vetter had been present at the baptism and ordination of my father, Eberhard Arnold. He said that it was the greatest event for the Hutterites in America. He witnessed that Eberhard Arnold was not just a preacher but an apostle. The three brothers spoke of him with warmest love. When they saw the picture of my parents on the wall, they were very animated and could hardly believe that my mother was so young at that time. Christoph pointed out that his grandfather wore a Lehrerleut jacket with buttons. Peter Vetter said with fiery love, "Arnold Vetter did everything. When he came to the Dariusleut, he wore hooks and eyes; when he was with the Lehrerleut, he wore buttons. That is just how he was."

You all know that Annemarie had a certain worry that we might become narrow and accept human laws. But when we were among ourselves, she said she too was willing to do anything out of love, and we agreed that the only hindrance lay in making it a condition of discipleship of Christ to accept certain rules and regulations. These brothers were in Woodcrest for about two hours and left very enthusiastic, saying again and again that John Hostetler was witness to this meeting.

When Jake Vetter and Jacob Hofer Vetter had made their surprise visit in March, we had been reading in the brotherhood some of Eberhard and Emmy's engagement letters. To indicate how Eberhard had been called by God many years before the first uniting in 1930 with the Hutterian Brethren, and how his life with Emmy and Else had been used, Heini had wanted very much to write a *Sendbrief* (circular letter) to all Hutterians. We had just finished assembling most of the materials for printing this

*Sendbrief* when these three Darius brothers arrived on June 6. It was a pretty fat book when typed up. One copy was given to the brothers and John Hostetler, and they read it in the car on the way back to John's house near Philadelphia. Eventually we published that manuscript as a book, *Seeking for the Kingdom of God*.

My own memory of this visit was that it was a very hot, muggy day. Soon Christoph came, all out of breath, barefoot, very hot, and in a T-shirt. (He had been down at the Rifton Lake property working with the Shalom group during rest time on some project out in the hot sun.) When we went over to the Forest River House, we were astounded by the respect and love these brothers showed, and by the reverence that came from them toward Heini, and especially toward "Emma Basel."

Peter Tschetter Vetter was deeply moved by the experience. He was a very close and dear friend of Sam Kleinsasser Vetter of Sturgeon Creek, the son of Samuel Kleinsasser Vetter who had visited Primavera in 1950 with John Wipf Vetter. (I have told how Primavera had not treated them then with the right respect at all and how Fred Goodwin had expressed sorrow at the disrespect we had shown them in Paraguay.) Well, Sam Kleinsasser Vetter the son, knowing about this and the affair in Forest River, was one of those who found the idea of a reuniting very hard. All of those brothers who before 1974 were in opposition to reuniting had experienced difficult and wrong things from us. We should not be surprised that there was in some a resistance and a feeling of "No, not again!" And Sam Vetter was one of those. Now he was a very dear friend of Peter S. Tschetter Vetter, and we are quite sure that during the months before the final meeting at Sturgeon Creek, Peter Tschetter's visit to us had a certain effect on Sam Vetter. Peter Vetter was also one of the Darius ministers who was there on January 7, 1974; he was a part of that meeting and wrote a very moving letter to Sam Vetter afterwards, referring to it as the "Year of Jubilee." All these different events fit together in a wonderful pattern.

On June 21, 1973, a letter came to Heini from Jake Vetter, requesting that Heini and two servants who had *not* been involved in the Forest River crisis come to Manitoba soon to speak with the Brothers. That did not happen then, as we know. The way had not yet been rightly prepared in our hearts. God had a different time in mind.

As background to the uniting, I quote from what Heini wrote afterwards to his son Christoph and to the brotherhood about his concern for unity amongst the Hutterian Brethren after the break.

> *Heini*: It has been a real torment to me ever since 1963, when I realized that the whole Forest River action in 1955 was wrong and sinful—we as a Bruderhof were unfaithful to Jesus. I saw no way of putting this sinful and disastrous state of affairs in order again before my death. We were too much used to unpeace before 1963; and because the brothers and sisters who joined us from there seemed so genuine, I at first believed that the Hutterites were more in the wrong than we. Since the Brothers demanded in the first place the return of all their baptized members, I knew no way to find a solution. If I had suggested sending those brothers and sisters back to Forest River, I would have felt I was committing a grave sin and betraying them. I beseeched God in deep prayer to open up a way, and God heard my prayer. In the end he gave me much more than I would have dared to think or hope. I now see the coming and the influence of the brothers and sisters from the Hutterites as a very special gift from God.

Heini then speaks of specific questions and struggles that came about in our circle because a few were afraid of the Hutterites, fearful lest we would have to wear different clothes and so on. Heini said:

I for my part want by no means to force anything, but the brothers in the West simply won't understand it if we are not willing to yield to them on some points out of love.

Several times in reasserting that he would never force anything, Heini would also add, "Out of love to the Brothers I would gladly wear five hats!"

It will of course get more difficult if ever anything is required of us that would bring narrowness or anything oppressive into our church life. On this point you must persist in prayer to God and listen to the brotherhood, and take great care that it never again comes to a break.

At the beginning of October 1973 we decided which brothers would go with Heini to the West. At the end of November the elders of the Schmiedeleut had a meeting in Sunnyside Colony looking toward the uniting. On the way home from that meeting Jake Vetter was involved in a bad accident. He had broken ribs and was in the hospital. He said later he didn't mind about the ribs, but he was afraid lest anything might stand in the way of the coming together with the brothers in the East—his heart was really set on that. Two days after this accident Mike Waldner Vetter and Dave Waldner of Milltown arrived at Woodcrest, as they were in eastern Canada. It wasn't a long visit, but it was a wonderful and important one. I am certain that when those two brothers returned home, they did everything they could to help along the cause of the reuniting.

For the further telling of the reuniting story, I next quote Don Alexander, Glenn Swinger, and Dwight Blough.

*Don A:* In speaking of the brothers in the West, Heini often said that there is no other people—visitors or groups that have come to us—who have responded so deeply and so sensitively to the presence of the Holy Spirit, and with such discernment of what is at work amongst us in the East. And I want to confirm this. We felt it time and time again when we were out there in 1974. What struck us was the humility with which the brothers were able to change from one opinion to the complete opposite. Not knowing what would be brought into their midst, fearing a worldly influence, fearing for their young people, many of them were anxious. For that reason some of them were opposed to being united with us as brothers. Mike Waldner Vetter from Milltown told us about it afterwards. He had pleaded with many who were opposed, who are now our most faithful friends, saying, "Reserve judgment until you have heard the brothers speak. Reserve judgment. Don't say anything until you have heard them speak in the meeting."

John Hofer Vetter of Riverside and Samuel Kleinsasser Vetter of Sturgeon Creek were two of those dear brothers whose minds were turned around. If the Hutterian Brothers had followed the rigid form, a church discipline for Heini would have been needed, which was the suggestion in 1964. But now in the January 7 meetings John Hofer Vetter was thrashing around trying to find the right answer. We heard afterwards from him, "Heini Vetter simply broke our hearts." He heard Heini pleading for forgiveness for love's sake and for the sake of unity in the church. He cast about in his mind how to get around this dilemma, and he suddenly remembered the story of King David, who pleaded before God and was ready to lay down his life. And he felt from Heini the same spirit: here was a brother ready to lay down his life. And he said, "That spoke to me, and there was the answer." From that moment on he represented heartily what was eventually given to the Hutterian Church, and the brothers all said it was a historic moment. The humility of these deeply serious brothers was a mighty challenge to us.

And it was refreshing to hear our beloved brother Joseph Waldner Vetter of White Rock in those weeks after the reuniting when the five ministers visited us in Woodcrest. He described to us how he experienced the visit of Eberhard Arnold on his hof when he himself was very young. But he got the names mixed up, and instead of saying Eberhard Vetter, he spoke of Heini Vetter all the time. And the same mix-up had happened in reverse when we were out in Manitoba for the reuniting. And the older brothers there especially, instead of saying Heini Vetter, kept calling him Eberhard Vetter. I can only believe it was because they felt the same spirit coming from them both.

The time before '74 had been one of deep searching for us in the East too. We in our brotherhoods were very uncertain, and we had many questions about what a uniting would mean, how it would affect our outward life, our meetings, our dress, and the place of women in meetings. Here again it was an experience for us all how we were led back to the New Testament, to Paul the apostle. He too strove with questions about the relationship of Jews and Gentiles, matters of the law, of tradition, and how these find a reconciliation in an experience of Christ where all are made one.

Many of us in our brotherhoods will remember that time in 1973 when Heini wrote letters to all Eastern communities, not in any way presenting his point of view but simply opening up for us a solution to these questions. Then when the time of uniting came, those questions simply disappeared. Knowing as we do now Heini's and also Dwight's great longing and innermost yearning, how slow we all were is heartrending.

*Glenn*: I could tell about our trip up to Manitoba in 1974. On the Friday morning of January 4, Heini, Dwight, Merrill, Don, Else [Heini's daughter, age twenty-three, a registered nurse], and I were given a very loving send-off from Woodcrest. In all the joy, we also felt a real seriousness as we left for Toronto. From there to Winnipeg was a very joyful leg of the flight. About thirty minutes before Winnipeg some of us were watching a very beautiful sunset out the south windows. We called Heini over, and he sat there and just looked and looked. Then he said, "I believe it has a meaning."

*Dwight* (in a letter to the Shalom groups of all hofs, dictated on the plane on that last part of the journey): We are quite interested to see who will meet us; Heini says that we should feel completely free to embrace any Hutterite. He is really full of humor as we go along, and amazingly enough gains strength each hour. We had a seat for him right at the front of the economy section where he could stretch out his splinted leg. (How nearly that had stopped the whole trip!) His leg was so long it reached into the first class, and the stewardesses joked about his foot traveling first class without paying extra. Heini has been telling us many anecdotes about his father's visit to the Hutterites. I feel very privileged to be with the beloved brothers and Heini and Else on this journey.

We will not argue about the different questions; through love the way will be found. If we are completely humble in this task for the brotherhood, it will all come right, with nothing of our own human effort hindering what God wants. I greet you all with much love as your brother and friend,

Dwight

*Glenn*: We received a warm welcome when we got to Crystal Spring. Grandmother Katharina Basel had very lovingly given us her house while we were there. That allowed us younger brothers to live upstairs. A living room downstairs adjoined a bedroom where Heini could withdraw, as the living room was never empty.

On Saturday, January 5, we toured the hof at Crystal Spring. Jake Vetter had gone away to a ministers' meeting, which we found out later was very difficult. He was so discouraged he even considered canceling the meeting on January 7. But he couldn't let Heini come all that distance in his condition and not go through with it. Crystal Spring very lovingly provided us with jackets like theirs because we, although simply dressed, were not uniformly dressed. They had no jacket that would fit Heini, so they went to work and made him one.

In the afternoon of Sunday, January 6, Jake Vetter said to Heini that he would like to propose that two of our brothers meet with ministers at Poplar Point, who had questions they wanted to ask us. Heini and Jake Vetter asked Dwight and me to go, and Mike Kleinsasser took us. Fritz Vetter of Poplar Point was present with his brothers Mike Waldner Vetter from Pearl Creek and Jake Waldner Vetter (mostly called Uli Vetter) from Huron. Glanzer Vetter from Huron was also present. They had many questions to us. Some of the main ones were about children's education, our young people, baptism, engagements, and weddings. Dwight led in answering, and in the end we felt very close to them all. It went well past midnight, so we were invited to spend the night with Fritz Vetter.

The evening after the reuniting, Heini wrote to Annemarie and the brothers and sisters at home. It is a very complete record except that Heini did not report about himself. Later the same evening Dwight and the others of us put together a report about how we experienced Heini in those meetings. To make one full story, I will alternate quotes from Heini's letters, from the other four servants' reports, and from a letter of Peter S. Tschetter Vetter of Mixburn Colony, Alberta.

*Heini*: I would like to give you a report about the historic events of today—a day that still leaves me completely overwhelmed. We only asked for forgiveness for our guilt.

*Dwight*: We could never have imagined what took place today in the preachers' meeting at Sturgeon Creek and what was given by God in that hour. Because we knew that there were many brothers there who were not ready to forgive, I had no idea how it would come out.

*Heini*: This morning, January 7, we were driven to Sturgeon Creek, where there was a meeting of a large number of preachers (seventy servants of the Word, I believe). Many of them shook hands with me warmly, but one said, "I am not shaking hands with you. We are not united." I heard later that he was a Darius brother. The Lehrerleut (I had never before seen a Lehrerleut preacher) were extremely warm and friendly, and I was able to recognize them immediately because they are the only ones with buttons on their jackets.

We were called into the meeting, and Jacob Kleinsasser Vetter (Jake Vetter) read to the elders an English translation of my letter (well known to the brotherhood). Then the Elder, Joseph Kleinsasser Vetter (Jake Vetter's uncle), stood up and read the same letter in German. Then each one of us was asked to speak. I stood up first and asked for forgiveness for everything that happened in Forest River.

*Dwight*: Jake Vetter asked Heini to tell the meeting what he had come for, which Heini did in a very moving and humble way. He promised he would accept whatever the brothers would decide. It was painful for us to hear Heini laying his life and his service completely and absolutely in their hands. We had no idea what they would decide.

*Heini*: I said I had had fear of men in the Bruderhof in Paraguay and in Europe, fear of the consequences, even though I was, at the very least, worried about the way things were going and had called Annemarie aside at Forest River and asked her, "Annemarie, is it really right, what we are doing here?" Then I asked for forgiveness again.

*Dwight*: Then Jake Vetter said each of us others should speak. We tried to share how Heini had grieved over this question, had sought forgiveness again and again (long before his trip to Manitoba in 1964), and how he had suffered all through the years in fighting for what his father had established.

*Heini*: Merrill, Glenn, Dwight, and Don were servants of the Word who had joined us after Forest River, and they testified to what they had experienced in Woodcrest, New Meadow Run, Evergreen, and Darvell. All the brothers were in tears— Jake Vetter was, the whole time we spoke. After my letter had been read and we had all spoken, I apologized once more.

*Dwight*: They asked Heini what Peter Hofer Vetter had said to him in 1964 at Milltown, because no one there could remember what had been accomplished in that meeting. Nobody had notes, nobody had any memory, even though there were people present who had been there. This put them in a dilemma, because Heini had not asked for only personal forgiveness from Peter Vetter, but forgiveness for all that had happened in Forest River. Yet Heini had been told that only he personally was forgiven, and the Bruderhof was not given the handshake or invited to the common table. Their dilemma was that they felt, on the one hand, they could not exclude Heini if that had been spoken out to him as forgiveness, and on the other hand, how could they give *church* forgiveness without exclusion? This went on—

back and forth. Several times they asked Heini to say again both in English and in German what he had asked for in that meeting and what he had said to the preachers and to Peter Vetter in 1964.

Finally it was clear that it was not only personal forgiveness from Peter Hofer Vetter to Heini that had been accomplished with Peter Vetter alone at James Valley before the meeting. For when Peter Vetter had called the meeting at Milltown, it could no longer have been just for personal forgiveness between two men, because it had thus been brought to the church.

> *Dwight*: After this point had been made as clear as seemed possible, Heini was asked by Joseph Waldner Vetter from South Dakota about the financial settlement at Forest River. (We learned later that Joseph Vetter was one of the very outspoken brothers from South Dakota who had stood very much against our request, especially on Saturday at the pre-meeting.) Joseph Vetter asked three questions: about the auction in Forest River, about the settlement of the debts, and about who took over the property. (This referred to 1957, when the Bruderhof moved back East from Forest River and began the Oak Lake community.) Joseph Vetter was completly satisfied with every answer Heini gave.
>
> Jake Vetter said to the meeting that if anyone had questions about other points, they should be addressed to him as chairman of the meeting. "Otherwise we want to consider only this main question about Heini Vetter and the forgiveness." We were asked to leave the meeting and were taken to the living room of Samuel Kleinsasser Vetter, the servant in Sturgeon Creek. We were escorted there by Dave Waldner, who stayed very much by our side, also by Mike Kleinsasser, who is a dearly beloved brother and friend. And Joseph Waldner Vetter from

White Rock in South Dakota came with us.

At this point Dwight asked Glenn to share what he experienced earlier with Joseph Vetter in the afternoon meeting in the church.

> *Glenn*: The meeting had already started when Joseph Vetter leaned over to me and said, "You know, in the Saturday afternoon meeting I opposed Jake Vetter." He said he opposed him on every point all afternoon. And then he said, "But today I have turned around completely, I am with you all the way, and I'm going to do everything I can for you." And that is exactly what he did. The meeting was supposed to have been in English. We had even agreed to it beforehand, but there was hardly anything in English. I leaned over to Joseph Vetter, who knew I was concerned about how it was going, and he said, "Just relax. It's fine. If it is any different, I'll let you know."

> *Heini*: While we were waiting (about two hours), Joseph Vetter inquired very closely of Merrill what was the best way to help conscientious objectors. He was very astonished by how much Merrill knew and what good advice he was able to give.
>
> Suddenly Joseph Vetter was fetched away, and the rumor went around that I would have to be excluded. Then Jake Vetter came in, and Mike told him of the rumor. Jake Vetter said he was not really supposed to give anything away, since the matter was not settled. He would only say this much, that they had decided that I was not to be excluded. After supper we were told please to wait patiently; they would decide now what should happen.

> *Dwight*: After supper they met for about an hour and a half. Then Jake Vetter and Joseph Waldner Vetter came back to Samuel Vetter's house and told us their decision: Heini Vetter

should shake hands personally with all those preachers who sat
on the front bench and ask for forgiveness; there were sixteen
of them. Then he was to turn to the whole meeting and
apologize. They had decided to close the matter with that.
Jacob Hofer Vetter of Woodland (the other assistant to Joseph
Kleinsasser Vetter) would speak out the forgiveness of the
Church. We were to sit at the back of the room during this
time. Heini then went in and spoke to each elder. He had been
told to say simply, "Beloved brother, I ask you for forgiveness,"
but Heini spoke in a very moving way and humbled himself
to each brother.

*Heini*: I can only tell you that it was a very moving moment.
I went to the first one and asked for forgiveness. How lovingly
most of them took my hand in both of theirs and said how
gladly they forgave me and what a joy it was that I humbled
myself so, and how much they loved my father, and I should
please never again do anything like we had done at Forest
River. Some things were especially moving: how Joseph
Glanzer Vetter of Huron spoke to me, how the Elder Joseph
Kleinsasser Vetter took both my hands—what a dear little
man—and said, "How glad I am to forgive you. How glad!
What a joy that you have come."

*Dwight*: To Samuel Kleinsasser Vetter Heini spoke with great
sorrow for how his father had been treated in South America,
which made Samuel Vetter break down in tears, and it was
like that right down the line with each of the elders.

There was complete silence in the whole room, an atmosphere
of reverence and complete forgiveness. It was an hour of God.
We from the East had known that Heini was again and again
taking on himself things of which he was completely innocent—I

mean especially the treatment of the two Brothers in Paraguay. Heini had left on a trip to North America several days before the serious meetings with the Brothers in Primavera in 1950.

> *Dwight*: It was really as Heini wrote you. Heini was greeted by each brother, "You, my beloved brother," and each took his hand as a brother. Then Heini turned to the whole group of preachers and again, for the last time, said how sorry he was for what he had done in Forest River and asked for forgiveness. All of the preachers there made some sign of spontaneous response, even rising in their seats, or saying aloud, "Heini Vetter, we forgive you." It was a wave of response to Heini standing there at the front of the room. It overwhelmed all of us, this hour that Heini has prayed and longed for and agonized over, when everything could come under forgiveness.

> *Heini*: When our apology was over, we were informed—we had not been informed before being called in—that they had decided that all those who had been baptized by them were to be placed in exclusion for a time because of having marched into the church and having moved East without permission. We were then also told that two [later this was changed to five] preachers would be asked to come to Woodcrest and Evergreen to carry out the exclusions and the church forgiveness and that this would make us Hutterian Brothers. That was a tremendous surprise for us. We had no opportunity to talk together alone, but we all felt that it was God's leading and that we had nothing to say. It would have been a second Forest River-type sin if we had said we couldn't do that without asking at home first. If you had experienced that atmosphere of love and embracing, you would understand.

> *Merrill*: One thinks back to 1935 after our beloved Eberhard's

death, when the unity he fought for was deeply hurt, if not destroyed. Today by the grace and mercy of God, this has been given back.

*Don A*: Jake Vetter then led Heini down the aisle out of the church building with several of the other elders, and we joined them in leaving the building. We felt a great joy and thankfulness as we went out and gathered again in Samuel Vetter's living room. We sat around in a large gathering with many brothers.

*Merrill*: There was a great press in the house; at least twenty came up to Heini one after another and embraced him, shook his hand, and expressed their love in a very moving way. This included Dariusleut and Lehrerleut representatives.

*Dwight*: There were at least three ministers who said to me that now Heini Vetter takes up the task where Eberhard Vetter left off. With the rift healed, they see Heini as fulfilling the task of an apostle. No one spoke about points or criticisms or questions. How love came from these brothers to Heini especially, but to each one of us! Earlier, there had been reserve in many of the ministers; now they were warm and loving, praising God that this could come about.

*Merrill*: When we arrived back in Crystal Spring, there was a large group walking outside in the thirty degree below zero temperature to meet us at the car. There was great rejoicing.

*Don A*: There was hardly a minute for us to be alone. Wherever we were, the room was usually full. We tried to phone again from Crystal Spring, but though it was late at night, the children were awake, and everybody wanted to be part of the phone

Else, Annemarie, and Heini Arnold before the departure to Manitoba

At the uniting—January 7, 1974

call. So it wasn't easy for Heini to share on the phone as he does in his letter. His innermost concern was that everything here is done with you at home, that we are led together, and that we understand it all as God's leading.

*Heini*: Here in Crystal Spring we from the East talked together very briefly, and all felt convinced that it would have been a great sin if we had not accepted. We would once again have sinned against the Hutterian Brothers and would again have had to ask for forgiveness.

Fred Kleinsasser of Crystal, who is known in Woodcrest as one of the five carpenters, inquired of Jake Vetter in my presence about the "points" of their traditional rules. Jake Vetter told him that he and the Elder had quite intentionally not brought up the points so as not to bring dissension. Unfortunately I cannot foresee what this will mean for us in the future.

It was said that the preachers who will come to us are given the task to abolish anything wrong they may find at Woodcrest, Evergreen, and New Meadow Run. That worried me a bit because I did not know what they meant. As I said, Jake Vetter had not found anything wrong on his visit—there had been singing and lovemeals and brotherhood meetings—and he had testified that he had not found anything wrong. The same goes for Michael Waldner Vetter and David Waldner Vetter. I cannot tell you who the preachers are who will come to us and what they may find wrong with our clothing, our head covering, and other things they may want to change. We have not committed ourselves in any way and know absolutely nothing of what is ahead of us.

You dearly beloved brothers and sisters, I ask you with all my heart to understand that it was not my leading or the leading of the five of us, but suddenly we were offered the hand. They set no conditions in regard to any points—not a single condition—but I think it is possible that this is still to come. Because all of us—Merrill, Glenn, Dwight, Don, and I—have the impression that this is God's will and his leading, I am not very worried as to the points.

Beloved brothers and sisters, a lot will depend on who comes and on what God will give. But let us accept it in trust. We were offered a hand. We were suddenly accepted as Hutterian brothers and sisters. With this in mind I greet you and plead with you not to be afraid, since it is so obviously a leading from God. I greet you in unity and peace as

your Heini

P.S. I want to tell you that Jake Vetter says he does not remember ever having experienced such a meeting. I really believe the Upper Church was there and that my father was blessing this gift. In this sense I greet you.

*Don A*: There was great jubilation, also on the part of all the brothers who came to greet us afterward. Yet in the midst of it Heini's first concern as he came out was, "Have I done the right thing? Will the brotherhood be in agreement?" And of course, you in the brotherhoods were meeting at the very same time.

Then we went over to Sam Kleinsasser Vetter's house and into a room packed with people. When Heini phoned the joint brotherhoods and asked the question, there came back a resounding, thankful "Yes!" This was only through God's leading. No one raised a question.

*Don A*: How Heini's whole heart was longing to put itself under our brotherhoods. He was full of concern that the brothers and sisters at home understand the situation, and that came out in his letter again and again. Those of us there felt his anguish that he might not have done it quite right.

*Peter S. Tschetter Vetter* (in a letter to Samuel and Rebecca Kleinsasser at Sturgeon Creek on January 13, 1974):

Dear Sam Vetter, with all those who are with you including all preachers in South Dakota, Montana, and Alberta:

The greeting of the devout shall be with you, for it brings peace with it.

We have come home safely under God's protection. We found everybody waiting for us. I must thank you very especially for your warm hospitality.

I am also remembering much that was said for and against. Many, many things should not have happened. But that is how mankind is.

Now, dear Sam Vetter, here is my humble insight: the Lord has led it, and we did not even think of it; God the Lord has guided our hearts, since the Arnoldleut prayed for such a long time.

Don't we feel that this is a centenary, yes, a year of jubilee, because those who prayed have persevered without ceasing—a jubilee year, a freeing year, a year of forgiveness and reconciliation, in which both the lower and the higher ones have turned their hearts through God's goodness and have been united in a new year, in a new life, which comes from God: from Jews and Gentiles one people has been made! For this I cannot hold up my hands high enough; a number of over one thousand people brought into the Hutterian Church, a whole people! Let us not give up; the Lord has done it.

For this our fathers have already broken the land, hoped, built, with an ardent longing and desire to bring the people to the right insight. May God continue to concern himself with us poor, weak men, for the sake of his praise, honor, and majesty, and may he expect us to become still more humble and thereby bring him a pleasing sacrifice. Amen.

Warm greetings to all preachers, of high or low station. I remain a very lowly

Peter S. Tschetter

For that January 7 meeting we had been seated toward the back of the room. All of the brothers in the front and Heini spoke German to one another. Yet it was as though I could follow everything, although I don't know German. Maybe it was from picking up a word here or there, but the atmosphere of God at that moment just carried everything in a way that we understood. In subsequent years when any of us went back to Sturgeon Creek, that room where the reuniting took place seemed as if it had shrunk to one quarter the size. Our impression and memory of the gathering was that it was tremendous, as if there weren't only seventy ministers there, but throngs of angels too. It was quite a shock to come there later and see a very small room.

*Dwight* (in closing these reports of the reuniting): I can hardly comprehend what this hour must mean for Eberhard, who fought for and was given, through the Holy Spirit, unity with the brothers whom men call Hutterian. As he put it, an inheritance was established for us. In the years after his death this uniting was destroyed through the sin of leading away from Christ — but not by Heini, our beloved Elder, who fought for his father's vision that our Bruderhof life be directed toward Jesus alone. God alone has prepared the way through all these years so that this falling away can be forgiven, also for Heini, freeing him and us all for what lies ahead. Heini's trip to Manitoba in 1964 was not in vain. May God lead us that his will be done in every part of our community life.

We have so much to rejoice about, to be thankful for. God has worked powerfully through our brother Heini, with great promise. May He also give him strength for all that lies ahead. Jake Vetter said, "Now Heini Vetter can speak out."

On January 8, 1974, at 10:30 a.m. a telegram was received, sent to Joseph Vetter, Jacob Vetter, and the ministers meeting at Sturgeon Creek:

> Our four *Gemeinden* in the United States and England are deeply moved by your uniting love and compassion. We praise God that he gave it to your hearts to forgive our beloved Heini Vetter after he humbled himself for our sin, and that he is recognized as our Elder given by the whole Church. We greet you in the peace and unity of our Jesus.
>
> From your jubilant brothers and sisters in Woodcrest, Evergreen, New Meadow Run, and Darvell.

It is wonderful that our joy and thankfulness were expressed the very next day. I hope that it doesn't at any time become confusing for anybody when we speak or read about Heini asking for forgiveness. Normally one asks for forgiveness for one's own sins, but in this case Heini asked forgiveness for what others had done. He received forgiveness as though he had done it, but he had not.

On a phone call to Christoph on Wednesday, January 9, Dwight said:

> Jake Vetter said your mother should come as soon as possible for a short visit—maybe ten days. . . . Throughout the whole trip your father has been given strength. But at no point on Monday could he lie down; in the meeting he was mostly either standing or getting up to speak.

The Brothers had repeatedly said to Heini, "Heini Vetter, you can speak from where you are seated, you don't have to get up." But every time, even if Heini was only going to answer yes or no, he stood up out of respect. He would struggle to get his splinted leg off the little stool, while Dwight and Don would take his arms and help him up and back down again. This is one of the things that moved the hearts of the Brothers so much. Then Dwight wrote home on January 14:

> Heini does not have the strength for much more on this journey. Yesterday he spent most of the day resting, and though he seemed a bit stronger this morning, he did not look very well. There are so many things he has promised, for which he does not have the strength. Only the love shown by the brothers here at Milltown and Crystal Spring has made it possible for Heini to continue. We could not match the love they have shown to us here. Mike Vetter and Dave and all here in Milltown have done everything they could think of for us.
>
> So yesterday evening we went to Sturgeon Creek. Heini stayed in Milltown with Don and rested and dictated letters. Samuel Vetter and his wife Rebecca Basel welcomed us warmly. Two Lehrerleut ministers from Alberta and Montana stopped in on their way to Michigan to arrange some printing. After supper we began to sing. Their young girls came in (the boys hardly dared to) and sang some songs. Then we sang. All got more and more into the spirit of it and more relaxed, so that even the Lehrerleut brothers were taking part. They knew some of the *Reichslieder*, and they did not object to our singing them in English. In fact, they praised the translation. Then Glenn, Merrill, and I told how we had come to the Bruderhof, which they were very eager to hear. The evening ended in a close and brotherly spirit.
>
> Samuel Vetter said tonight he feels there is a movement

going through the Hutterites, and he hopes it will bring everything to a better direction. I had to think what it will mean for us. May God truly lead us in everything ahead. I greet you in peace and unity.

How joyful Heini was when Annemarie arrived; it meant so much to him. Our room filled up again with brothers, sisters, young girls, and children, while Heini and Annemarie were having a cup of tea. On January 15 he wrote to all brothers and sisters:

> Annemarie and I and all the brothers with us send you the greeting of peace and unity. Apart from nursing me, our daughter Else spends the whole day with the young girls of the different communities. This gives me the possibility to hear what the young people think, want, and seek. She informs me again and again that the Hutterian communities expect a revival and a renewal through the uniting with us and that the young people are extremely hungry for this inner relationship. My heart burns with love for them and for our own young people that God may give this. Apart from our expenses for daily bread and building, I think it is right to invest everything we have in this one thing: to help the awakening that is already taking place here among the young people.
>
> Michael Kleinsasser serves me as a male nurse. He stays right by me, watches that I don't fall, takes off the brace and fits it on again, and shows his love from morning until evening.
>
> I do not know what lies ahead of us; I only know that God has led us until today. I was asked only one question before the uniting and gladly promised only this one thing: never again to take baptized members from the Hutterians into our communities without permission. There were no questions, no "points"; everything was left open. And I was so fully accepted that, after the forgiveness was spoken out, I was recognized

as your Elder, and all the servants here are recognized in their services. This morning Dwight held the *Lehr* (teaching) in the Gemeindestunde, and Merrill read from Andreas Ehrenpreis about love to the brothers. Dave Waldner came to me, also Mike Kleinsasser, and they were very moved and touched.

I have only one hindrance, and that is that my body is not as strong as I wish. Else does everything she can think of, and the brothers are most considerate. But some, in their great love and wish to meet Heini Vetter, give me a very strenuous day. Then Mike Vetter keeps people away so I can rest. Dave and Mike Waldner do the same. Unfortunately in spite of all this, I am not strong enough to do all that I want so very much to do. It distresses me that when I am especially tired and not feeling well, the brothers can't understand my speech. But I have to accept it.

Since I am now very much loved and my name is known in all colonies, even where I have not been, I believe that my task will be to write *Sendbriefe* (circular letters) to be printed for all Hutterian Brethren. My hope is that after the visit of the ministers to us in the East and after the church discipline of all those who came to us from the West, a brother can spend several days with Jake Vetter and write down the name and address of every Bruderhof in the West and also of each family and individual. This will enable us to write in a much more personal way to the colonies.

We should be aware that we are being received with such enormous love that I am not sure if it is not more loving than the way we received them. Even when they come only to sing, they are so overjoyed. For Else they do everything they can. I do not think we can talk over anything here about the future until the visit of the [five] ministers has taken place.

After the reuniting there were several journeys in Manitoba

during January, but Heini was himself able to travel very little. One day we did go together to Huron. Another day Dwight and I went to Forest River with Mike Vetter of Milltown. It was wonderful to spend the hours in the car talking with him on the way there and back.

Another visit was with Dwight to Lakeside. We were aware that Heini had very much on his mind and heart that Forest River had borrowed money from various Western communities, one of them Lakeside. Because Forest River was in a poor financial position, this money had never been paid back. So the brotherhood decided to make out a check to Lakeside; Dwight and I went there and spent a very wonderful hour with Jörg Wipf Vetter. He was quite weak and unwell on this second visit (the first one had been with Heini in 1964). He was very loving and refused to take the check. He said, "You brothers don't owe us anything; that is all forgiven, settled, and over with." But then Dwight said to him, "Jörg Vetter, we were asked to do this and we want to. Maybe someday you can help us when we have a need." Then he accepted it and later wrote a very loving letter to Heini in thanks and in joy over the whole thing. Jörg Vetter had been too sick to come to the January 7 meeting at Sturgeon Creek.

On our last day there (Saturday, January 19), Heini was quite a bit better; he must have been, or we couldn't have traveled. On Friday many people came and said, "Could I just say good-bye to Heini Vetter?" and he couldn't turn anybody down. That evening there was a joyful farewell supper and a singing time in the dining room. Some had to travel for hours to get there. We sang our spirituals, also "There is a balm in Gilead," which we had sung everywhere we went.

The delegation of five ministers to make suggestions for corrections and improvements arrived in Woodcrest on the 27th of January. They visited our three places in the States. It was an experience of great love, especially the exclusions. There had been a lot of fear and trembling from different ones of us. Afterward everyone wondered what the fear was all about. In Woodcrest in 1986 Jake Vetter (one of the five) shared about this visit:

> Five brothers were to come to Woodcrest to work out the suggestions agreed on at the reuniting. This was all thoroughly dealt with. Then Heini Vetter experienced another great astonishment in how these five brothers led in a wonderful reconciliation. I don't know where that power came from, and all that wisdom. Nothing was left undone; they did everything.
>
> Who got rid of all the fear of rules among you? I didn't. None of us can say we did. But God knew the uniting Spirit was there, making us all of one mind and one heart like the early church. Then even a united dress fell into place. Wanting to be different disappears when God sends the spirit of unity. In John 17 Jesus prayed, "Father, make my disciples one as we are one." This Spirit is what we need. This is why at Pentecost they were all of one heart, one mind, one soul, and one accord. The Spirit did it. I still marvel at the real, true, honest forgiveness from our wonderful God. Before, we could have written a thick book about accusations and guilt. Now they are all gone. The Christlike spirit brought us together and made us forgive each other and bear each other. I thank God all the time.

My calendar entry for February 6, 1974, was: "mtg re 'points' NO demands." And Heini wrote in "A Printed Sendbrief" to the Western Brothers in March 1974:

> I want to thank you and the Schmiedeleut *Gemeinden* for sending us the five representatives from Manitoba, South Dakota, and Minnesota. The visit of these elders has been of

the greatest importance to us. We feel that God wants to do something at this hour. We feel we need you, and your beloved brothers said that we need one another. The visit with your representatives was full of harmony and the grace of God. We are deeply touched by the humililty and love represented by all five brothers who were with us.

The whole question of the united dress was still difficult in that year of 1974 after the five ministers visited, because a few found it hard to face up to that question. And so there were other trips throughout the year (including those to and from Darvell) for the inner fight in our own communities. But God did give us unity, and we did purchase the "Sunheart" airplane out of our longing to make faster trips to our brothers in the West, which then bore out what Heini had said in his March *Sendbrief*:

We cannot express strongly enough how thankful we are that this visit draws a line under the terrible split that took place in 1955. It is a grace of God that full forgiveness of the Church was given. God worked mightily among us while you brothers were with us, and he is continuing to work among us and among you.

# 13
# *We Would Be Building*

We have looked earlier at our time of unprecedented collapse in the year 1961: Primavera in Paraguay was closed down and moved to the northern hemisphere; Sinntal and Wheathill in Europe were both closed as functioning Bruderhof communities. It was the fruit of years of not being centered enough in Jesus Christ, years with lots of goodwilling human effort. People did certainly join the Bruderhof in Primavera and in England during the 1950s and earlier, so these years were not fruitless. But the erosion of the foundation—not any wrong form or lack of goodwill—led to the crises of the years 1959, '60, and '61. To put it in Hutterian terms, the lantern was there but the Light within the lantern had flickered very low.

After 1961 in our story, we jumped to the 1964 and 1974 journeys of reuniting with our Western (Hutterian) brothers. The closing of Primavera in '61 had brought to an end the need of supporting those hofs and of staffing them with responsible services. But as the year 1962 began, there was still no solution for the service of the Word in Bulstrode. Young brothers, witness brothers from the States, were still coming and going in relays until shortly after Easter, when Georg and Moni were able to

231

take up their services. Again one could recite a list of many journeys back and forth, each a number of weeks in duration. I experienced such a time in Bulstrode in April and May of 1962 and remember it vividly. One of the witness brothers, Jack Melancon, had gone over with Don Noble to replace the Bloughs. There came a crisis into Jack's personal life, and I was sent to replace him. Don Noble was responsible for the service while I was there, though he had not been appointed as a witness brother. But he was able to carry that kind of service as well as any.

With the closing down of Primavera and many families coming to England, there came every day a deluge of letters with requests, complaints, or bitterness—or longing for contact. People who were away from the community had many needs after being absent from England for up to twenty years. And there were the needs of others away from Wheathill, Bulstrode, or Sinntal. All these letters would stack up on the desk, and it was almost impossible to turn to them because of the needs in the household of Bulstrode itself. Each day the pile would grow. It was a time of unspeakable difficulty and distress, and of not knowing how on earth to cope with it. Heini, Annemarie, and Christoph were also there for a month before Easter, and that was a great help. If only Heini had been there all the time, he would have found a way. He would have assigned to different ones the responsibility to answer this letter or that, but we younger people were just snowed under.

It was in the middle of my visit to Bulstrode that Heini and Annemarie and Christoph were first able to visit and be greatly strengthened by two daughters and three granddaughters of Christoph Blumhardt. (His father's name, Johann Christoph, had been chosen by Heini for his own son.) All these sisters were still living in a fresh yet quiet spirit that reflected the life and witness of their two forefathers. We have been able to maintain a warm and mutually rewarding contact.

For Easter 1962 Woodcrest had the experience of singing

Mendelssohn's *Elijah* for the first time, with Dwight singing the beautiful tenor solos. The wedding of Klaus and Irene Meier in June was the first in nearly two years. In July we had our very first joint brotherhood meeting, when we met together at Woodcrest from all three American Bruderhofs. That was our first conference after Primavera had moved up north. In that conference on July 13 Heini was at last appointed and confirmed as our Elder. Many people have had the idea that he was the Elder before, but he had never been given that service or that name previously. And only then were Art and Doug confirmed in the service of the Word and Don Noble appointed on trial.

In August there was the baptism of ten people—the first Woodcrest baptism in three years. Now the fact that there had been no baptisms there for three years and no weddings for two, was indicative of the time the hofs were passing through. Heini and Annemarie made another trip to Bulstrode in November, and in December came the final sale of the Sinntal property.

The year 1963 was a year of increased reaching out to brothers and sisters who were away, with trips to South America and to England to visit and help as many as possible. In October Dwight Blough and Dick Domer were appointed to the service of the Word, and at the end of the year Dick Domer, Howard Johnson, and Stan Ehrlich made a trip to South America to visit those no longer with us.

In 1964 we considered seriously whether we should vote in the Johnson/Goldwater presidential elections. Heini had first introduced the question in a household meeting on July 19: "Since the Goldwater convention, I have asked myself if we do not live too much to ourselves. And yet we have only the authority of Jesus—defenseless love like sheep among wolves—not to preach hatred but love to the enemy (also to Mr. Goldwater)." Then after more than a week of serious searching for unity, Heini summed up our united feeling in a members' meeting on July 27:

We have come here to exchange from heart to heart what
our responsibility is in this hour, especially for this country we
live in. It will be very important that we all express what we
feel—also that we listen, inwardly listen, to what God wants
to say to us. The question was brought up in this brotherhood
by two or three people: shouldn't we consider voting this year?
Have we not a responsibility that extremists do not take over
this country?

There have also been other suggestions, from an urge that
we do something and make a witness. We heard the question
yesterday: Has not the hour come when the brotherhoods have
to ask God that he may give something of the apostolic
mission—even in the most humble way—not that we can bring
it about? Even though we never dare to name it, that is what
we should ask for. It is an hour when we should not go to
sleep. We should not be depressed but seek the joy in God. . . .

It would be good if we could get clear on a direction about
voting. My feeling is that the longing behind this question is
that we do something and don't live just for ourselves. We
don't at all feel united to go out and vote. I would even go so
far as to say that I would have a bad conscience to do it—but
I would also have a bad conscience if we were to think only
of ourselves. I do find it responsible to ask the question; it
should bring us face to face with the hour. The government is
always bound together with the police and the electric chair,
and it is not what we are called to; it has not the sheep's nature.
But I feel that behind this question, since it came so sincerely,
is a feeling of responsibility for mankind.

Every individual brother and sister has a responsibility in
this hour to return to our first calling, cost what it will. We
must not go to sleep, we have to watch. We have to give
ourselves. It has to come about that at least two people from
every Bruderhof—even from the weakest Bruderhof—are sent

out. It has to come that we dare to appoint people for the service and give them our whole support for this kind of mission—in whatever way God might give it. I hope very much that the younger people are also included in this outreach. It is a serious hour. In England some strongly believe that if Goldwater comes to power, it could mean a world war. We might be protected from war, but it could still mean that horrible things are done. This should challenge us to give our hearts, our souls, and our lives in love.

Since the first Manitoba journey seeking reconciliation with the Western Brothers has been covered, I will skip to 1965. The Civil Rights movement came closer to us in March of that year. Heini and Dwight's concerns led us in our involvement. I quote from Milton Zimmerman's report, based on his diary:

This whole movement for justice for blacks in the South had been going on for some years. We had become involved in the spring of 1964 when Michael Schwerner and two other men were murdered in Mississippi as they worked among the blacks to support them in their striving for the basic civil rights that everyone else in America takes for granted. In February 1965 our Congressman from New York went down to Selma, Alabama, with fourteen other Congressmen because blacks were having a very hard time getting registered to vote. Two weeks later Jimmy Lee Jackson was shot by a state trooper. A week after that on February 25, a federal district judge in Mississippi threw out the conspiracy charges against the men in Mississippi who were about to stand trial.

Later seven of the charged were found guilty (by a jury of Mississippi whites) of conspiring to deprive Mickey Schwerner, James Chaney, and Andrew Goodman of their civil rights.

According to Cagin and Dray in *We Are Not Afraid*, Macmillan, New York, 1988, they were sentenced variously from three to ten years, and after losing their appeals, began serving sentences on March 19, 1970, five-and-a-half years after the murders.

Christoph and Art Wiser were in Atlanta and could go to the burial meeting for Jimmy Lee Jackson in Marion, Alabama. Then on Sunday, March 7, came the first attempt by the blacks to march from Brown's Chapel in Selma, when they were brutally attacked at the bridge by the police. Scenes from this attack were on television all over America. Everybody was aghast at the brutality they could see right there on their screens. Two days later Dwight, Doug, and Mark went off to Birmingham and Selma. There was continuing violence; a minister named James Reeb from Boston was savagely attacked in Selma and died as a result. Our brothers returned home a few days later because it seemed the march would not soon take place.

Dwight told us most enthusiastically what he had experienced. The main action was still centered around ministers like Martin Luther King. Their meetings were in churches, and they sang spirituals over and over. There was much in this mass movement that had reference to faith and hope and to the justice of God. I remember Dwight saying they felt heart and soul with these songs, especially "We shall overcome."

Later Stanley Fletcher arrived from Bulstrode. A few days after that there was a communal brotherhood meeting in which we decided to send brothers to Alabama, because it looked as if the march from Selma would be possible after all. Dwight and others had made contacts with the S.C.L.C. (Southern Christian Leadership Conference). We had some reports about what was being planned and hoped for, and we all felt with Heini that we should send representatives from the brotherhood.

Five of us went down with Heini in time for this march.

Heini marched the whole way that first day. It was eight miles, and it was hot. But it wasn't fast walking and we stopped often for a little rest on the side of the road. We met many of the people—there were thousands marching. Since Heini had already had so much heart trouble, it is amazing that he walked eight miles that Sunday. He wanted contact with all the blacks who longed for justice and peace—at that point, still in a nonviolent way. (The Black Power movement became widespread only later.) On the day the march came to an end, Mrs. Viola Liuzzo was fatally shot. There were several who paid the whole price.

Dwight Blough was one of those brothers who was relied on heavily when the year 1961 came with great upheaval: In June he was in England for six weeks, and then again in November— this time with Norann—for thirteen weeks in Bulstrode, responsible for the service of the Word although not appointed. Although very new in the community life, Dwight was totally dedicated and worked very closely with Heini at every step. In many ways one thinks of them together: our brother Dwight and our Elder Heini. What they have meant for our life together in all that has taken place through their services is staggering in its significance to us.

Then in 1965 there came a time with Dwight in Oak Lake/New Meadow Run that was important for the whole church. Kathy and I and our family had moved there in 1962 and remained for a period of six years. But before the Bloughs came in 1965, we had been given a three-month rest in Woodcrest. Even though Dwight was still teaching in the school, he and I worked together on the Carriage House extension of the dining room (later the brotherhood room) and on the extension for the offices at the north end of that building. That was a great joy. The use of blue

Heini and Annemarie have
a gemütlich hour with the
Blumhardt descendants

On the way to Selma, Alabama—1965

Brown's Chapel before the mar

and orange paint as at the Rhön Bruderhof was a completely new idea. Our dining rooms were all pale pastel colors, and there were quite a few who were not sure they were going to like the change at all. Well, it was the right color for then, as we all know, and this blue remained for over twenty years.

Our two families drove out to Oak Lake together. At our farewell lovemeal from Woodcrest, Milton gave Dwight a long package, a plaque with big letters and numbers, the Woodcrest telephone number, as a reminder for Dwight to phone Woodcrest. (In those days there was no such thing as a direct line; we had to place all our calls through the operator.) Dwight said:

> It is not only numbers that are on this board that Milton gave us tonight: one cannot see it with the eye—this overwhelming love that carries us. I hope that we can fully serve it. To be gathered in this room is a tremendous gift: brothers and sisters through love. I look forward to the summer in Oak Lake, and we will feel the unity and the going forward with you.

If we today walk round the New Meadow Run hof and look at what was once the resort hotel (the old main building of Oak Lake), we may see a lot that still needs doing. But if we think of what was there at the beginning thirty years ago, there is no comparison. It is fantastic what God has given since then.

Before we had legal possession, the resort hotel had several bars for the sale of liquor, a chief source of income. What was a "grand ballroom" for dancing became our school, and what was a boathouse was for years our Children's House. There was no play space for children except the little lawn between the hotel and the boathouse, a small ball field out back, and a small hill clearing in the woods that we named the Indian Festival Ground.

And there was an atmosphere on the place that had an effect on brothers and sisters. Already in 1962 a servant and family had been sent there with very great enthusiasm by Woodcrest. The fresh wind they brought was met with coolness and resistance, so Heini asked them to come back. Later on the family returned to Oak Lake, but the struggle against the atmosphere of that place was a continuing one.

In this fight for a new time, even donkeys had a part. We had several in 1962—Eeyore, Sheeyore, and Acorn. One of them had a terrible problem with her hoofs; they were like overgrown fingernails. They were splitting and splaying out, in very bad condition. Heini saw this on a June visit, and he knew exactly what to do. We got together some tools for him—different kinds of knives and chisels. When we had approached the donkey, Heini reached down and pulled up a hoof and went to work. He wasn't very strong at the time and was soon winded. Even though with his agricultural training Heini knew how to handle an animal, this donkey was scared stiff, and she began to lie down on him while others of us were holding her up. He worked away and gave the donkey a very nice manicure. It all turned out well in the end. Eeyore was given to Woodcrest that year and welcomed in family meeting the first Sunday of June 1962.

The new time for the hof really began when Dwight arrived in June of 1965. The first thing he wanted to get his teeth into was the dining room. Dwight always had renovation in mind. He was not one to tear down something just to get rid of it. He always wanted to renew, even though he did once look down the second-floor hallway in the Main House—240 feet of rug—and say, "I wish I could drive a bulldozer down this!" The dining room was a pale green color and had enormous plaster pillars, huge things, two to three feet in each dimension— tremendous— and they led up to big plaster beams that ran along the ceiling. I think the ceiling was a shade of light green also, and between all these pillars were great lighted milk-white globes. Originally there had even been sickly pastel-colored Chinese murals—

pagodas, lakes, and trees—and silk bags with silk tassels hanging down over the lights; all these had long since disappeared. But there was still a carpet on the floor with quite a complicated pattern of green, yellow, orange, and purple! For years there had been a running battle to get rid of the carpets (first in the corridor upstairs), but the ones on the dining-room floor were still there. There were two big windows in the room, each with wired glass in them as fireproofing. The fire escape came right down across one of the windows, and if you opened that window to get air, there was an impossible cat that used to come into the room. Nobody would do anything about it as he stalked into the brotherhood circle.

So there was plenty of need for renovation, and when David Maendel left to go to Woodcrest for his wedding, Dwight had a real sparkle in his eyes and said, "Let's get this place completely renovated and changed by the time David and Maria come back from their wedding trip!" (Since Dwight had rehearsed Haydn's *Creation* with the Woodcrest choir and had promised to sing the tenor solos for their wedding, the work had to proceed without him for a week.) The renovation question was brought into the brotherhood, and straight after the meeting Dwight went for the sledgehammer, and we had our first work evening getting rid of those pillars then and there. As Kathy said, "They were full of pipes and plumbing and wires and . . . oh, what a mess!"

All this was just the thing for Fred Goodwin's training as an engineer. He really enjoyed that renovation. We took that room completely apart. Fred calculated the weights so the building wouldn't collapse. The new metal posts had to be extended right through down to the basement. We had to dig big holes in the basement floor for great concrete piers to bear the weight of the whole building above. Then we took out all the windows on the south end and knocked away all the plaster. We were sure we would find a steel I beam right in the middle of them, and we

Family meeting
welcomes Eeyore

South entry to the New Meadow Run
dining room—1965

We took out all the windows . . .

put in
French doors,

a porch,

and steps . . .

to gather
on the lawn

were going merrily away at the hollow tiles with our sledge-hammers when we found out that there was no steel in there! We had to do some emergency shoring up—fast.

But the aim was—our new dining room (later the brotherhood room). We were meeting twice a day in it for our mealtimes, and for all our meetings. It was a long room and tended to be dark and airless. Dwight's aim was to have French windows that could open up the whole south end to a porch with steps going down outside. Then we could gather before a lovemeal on the lawn outside. That was a radical change. Those doors look a bit old today, but they were a breath of fresh air in 1965 in more ways than one.

Emy-Margret had a little piece of the original orange-painted plaster from the dining room at the Rhön Bruderhof. We tried hard to match it. We looked and looked and looked for orange paint that was truly orange and for fluorescent lights that didn't make it look like mud or people look as if they had jaundice. But finally some meat-counter lights were just the right thing. In Kathy's words:

> We painted and painted, but the brothers had all the lights down and all the electricity off, and we couldn't really tell what it looked like. But finally we were pleased to see how bright it was.

The next big change at Oak Lake that summer of '65 was recently described by Kathy for the children:

> We all knew that we could bring our problems to Heini, whether they were problems in the brotherhood or problems you children had. He would help us see whether our problem that we thought was big was actually small and whether we were not even seeing the big problem. Often Heini would have quite an unexpected answer, usually simple, clear, and direct.

Because he lived so close to God, he had a much bigger vision. I always think of Dwight in this, because Dwight listened carefully to those ideas of Heini's and would respond enthusiastically.

In the middle of that summer—it must have been in July— Heini and Annemarie came out to visit us. Dwight and Norann, Dave and Maria (just married), Christoph, and Merrill and I went to Somerset to meet them in a little diner for supper. During the meal we were pouring out all the problems at Oak Lake—I remember us all talking at once and Heini just listening. After supper he shoved his chair back, and I thought, "He is going to tell us the answers to at least some of these problems." He said, "Well, this is maybe a crazy idea, but what would you think if we were to drain that lake?" Well, we just could not believe it; that was the last thing we expected him to say. We could not understand at all how that would solve any of the problems. Some of us thought the lake was rather beautiful, and the children enjoyed it.

Now we all lived together in the one big house: the school, children's house, kitchen, laundry, and meetings were all in that one big building. You could go to supper or meetings in your slippers. You could put your laundry down a chute. You didn't have to pick up your children; they just walked upstairs when snacktime came. You didn't even have to put boots and snowpants on your children to go to school. And so we got pretty lazy; we got used to things being easy. And there was a lot of ungratefulness for all we had and lots of complaining and saying no to change.

Until the summer after we had built the new shop and had moved the baby house into the former boathouse (February 1965), we had had the lake on one side and the highway on the other. All the big trucks coming to us had to come off Route 40 right through the little children's playground. So

Heini's idea of draining the lake wasn't so crazy after all. It would change the whole hof: we would have a place for the children to play and could build a new road all the way to the shop without going out on Route 40. Within a very few minutes, while some of the rest of us were still thinking this idea over, Dwight was very enthused and was ready to go pull the plug on that lake. The rest of us were so easily halfhearted or stingy or lukewarm, with a real resistance to the Spirit.

As you can imagine, it was a very exciting time when we decided to pull the plug and drain the lake. There was a huge pipe about two feet in diameter at the bottom of the dam, with a big wheel that you could crank around and around and around for some minutes. That would open a valve and the water would shoot through. At first the meadow was not so romantic — it was acres and acres of mud. Not only that, the contour was wrong; it followed the original stream bed, which meandered all over the place. The stream that was later on the west side of the meadow had to be put there. This was done by a great big backhoe, from the causeway-to-be on down to the dam. But upstream from this causeway there was nothing for a backhoe to stand on to divert the stream; it would have sunk down into that chocolate pudding.

So the delights of dynamite came in. Dwight had already shown his joy in dynamite when the first barn for the school was built in Woodcrest where the Rhön dining room was later. But going around with Dwight when he dynamited stumps for the new road from the causeway out past the shop made me nervous. To see him ram a hole in the ground with a big rod and then peel the paper off a couple of sticks of dynamite and push them down the hole, then take the handle of the sledgehammer and tamp that stuff down into the hole — you wondered how close to stand. Then he would set the cap. He very strictly told us we must not run for cover and risk falling down, but after the fuse was lit, we must walk. So we would steel ourselves to walk away and then hide behind a tree. The thing would go boom and the stump would jump out. And each time we over in the office would get a phone call from Mrs. Gorley, the previous owner who lived up the hill from us. (On one or two occasions rocks had come down on her roof—rocks from the other side of the lake!) All this was to move the entrance to the community so the trucks wouldn't come in through the children's play area.

Dynamiting a *ditch*, however, was one thing that Dwight did not have experience with. We had heard that you could make a very nice ditch with dynamite, and that it was much easier than digging. So Dwight laid out the dynamite upstream (to the south) from where the causeway was to be. It was relatively easy to make the holes for it; you just rammed the rod in and reached down with a stick of dynamite the length of your arm and set it in there. What we did not know was that you are supposed to pile the dynamite sticks on top of each other all the way up to the surface. The first time around, Dwight just put one down at the bottom. We had the holes all lined up, a foot apart, for over a hundred feet. The first stick would be set off with a fuse and cap. The rest would go off by a chain reaction from the concussion.

Well, it worked beautifully. We stood back and watched that thing go off and watched a hundred tons of mud go straight up into the air about thirty feet, and then fall straight back down into the ditch! Until then, we could get around by laying down boards to walk or crawl on. Now it was really *soup*, and we had to start all over again. Eventually it all got cleared out, but then when the blast was done right, the mud was plastered nicely on all the leaves of the surrounding trees.

Dwight's threat about driving a bulldozer did not remain only a threat (though not down the hall). We got a bulldozer and a dump truck, and they worked for months and months and months.

The bank at the back of the ball field provided us with the fill for the lake and the causeway. Different brothers usually operated the bulldozer. We let a neighbor drive the dump truck, and we told him if he worked so many hours for us, he could have it. He worked off the hours, and so we did not have to figure out how to get rid of it.

After the causeway was finished and the lake filled, we hired a bulldozer to push this dirt (mixed with the mud) across the meadow. This gave it the contour it now has, with the water flow moved from the east side to the west side. That took a tremendous amount of work, but it was a lot of fun.

Later, when the new road was built, what work projects we had there, gathering and burning the branches! There was a spirit of vigor about it—the same spirit that came from Dwight. He also had a lot of daring, but he was not foolhardy. Very seldom was there an accident. I think it was because his life was centered in Jesus. He built tree houses with the children, and they dove off high places, had fast sled and go-cart runs, and so on. We have heard how Eberhard also liked children to be daring and to do daring things, but he would not allow them to endanger themselves unnecessarily.

Dwight and half a dozen of the boys caught the last of the fish that were left in a little pool at the bottom of the lake. Some conservation men came out with a truck and sorted out the good fish (the game fish) from the bad, and the boys and Dwight were a sight—all mud from their necks down.

All these changes had also a strong and important bearing on the inner life of this Bruderhof. As we tell further about what happened in the autumn of that year, it will become clearer. But it was not only this hof; this kind of comfortableness that Kathy mentioned is a danger everywhere. If we are comfortable, we tend to like it, and there is something about wanting to be comfortable that just plain opposes Christianity. It got so bad that

Drained lake—summer 1965

All mud from the neck down . . .

New Meadow Run
—1983

Dwight helps go-cart repair . . .

His bulldozer dream became reality . . .

. . . He lays
dynamite as Fred
watches and Merrill
and Ian take cover

someone from the backwoods of our Primavera hofs (without any bathtubs) found it unbearable that a bathtub was removed and that he had to walk fifty feet down the hall to the next one. Yes, we even had a crusade against bathtubs. They came out by the dozen. So did many of the wash sinks that were in every room— oh, many things! You can't look down the 240 feet of corridor in the Main House anymore; it is full of jogs and jigs that have been put there to make the rooms more usable on each side of the hall and to give a more homey feeling to that second floor.

We didn't have the lake after this summer of 1965, but we still called it Oak Lake, and that didn't quite fit anymore. For a new name, we thought of "Meadow Run" because of the little stream in the meadow. If I remember right, it was Emmy (Arnold) who said, "No, it should be called New Meadow Run." I think we shouldn't forget that—our Bruderhof is located at *New* Meadow Run.

While Heini and Annemarie were with us that summer of 1965, telephone calls had come from Bulstrode saying they needed help. Heini returned to Woodcrest with Annemarie, and after a few days they left for Bulstrode. Over the years they had been absent from the family so much that this time it was felt that their girls should go with them. They went by boat and I wished such journeys could have taken place more often. It was a long one for Heini and Annemarie, but the girls had to return early for college and high school.

Heini and Annemarie had not been long in Bulstrode before it was clear there was a need for more support in the service over there, for someone to carry the main responsibility inwardly. The servants here in the States met at the Top Motel to talk over the situation. Those were mighty lively meetings. I mean there was fun too, with Dwight and the other brothers. It was during the camping season, about the middle of August. When we decided to send the Nobles to Bulstrode, they were with one of our school groups down in Maryland at Swallow Falls. I drove Pete and Sarah Hofer down there and informed them; they had to pack up. The Hofers stayed with the school group, and a week later the Nobles were on their way to Bulstrode for a long period.

Don had been part of the team helping Dwight, so before he left, Dwight had the idea of an outing with the witness brothers on the Yough Reservoir. That was the first time we ever rented one of those pontoon boats. That was quite a thing, to go out there and spend a day with the brothers, eating and celebrating.

When Heini and Annemarie returned from Europe in October '65, Dwight and Norann, David and Maria, Christoph, and Kathy and I went over to Woodcrest to welcome them home and to celebrate with them the engagement of Christoph and Verena. We were also looking forward to the wedding of Seppel and Christine in New Meadow Run and began preparations for it.

About that time the new entry road for New Meadow Run was completed. The previous entrance had been a terrible hazard— right off the highway past the school library. Cars or trucks coming down Route 40 from the east had to turn midway on the hill into our entry, with the risk of having the high-speed traffic behind plow into them. So one of the high priorities had been to get that new causeway road finished. In the middle of October we had a real ceremony. We formally closed the old entrance by putting a white picket fence across. (Later on a stone wall was built there.) At the shop there was a ribbon across the new road. Fred Goodwin, our engineer, had to cut it with a pair of scissors. He wore a top hat and tail coat, and it was all done with ceremony. This was the sort of fun Dwight and Fred and all of us enjoyed.

Something else very much on Dwight's heart was to find ways to cut down the distance—those four hundred miles—to Woodcrest. As I mentioned, we did not have a direct phone line, and on every call to Woodcrest you were conscious of running up the cost. It was quite a strain on Dwight, who wanted the maximum sharing with Heini about all questions pertaining to our inner and outer life. So Dwight, who had once been a pilot, had himself checked out at an airport near Scottdale. After a few flights, he was approved for handling a small plane, and we planned a flight to Woodcrest, which turned out to be a landmark in New Meadow Run's history.

November 1, 1965, was a bright day even though the sky was fifty percent cloudy. First thing in the morning Dwight placed a phone call to Heini at Woodcrest. We servants talked about this and that, quite calmly, and then hung up. Dwight, Andreas, Mike Brandes, and I jumped in a waiting car and drove to the Scottdale airport. We had planned ahead that Sibyl was to meet us at New Paltz, five miles from Woodcrest.

We arrived at twenty minutes to twelve, Sibyl met us and drove us up to the hof, and we walked in just at dinnertime—three and a half hours before that, Dwight had been talking with Heini! Such a thing had never happened to us. It may not seem strange now, because there has been quite a bit of small-plane flying back and forth, but that was our first time. My, oh my, if we only had a picture of Heini's face when he saw us walking in. It was magnificent! He welcomed us warmly, "Now that you're here, let's use the time."

There were certainly things to talk about; there were meetings with the Woodcrest witness brothers that afternoon and with the brotherhood that evening. The next morning we met with all the services—brothers and sisters. For about twenty-four hours it was quite an intense and important time, like a conference.

Next day we left at noon and flew back home. On the way there, I might add, it had been very bumpy riding in the plane and some of us were more-than-enough queasy at moments. But we made it fine, and it was a joy to do that with Dwight. To our surprise, a special meal had been prepared to welcome us back, because it was felt how significant this was—to cut the time on four hundred miles and make a round trip in twenty-four hours! That evening we reported in the brotherhood. Unfortunately there were negative ripples too, and this was connected with the whole problem we had felt over the years—something of the old atmosphere of the place. I think someone had even commented, "Why have a lovemeal? They've had their fun."

It soon became clear that the small-plane flight wasn't really the main issue. When we talked all this over with Heini and the Woodcrest brothers on the phone, it was seen most seriously, not because of the plane flight, but because of a spirit of opposition to the oneness that binds us closely together and to the vitality and fresh wind that Dwight lived for.

So a joint brotherhood meeting was called, and the brotherhoods from Evergreen and Woodcrest got in rented coaches and came out to New Meadow Run and met with us for five days solid. I remember one comment that Sarah Hofer made at that time. She said, "In the laundry there's such a chairy atmosphere." (Cherry atmosphere? One thought first of a fruit.) And she explained, "Well, someone is always bringing a chair and putting it under you and saying, 'Aren't you tired? Don't you want to sit down?'" It was a sort of mutual self-indulgence. When Annemarie came out, she made the comment in quite a disgusted tone of voice, "They act like old *Knackers* (fuddy-duddies) here." That was a marvelous term, and it stuck. Pretty soon there was a little club of the old *Knackers* on the Bruderhof. You had to be fifty years old in order to get into it. I tried but never made it—nor did Dwight.

We had this serious conference lasting five days, but we were definitely not through the struggle. We had a breather; everybody went home for Advent, which came eleven days later. On the Tuesday following Advent, back came the brotherhoods in the buses—this time for four days. Don and Eve came over from Bulstrode to take part. They were a newly engaged couple. That

Dwight's flight to surprise Heini—November 1, 1965

Chartered bus leaves after Advent Conference in New Meadow Run—1965

conference was a real fight for the inner atmosphere. Its ripples spread way out from Oak Lake, or New Meadow Run as it was called by then. There was a follow-up conference in Evergreen in January, and then a trip to Bulstrode that eventually led to its move here to the States. All this was set in motion by these two joint brotherhood meetings, in which the thing that tipped it over the edge was Dwight's wonderful flight to Woodcrest.

When the brotherhoods had gone home after Advent 1965, New Meadow Run started the rehearsal of the little play-within-a-play in *A Midsummer Night's Dream*. This may seem incongruous, but something so stiff and stodgy there needed to be broken up. And that was the perfect play. There was great joy and pleasure in repeating it in Woodcrest before Christoph and Verena's wedding the next spring.

During the January 1966 follow-up conference in Evergreen, Doug and I were sent over to Bulstrode. One after another, others were also sent. We felt the problem there was very much the same as we faced in the States. I don't know what to call it—a stuffy atmosphere? Not that the house was stuffy, it was even a bit drafty and cold, but there was an inner stuffiness. The inspiration came to take down all the bookshelves that covered the walls and to redecorate the dining room in bright orange. There was a grand project to get this done. Meanwhile the situation at Bulstrode was seen as so serious that first Heini and Annemarie came for another visit and then all the servants for one week. That was in early March.

There was indeed an inner struggle there in Bulstrode. It took various forms. The dining room had a huge fireplace. Sometimes to have the fire burning was a necessity, but the many armchairs and footstools were not. Dwight got his teeth into all that too. We used to sing a song very often in those times in connection with the Civil Rights Movement, "Oh Freedom, Oh Freedom," and that song has in it the line, "No more weeping." Once when we were together, Heini enthusiastically suggested a few more lines like, "No more footstools over me" and "No more armchairs over me," and we sang them lustily.

But there was something inorganic about helping in the struggle at that distance across the Atlantic Ocean. Since there had been such a benefit in drawing closer together after Primavera closed in 1961, it was felt best for the whole church to gather now in the States. On March 20, 1966, the Bulstrode brotherhood and the three brotherhoods in the States decided to move the Bulstrode community. And so the U.S. hofs were built up, room was made, and by December of 1966 Bulstrode was closed and all had moved to the hofs in America.

Before going to Bulstrode in early March, Dwight had ordered for New Meadow Run the music to *The Seven Last Words* by Schütz. We had sung this at Woodcrest and it had meant much to us all. So Dwight was very chagrined when he came home from Bulstrode to find that the company had sent another composition with the same title but by a composer named Theodore Du Bois. Well, I had thought it was ordered on purpose, I was familiar with it already, and I was quite enthusiastic; together we took a second look and used it. Dwight sang the solos, and that was a wonderful musical and inner experience, singing that on Good Friday.

In February 1966 when Heini and Annemarie came over to Bulstrode by ship, they landed in Antwerp, Belgium, and the Nobles and I went over to meet them. One of the things we did in Antwerp was to go shopping in some huge department stores. Many of us have enjoyed the wonderful relationship between Heini and Annemarie and the humor that often came to the fore. One of the points of friendly, happy contention was often the issue of shopping. If there was anything Annemarie loved to do, it was to shop, and if there was anything Heini couldn't stand, it was to shop. The sisters enjoyed their shopping, and I stuck with Heini and enjoyed all of his comments. Of course he tried to get the sisters to wind it up, but no, there was something else to see on this floor, and something else to see over there, and so on. It was great fun.

The next night we stopped at a little village in France not far from Dunkirk, a bit inland, and found a hotel for the night. In Belgium we had found that nearly everywhere you went you could find someone speaking English. But in that little village nobody spoke English or German—nobody at the hotel, nobody at the police station, nobody in the stores, nobody on the street, and not one of us could speak French. Annemarie said that she had had French in school but couldn't remember much of it, at least not enough to be very useful. Also our hotel wasn't very clean and there were a few choice comments about that. But at supper we again heard wonderful stories and enjoyed being gemütlich. Then we went upstairs for a good night's sleep. But that night was the last before the beginning of Lent, and there was a big party downstairs, a party that really roared. They were singing and clapping, and it was loud. Our rooms were right above it. I think it was after one o'clock when things started to wind down. Remarkably enough they sang some songs in English. "It's a long way to Tipperary" was one of them. I don't know if they knew what they were singing.

In the summer after Heini's return from Bulstrode, we had many meetings at all our places on the question of federal income tax, looking at it closely and very seriously as to whether it was right to pay the taxes when they go so much for defense purposes. We felt that with these taxes it is not possible to separate what goes to the military from what doesn't; even if you pay only part, that part is distributed as if you had paid the whole. Therefore we did not feel to withhold even part of our income tax.

The Plough Publishing House had been expanded in the years following 1963. We had to enlarge the print shop in New Meadow

Run. Christoph, Rolf, David, and quite a number went there over the years. It was a real blessing to maintain the publishing work; we brought out a number of books in the 1960s and 1970s. Dwight took a strong interest in the publishing and worked closely with everyone in it. The little red booklets, *Living Churches*,* were brought out as a surprise for Heini.

When we were working on *Salt and Light*,† however, some of us—and that includes me—began to get opinionated and un-brotherly about the way Woodcrest had prepared the manuscripts. We would get together in Dwight's office and talk about it. I don't remember exactly what Dwight said; I think he tried to bring understanding. But on one particular phone call with Heini, we said things that were not right and Heini said, "Brothers, you had better come over." So on very short notice Dwight and Norann and Mike Brandes and I drove to Woodcrest. That was in September of 1966. I was in real inner agony during that trip, because I knew my attitude had been wrong. When we arrived late, we were given supper in the snuggery. Heini came in, and I'll never forget his outreaching love in that moment. He could see the misery I was in right away. We had talks and came very quickly to an understanding and were treated with the greatest love. There was a meeting in real unity before our return to New Meadow Run.

Dwight's urge to put into action his concern for the poor was again something very new for New Meadow Run. There was a family nearby whose house was unfit to live in. I think they had had a fire, and Dwight's idea was to build them a house. Nothing like that had been done before. I will not forget the day we got sixteen men together. The owner of the house, Mr. Teets, had

---

*Eberhard Arnold, Plough Publishing House, Rifton, N.Y., Vol. I, 1973, Vol. II, 1975.

†Eberhard Arnold, Plough Publishing House, Rifton, N.Y., 1967, 1977, 1986.

already built a cement block foundation, and we went there with lumber and in one day built a house. I tell you it went up with speed. Dwight was everywhere and directed the whole thing. He knew what to tell every man to do, all busy with hammers. The racket was deafening and we didn't have such things as ear covers. The house just rose up, it was that harmonious a working together. (A crew did go out later to put on the finishing touches.) I remember a little boy there, around seven years old, who stood and watched us with open mouth the whole time. He said, "I think you are the best carpenters in the whole world!"

All this new time that we experienced with Dwight and Norann in New Meadow Run lasted only a year and a half, but I have never experienced anything like it again. Kathy expressed it recently in this way:

> We can't be grateful enough to Heini and Annemarie and to Dwight and Norann for how they struggled for a lively, joyful, and wholehearted way in our communities. I know it was painful for some of us there, who during that time were just comfortable and lukewarm. The fight was not against people but against a stifling spirit that tried, and can still try, to take over. That struggle set a direction for us—we need to be called back again and again to a joyful and active way that leaves no room for the opinionatedness, touchiness, and small vision that can destroy what we want for our life together.

Those were wonderful months—the renewal, the new life, the spirit that came in—but it took a battle. Something was brought to us that must be kept alive, a spirit closely linked to Dwight and Heini and their services; they were as united as two men can be.

. . . as united as two men can be

Bruderhof's 50th anniversary at Woodcrest—June 1970

# 14
# Near to the Fire

"He who is near to me is near to the fire;
He who is far from me is far from the Kingdom."

These words, a "Lord's Saying" recorded by Origen and
Didymus, were carved on the beams of the main house at the
Rhön Bruderhof in Germany (as were Martin Luther's words
introducing our earlier chapter "Of One Mind"). These beams
were removed from the ruins and sent to our various dining rooms
in the States. They arrived in March of 1969 in time for a joint
brotherhood meeting on mission.

Over the years Heini said again and again, "I wish to confess
that mission is the greatest longing of my heart. I believe that
Jesus first called me only for that. I have stood in his way." And
he said:

> We cannot escape the command of mission. It belongs to a
> living church that missionaries are sent out two by two. That
> is how it was in the early church. That is how it was in the
> early Anabaptist movement. With glowing love and endless
> courage, Jakob Hutter returned again and again into the

261

dangerous Tirol until he was captured and gave his life as a martyr. The City has to be on the hill and the light has to shine out. Does the world really recognize today by the Church that the Father sent Jesus Christ into the world? Do we not have an enormous responsibility?

Then the fiftieth anniversary of the Bruderhof was celebrated at a conference of all brotherhoods over the summer solstice of 1970. And we decided to translate Eberhard Arnold's *Innenland* as an expression of his life's witness and also as mission.

Kathy and I were very grateful to be at the Evergreen/Deer Spring Bruderhof to experience with them a time of healing. Because humankind had fallen away from God and had come under the destructive power of Satan, whose wounds could be healed only by Jesus, Jesus' main mission when he came to this earth was healing from sin. Since healing was his mission, it is also the mission of the Church. So there was no reason for the Evergreen Bruderhof to be discouraged over their struggle of the previous eighteen months or so. We have a God who does not let go of us, and we can be thankful to be able to struggle and fight for something new. It is not very often that whole groups of people are given that chance. I say this to encourage all of us. We will need to remember it.

While we were at Evergreen, a sister spoke to me about the spiritual struggles of our Bruderhof history, asking when these constant battles will stop, or how long they will go on; just when one feels that a time of peace may be at hand, we are again plunged into struggle. Even though all of us long and wish for peace, I think we just have to accept that if we are going to associate ourselves with the Church of Jesus, then we are making a decision for struggle for the rest of our lives. In 1968 it had been decisive for all of us to hear our history and to begin to picture the spiritual struggle over the years. On the request of a baptism group that August, Heini began to report for the first time our brotherhood history as he had experienced it. This report was so important that it was very quickly moved from the baptism preparation group into the brotherhood. Heini always presented it in a way that emphasized his mistakes and weaknesses, and all glory went to God.

This answer—also to the Evergreen sister's question—is in the words carved on the beams in each of our Bruderhof dining rooms from the sayings of Jesus: If we are near to Jesus, we are going to be near to the fire. That's the way we have chosen. But the words also say that it is the only way to be near to the Kingdom.

From what little experience I have had of studying and thinking about the word of God on this earth, particularly the study of what is called church history, I found that each time God breaks in on men with his wonderful power, it means a struggle; again and again it means people going out on a limb, being willing to take risks, with the conviction that they are led to it by God.

One can find this not only in the early church or in the Hutterian or Anabaptist movements; it is much more widespread than that. You have to include Francis of Assisi, Martin Luther, John and Charles Wesley (Methodist Church founders), George Fox, the founders of the Baptist Church, and many, many others. God broke in, there is no question about it. It wasn't just that they *thought* God was speaking to them. God *was* speaking to them!

But if we look at history (at least to the small degree that I have), almost every movement of God breaking in follows a pattern, a pattern in which movements start with enthusiasm and power and then fade into a decline until they cease to exist. They become a rigid institution or so completely worldly that within a generation, more or less, they have nothing at all from God, or very little, and are completely changed from the original.

There are examples in history where this did not happen. The most striking and wonderful example of it is the Hebrew people.

If you read the Old Testament, the wonder and the glory of it is that here you have a people who were no better than any other. They weren't a different kind of people. They were just like anybody else in the world. But there was one difference and that was that God chose them, and God chose that they should be continually called back. So it was not a steady decline from the time of Abraham on. Instead, there were constant renewals and revivals—with Moses, with Samuel, with the prophets, each of them in their turn. God came in and spoke, and they were lifted up again. It was a history of constant struggle. And there were other examples in history.

In the 460 years of the Hutterian Brethren we also find a history in miniature where there were periods of decline and of giving up their life in community, but for some strange and humanly unexplainable reason, they did not just go out of existence or turn into something different; no, God called them back again. Then too our short little Eastern history of sixty-six years is like that. But there is nothing about us that would make us the least bit worthy to be anything special. We are not. But for some reason God keeps pointing out and pointing up and calling us back. And I feel we have to have a deep respect before all this because it's pretty unique. It doesn't make *us* unique, mind you. It does not make us a bit unique. It should make us very, very humble. In spite of what we are, it happens. But it also gives us tremendous reason for rejoicing. I feel that this hour is an hour of God, when he is calling and reaching out and asking for a renewal of the first love. And there is no doubt that our brothers in the West also feel this.

In the year 1970 all those away from the communities were also deeply on Heini's heart. Some of them were on the other side of the ocean and could not come back to us because of the very stringent U.S. immigration laws. It was, for instance, a great pain that after it was decided that the Greenyers should return, it took so long for them to arrive. We had known that Kenneth Greenyer was critically ill, and he then had only a matter of months in the brotherhood at Woodcrest before he was called into eternity. Heini brought this concern to the brotherhood early in 1971, and out of that came the establishment of Darvell as a Bruderhof in Europe. Starting with a household chosen from the other hofs, Darvell was an outreach point very specially for our members away who wished to visit, and it has functioned in that way all these years. Heini's own words in 1971 about Darvell were:

> The main reason for starting a Bruderhof in England was to find the way to those who once belonged to us, to find a new relationship. We felt our door should be open to everyone who is really called by God. So we felt we should go to a country where there is more of an open door for all foreigners, and England seemed to be that country. We long very much to come into real inner contact with more people, also with former members.
>
> We will need a deep inner clarity and leading from God for this task. In many places we felt that God had worked in the hearts of people. It was quite surprising and touching to see Ria Kiefer. When we first saw her again, she shook all over and said that she had had a terribly bad conscience but had experienced repentance and was asking to return to the English Bruderhof. It moved our hearts because she is eighty-two and fragile, and she said, "I hope I live long enough to experience this." [She did.]
>
> Repentance is not something that is *forced* in the heart . . . but repentance brings joy even in heaven. So when we call one another to repentance, we do not call to self-circling and self-torment, but to something that leads to the greatest joy, and that is also a joy to God. We will have to build up the new

Bruderhof with speed, building a dining room and housing for people; and it may mean that we have to live poorer to make this possible. But all will do that with great joy, I am sure.

Darvell has the special task for—if I may use the word—lost sheep. Every Bruderhof has this task. We were all lost and had to be found—and have always to be found. And for those who are not with us anymore, I have often to think of the words: They are His. They belong to Him, and we should carry that on our hearts. There are some in America, but they are mostly in England and Germany.

We long for our way and life on all places that Christ is really everything. And we wish for our young people and our old people to experience the deepest interchange with Christ: that he gives us his righteousness and goodness and on the cross takes our evil and injustice upon himself—this leads to the deepest unity and communion.

Because we want to send off brothers and sisters to England for a new Bruderhof, I feel that God is wanting of us a complete and unconditional surrender to Jesus, our Lord, that he may lead the new community. There will be very many joys in Darvell; but there will be also many pains. The contacts with former Bruderhof members will be partly very painful, and sometimes a great joy. Perhaps the first great joy will be Ria. It will be very important that this new beginning is inwardly— certainly outwardly—carried by the three communities, because it is for all of us that the brothers and sisters are going.

On August 22, 1971, with families and some to carry the services going to Darvell the next month, it was decided to appoint Christoph Arnold to the service of the Word.

In February 1972, Christoph, Stanley Fletcher, and Andreas Meier went to a community conference at the Reba Place Fellowship. At that conference they heard from somebody from

Kansas that Bennie Bargen was a seriously sick man. This report was brought back to Woodcrest, and Heini was immediately very interested. Bennie and his wife Esther had been with us in Woodcrest in the years 1955 to 1957. He was a professor of economics and bookkeeping at Bethel College in Kansas and had a lot to do with setting up the bookkeeping and order processing system at Woodcrest. I think all of our hofs today follow in some measure the systems that Bennie set up at that time.

Bennie and Esther were novices, but they had not found the basis for a fuller commitment and had returned to Kansas. He had been crippled by polio since boyhood and was marvelously efficient on a pair of crutches. He could get along just fine up and down the hill to the shop at Woodcrest. He loved to do inspection work; he would sit right on top of a table with a stack of things to inspect on one side, and the stack that he had completed on the other side, and all his tools and materials there with him.

Now this report of Bennie's serious illness came some fifteen years after they left Woodcrest. Immediately Heini wanted to get into contact with him and wrote to him, and quite a lively correspondence began. He was in a nursing home, paralyzed from the waist down. He could not get around anymore and had to have help from others. He could not use his crutches anymore. His letters always came in the form of a cassette that we would transcribe for Heini. Later Heini wanted to go out to Kansas to visit Bennie, and I felt very unworthy to make that journey with him. We flew out at the end of May and spent three days in Newton with Bennie and Esther. Bennie wanted to talk over things that needed clearing up, and he asked to return to the community.

In July Dwight and Charlie flew out and fetched him to New Meadow Run to spend his last four months there in the brotherhood life. That became well known because Dave and Neta Jackson, who were visitors when Bennie arrived, wrote it up in their book,

*Living Together in a World Falling Apart,** and we often hear
about it from seeking people. That was Heini's love and his
reaching out. As long as he felt that a contact was not wanted,
he never pressed, but as soon as there was a special need, he
wanted even to fly. That was all a very wonderful time with
Bennie—the children were often at his wheelchair. Bennie
became a full member early in September and was called into
eternity on November 14. His death and that of four other beloved
members all came within the year: Kenneth Greenyer, Hans Uli
Boller, and Hannes Boller, and then Hans-Hermann Arnold on
the third Sunday of Advent.

In August 1972 there had been joint brotherhood meetings for
the baptism of seventeen and the confirmation of the service of
the Word of Christoph Arnold and Don Alexander. In Darvell
and Woodcrest that year there were many reunitings with members
returning after years away. Hans Meier came back after a very
special visit to Woodcrest in November. We were having a joint
conference with Hans-Hermann, who expressed a special concern
for all members away from the Bruderhof but actually belonging
to us. Many letters from brotherhood members were written to
them then and sent out. Again our history was brought into focus
and became very important for us. That happened in the last
weeks of our brother Hans-Hermann's earthly life. Heini said of
this time:

> In his last days Hans-Hermann thought with special love of
> all those who were once in the brotherhood. What moved us
> around his bed was that in spite of his physical agonies,
> especially his hunger for air—he had cancer of the lung—he
> was more concerned with what answers came to our letters sent
> out to all brothers and sisters who were once with him in this

---

*Creation House, Carol Stream, Ill., 1974.

life. He was more concerned with his love to God and to men than with the salvation of his soul. That Christ saves the soul is a great thing, but God's love is very much greater.

In this short history there is space for only one letter that came from a baptized member away from the community. Ilse von Köller began her letter in early December 1973 and completed and mailed it in March 1974.

Dear Heini! Dear Brotherhood!

Today I want to write you a long overdue letter. In my thoughts I have written to you often but never put it into deed because writing is very strenuous for me. The most recent incentive for me to write is to answer the letter of September 1973 from Evergreen, "To Brothers and Sisters."

I cannot agree to the quotes in that letter from a member away: "Heini and the American brothers destroyed everything."

What happened in 1960 and 1961 came as a stormwind sent by Christ, which I felt almost physically and which had to come, to sweep out what did not belong in the community.

Since God needs human beings to carry out his tasks, and since men simply are men, this sweeping-out also came to people who belonged to the community—and perhaps not to some who do not belong to the community??

It is my unshakable belief that people who have once died to themselves out of love to Christ and who began a life on the Bruderhof will come back and be reunited with you. And in fact you are now in process of helping all these people to do so.

What then is my situation? I came to the Bruderhof because I was inwardly compelled. On a visit to Wheathill I realized that this is the only life worth living and that only this kind of life eventually makes this world a Paradise. I was fully aware

Hans Hermann
and Heini Arno
. . . a special concern for all
members away—October 19

Ria Kiefer

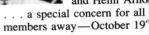

Ilse von Köller

Bennie Bargen

that God calls men to such a life and that this life demands much and is difficult.

It took me months to figure out what advantages and what disadvantages this life would have for me (for I always think first of myself in everything). I then made the decision to go to the Bruderhof. But this was never out of love to Christ, but more out of fear that he might punish me and things might go badly with Y. unless I carried out what I had recognized as right.

I came to the Bruderhof and never made a secret of my motives in coming but always spoke openly about that. I should never have been baptized. In my opinion, only those who want to lead the life of brotherhood out of love for Christ and die to themselves should be baptized. (What the latter, dying to Christ, means is something I never understood until shortly before I left, when I got a glimmering of it.)

Hans baptized me because—I believe—he wanted to gain members, to enlarge the number of people on the Bruderhof, to found new Bruderhofs. He needed people for this, and Ulrich and I were people able and willing to work, people who to Hans's way of thinking were a gain for the community.

It is true that there were brotherhood members at that time who realized that we ought not to be baptized; but they did not dare to raise a voice against Hans. Now a word about Hans Zumpe too. In the world, Hans could have been a manager and thus a well-to-do man, highly regarded by the world. These characteristics and tendencies of his, which ultimately he received from God, could have operated for the good of the community. For the fact that these became diabolic in the community (to express it very harshly) we all bear the guilt, and therefore I do too, to a high degree. Hans became what he was through our admiration, bondage to a human being, cowardice, seeking our own advantage—these things prevented us (myself very much included) from fighting through with him what I recognized as wrong. Because of this it is a great comfort to me to know that God's love and mercy also work beyond death, that all of us without exception (all of mankind) will at last be redeemed and will worship God unitedly.

Although I never truly belonged to you, I feel that I share the guilt for what had to lead to the conclusion in 1960 and 1961. I do not think it is a real excuse, either, that I only got a glimmering of real brotherhood life shortly before I left and know only since I have been away what it should be like—but did not experience it while I was still there.

I therefore have no right to accuse, since I share the guilt. Still it corresponds to the truth that I was strengthened by Emi-Ma in the opinions I had at that time about brotherhood life: for instance, that there needs to be a leader; that the leader, if he goes about it cleverly, can and even should put through his will in opposition to the will of the community; that there are privileged people and disadvantaged people; that there will always be sympathies and antipathies; and that all these are taken for granted—just the very things that are usual in the world. Often I was horrified and had a bad feeling after talks with Emi-Ma, and said to Ulrich, "It's just exactly the same way here as in life outside." But I was too comfortable, it suited me to know what was going on, I wanted to stay among the privileged, and I was silent. Today I know it would have been my duty to speak about everything I felt was wrong.

During my time at the Bruderhof I really believed it was enough to give one's best—the best gifts and knowledge one had. I thought it my duty to concern myself with a better life, i.e. prosperity, for the Church. I wish for you that you grow in clarity and in love and that God will give you the strength for this. But here too I must admit that I cannot wish you all good things from a free heart, but rather always have to say at the same time, "Christ, come into my heart and wish it with me"; for I cannot do it by myself. I often have bitter feelings and regard it as a misfortune that I went to the Bruderhof (and that we were baptized), even if only on account of Y. She did not find her way to a conventional life because she was affected by how it had been on the Bruderhof. She does not believe in Christian brotherly love, after having experienced how people who were faithful to the Bruderhof for years, even decades, were sent away and left without any help (inner as well as practical) for years. She does not believe that Christ is the Son of God. She mixes all the religions in the world up together and tries to pick out of this what suits her.

In spite of all this I know that God is love and mercy and that I—who certainly was called but was wrongly accepted by you—will always remain your sister. In this sisterly bond in spite of all contradictions, I thank you for not having forgotten us. I greet you in the love of Christ and wish you a blessed new year.

March 1974

I didn't send this; it strained me so much to write it that my illness got worse for many weeks. Ulrich, who is always lovingly concerned about me, advised me against sending this letter to you. Any possible answers from you would make my illness worse. I therefore ask you not to answer this letter, but I thought it right to put down what I think in writing once more for you, dear Heini. (I have already expressed it in personal talks with Brotherhood members who have visited us.)

God's love stands above everything!
God's clarity be with all of you!

Your Ilse

Ilse returned to the Darvell Bruderhof on January 31, 1978.
For Christmas 1973 *The Universe Sings* was first prepared and

sung as a cantata at the opening of the new Rhön dining room in Woodcrest. The kitchen wasn't ready, so all the food was transported from the former kitchen for a time. While we had our meals, a gigantic mobile hung from the ceiling. All the planets were represented—illuminated and circling slowly, reminding us of the rotating galaxy. *The Universe Sings* was done beneath that mobile.

In the midsummer of 1974 we celebrated the twentieth anniversary of Woodcrest. At that conference we also asked Christoph to assist his father with the elder's service. That fall a visit was made to Darvell by Heini and Annemarie, Christoph and Verena. After Heini's death in 1982, so closely following his beloved Annemarie's in 1980, this visit was recalled by three of those present:

> *Josef Ben-Eliezer*: The visit in September 1974 started off with a struggle in the brotherhood and led to a very shaking time, which also brought all brotherhoods closer together. The servants from all our communities came.
>
> On September 2 Thomas and Audrey Ann Jefferies returned home to stay, after living outside the community for many years. I know how much the outreaching love of Heini and Annemarie meant to them here. Then Heini suddenly became very ill on September 10, and the brotherhoods in America were informed. It was quite difficult in England to get oxygen in the night. At about 6 a.m. the ambulance came, and Heini was taken to the hospital. We met in the brotherhood, interceding for him and for his family.
>
> We were deeply relieved and grateful when Heini did recover and was able to come home. Those of us who participated in the brotherhood met with Heini in the Arnolds' living room. The whole brotherhood stood there as we united in prayer. I

The new Rhön dining room in Woodcrest

Our Elder Heini and his helper Christoph visited . . .

Darvell in the fall of 1974

will quote a little of what Heini said to the brotherhood at this
meeting on September 17:

> What matters is to experience Jesus together. I had hoped to
> come to you, but instead you came to me because Milton did
> not allow me to go out.
>
> Whenever we have come to found Darvell anew on the
> foundation of Jesus Christ, this attempt was attacked. It must
> be very important, because each time we come closer to it, a
> new attack comes. So the words, "He who is near to me is near
> to the fire. But whoever is far from me is far from the Kingdom,"
> speak to us again. What we need as a brotherhood is the wind
> of the Holy Spirit, the fire that Christ brings. We need to become
> so united with Jesus Christ as if we were to eat his flesh and
> drink his blood—he gave us this picture. There is no stronger
> picture for our becoming completely one with Christ.
>
> I hope we can celebrate the Lord's Supper as a brotherhood
> that is spiritually poor. Jesus said, "Blessed are those who are
> poor in spirit." A couple confessed to me that even when they
> are joyful, there remains underneath a pain of emptiness. For
> them I also want to say, "Blessed are the poor in spirit." But
> it has to come to an encounter with Christ, to a complete
> surrender. Inner emptiness cannot just be accepted. So it is my
> prayer for this couple and for all of us that we all hear the voice
> of the Good Shepherd.

During that visit Heini felt urged to translate freely from
"The Living Word" by his father. He took the German *Innenland*
and read out of it in simple English, just as it struck his heart.

On September 25, when we celebrated the Lord's Supper in
the Harvest House, we felt that God had overcome the
resistance. I can still see Dwight, after the Supper, singing
"Jesus is victorious King." It was just three months before he
was called into eternity.

It was so crowded in that narrow, long room, with the tables arranged in a rectangle, that it was impossible to walk from one end of the room to the other once people were seated. Dwight would go around the outside of the building, come in the back door, pick up the bread and the wine from the far ends of the tables, and then go back around the outside to bring them to Heini.

> *Christoph*: Verena and I and some of my sisters had gone with my parents to Darvell for that visit in 1974. Things became very serious when my father had to be rushed to the hospital in an ambulance. We didn't know if he would arrive alive. All the servants came over with the rest of my family.
>
> Dwight had great joy in bringing along some broad-brimmed black hats. One day when my father was feeling a little better, and he and my mother were in the living room of the Alm House (named for the Alm Bruderhof), those thirteen brothers marched up in their black hats, Dwight in front. It is a miracle that strength was given back to my father to lead us in the celebration of the Lord's Supper.

Soon after this, Annemarie and Dwight were with us on the trip to the Cotswold and Oaksey Bruderhofs. We had on our big black hats. The field that surrounds the Cotswold burial ground had barley growing on it and also a mass of bright red poppies— Annemarie took great delight in them! I still have a vivid picture in my mind of Dwight with his big broad-brimmed hat, loaded all round with red poppies.

> *Christoph*: We were quite a big group flying back to the States: all the servants, my parents, and our family. Dwight had the idea of renting a big coach—it really was big—to get us all to the airport. A number from Darvell went along, including Thomas Jefferies, who had recently returned to the community.

On the way to the airport Dwight started one Negro spiritual after another, and we all sang together. He called out verses of "We shall overcome": "Black and white together," "The Lord will see us through," "We are not afraid," etc. Then Dwight made up verses: "Jesus is the Way," "We shall live in peace," "Peace and unity." As we sang, Thomas was deeply impressed because it was so different from what he had experienced in the community life before the 1961 crisis. To give him joy, my father got up while we were driving along, took off his black hat, and put it on Thomas's head as a gift to him.

*Thomas Jefferies*: Something changed in the atmosphere; something was won. I remember how much the task of the Church was burning in Heini's heart. He could not sleep at night for thinking about this. Heini impressed on us very much that the song "Look Away" should mean to look away from ourselves, away from our own Bruderhof to the whole world, to look more at the cosmic, historic task of the Church. We should take up and fulfill this longing of Heini and Eberhard's hearts—the longing that God may give mission and that men may know that he sent Jesus into the world and that we are united by him.

Six weeks after this Darvell visit Heini wrote to me, "What we and the brothers in the West need is to know there is only one thing that corresponds to the greatness of God's kingdom: the readiness to die for Jesus, a readiness that must become newly alive again and again." And just four weeks before Dwight's death, Heini said to me on the phone, "What comes to us from God must be kept alive in deeds and never become a dead letter. Jesus was the greatest opponent of outward show in religion." Dwight had always taken this warning seriously, and two of our young men, telling of a late night rescue party that December of 1974, remembered:

> Early in the afternoon of the first Sunday of Advent, December 1, 1974, it began snowing heavily. By late afternoon, the storm had turned to thunder, and lightning flashed through the whirling snow; trees were whipped about, branches cracked and torn. After the evening meeting, we shovelled one foot of snow off the shop bridge—this was the only road out, as fallen trees and cables blocked our two drives. After making sure that our generators were working and everything else on the hof was in order, Dwight set off in the four-wheel drive suburban to see whom he could help on the roads. The tractor plowing the meadow path was stuck, but Dwight charged past, snow up to the axles.
>
> Later for a second trip, Tim, Martin, and Benito joined Dwight, Stephen, and Peter. We stopped at any stranded car to offer help. The roads were deep in snow, and very few vehicles moved at all. There were many cars on the sides of the road, with people sleeping in them. We found one old couple sitting alone in their car in a snow bank. They were trying to get to Uniontown to spend the night. They'd been on the road for thirteen hours, nine of them spent on the last thirty miles. Dwight got in their car and drove to Uniontown, and the rest of us followed. We finally found a hotel with room for them and some others. We had to try quite a few different places before we found empty rooms—Dwight was determined to find shelter. In one gas station there had been eighty-some people spending the night. We were up till 3 o'clock driving and stopping and asking if help was needed. On the way back Dwight treated us all to a hamburger and coffee after we had hunted Uniontown up and down and found the only restaurant open. A joy always went with the task.

Heini's wonderful correspondence with children would be a complete chapter of another book. I will share just one of these exchanges. Sometimes we can see a person more clearly through the eyes of a young child than through our own. One child wrote of going to the Gemeindestunde and then asked some questions and Heini answered:

> You ask why we talk about a brother or sister passing into eternity, instead of being killed or dying. I would not know a truer word for a brother dying than to say that he passed into eternity. That is the remarkable, deep fact: when a brother passes away from us, he goes into eternity. Those who believed in Jesus have gone into the eternity of God, and those who did not believe in Jesus and have done evil, have gone into the eternity where there is darkness. Ultimately Jesus will come and judge them, and he will judge all of us.
>
> I think in great love of you.

On December 30, 1974, our beloved servant of the Word Dwight Blough and our novice brother Jerry Kadish were called into eternity in an accident while on a practice flight for intended outreach journeys to the far West. At 3:30 a.m. on December 31, after hours of anxious waiting, Heini said to the gathered brotherhoods:

> We have to tell you that our brother Dwight and our brother Jerry have been called into eternity. God is speaking very seriously to us on the last day of this year—I do not know what he is saying. But we want to listen. I cannot imagine that this happens without God having something very serious to say.

In various meetings with our visiting brothers and sisters from the West in January 1975, Heini said:

> We have lost two of our most beloved brothers, one who served Jesus for almost twenty years and one who was just new in giving his life to Him. We are in great anguish in this hour with our two sisters and their children. We especially greet the brothers who came from Manitoba, South Dakota, and Minnesota. It is very, very loving of you that you have come to be with us.
>
> That Dwight was taken so suddenly out of this life is a complete mystery to us. But God did it, and no hair falls from the head and no sparrow falls from the roof without his will, so we believe that he is in the arms of Jesus, whom he wanted to follow with all his heart and being and to serve with greatest joy.
>
> I know that here in New Meadow Run Dwight meant a great deal. He did not spare himself. He served his brothers and sisters and the children. He will be enormously missed, and I want to ask all of you to see this happening as a call to follow Jesus more fully, to give your hearts to Jesus more fully. It is a call to believe in the rebirth of the Holy Spirit, which unites us with Jesus as if we drink his blood and as if we eat his flesh. It unites us so closely with the person of Jesus that we become one body, the body of Jesus Christ.
>
> I want to express our deep longing that Christ may become more alive in all communities, here in the East and in the West. We are so very, very thankful to have brothers and sisters from Manitoba among us, and I hurried here from New Meadow Run to be with you. We had planned that Dwight and Norann would be traveling now in Manitoba. And God led it completely differently. *You* came *here*. Love brought you here, and we feel a very deep love to you, to you personally and to the Hutterian communities. We long that Christ may be revealed

in this world today through the fact that his disciples are united, as he himself expressed it.

If I were to start to speak personally about this calling into eternity of our beloved brother, our servant of the Word Dwight who means so very much to us all, I could say very, very much. But we want to hear God's language, what God wants to say. And we want to hear it with our hearts. Because of that I have chosen to read tonight the parable of the ten virgins. After the parable Jesus adds: "Watch, therefore, for ye know neither the day nor the hour wherein the Son of man cometh" (Matthew 25:1-13).

Jesus does not speak here of all the world, but of those who went to meet the Bridegroom—who were decided to meet the Bridegroom Jesus. And five of them were wise and five foolish. The oil of which Jesus speaks is the Holy Spirit, and the lamp is our heart and the outward form of our life. As I understand it, if they were all virgins who went to meet their Bridegroom, they were all Christians. Some had the outward form, the outward vessel, but not the life, the life that comes from God.

At supper we heard about the Beatitudes, and there we see how the heart that has the Holy Spirit should be—in those who are poor in spirit, those who mourn, those who are meek, those who hunger and thirst for righteousness, who are merciful and pure of heart, peacemakers, those who are persecuted for righteousness' sake. The whole Sermon on the Mount expresses how we should be if we are awake—we should *never* come to prayer if we don't forgive our brother; we should love even our enemies and bless those who curse us; we should not collect money or treasures on this earth; we should put our whole trust in the Father; we should use no force. This parable is very sharp on the foolish virgins, who are not allowed into the Kingdom of Heaven, and it is a call to us. It is a twofold call: first to watch and wait for the Holy Spirit to change our soul and our being, so that we become reborn and are daily in contact with Jesus. The second is to live for our brothers who are with us on the way to meet the Bridegroom, to call them and challenge them to have oil in their lamps, to be watchful and to be ready.

The fact that Dwight (and Jerry with him) was so suddenly called out of this earthly life is a very great challenge to be ready at all times—to watch and pray. The outer form is not enough. It is not enough to live in community. It is not enough to follow the outer form to the end, and our readiness must come from a living heart.

The *living* Word moved us very much in the last year: we do not have a silent God; man does not live from bread alone, but from every living Word that comes out of the mouth of God into the heart. And that is what we need, our whole inner life must be reborn so that we have oil—not only the outward lamp. The lamp may be very beautiful—it is not enough.

So we are called in this hour to rededicate our lives to Jesus, to have a daily contact with him in our hearts, a living contact— to have real community in him. The experience of the Holy Spirit is the experience of community. It is not only an individual experience. After Jesus promised the Holy Spirit, the Comforter, to his disciples and told them to wait in Jerusalem, they stayed together and prayed and prayed, waiting. And when he came, they became of one heart and of one soul. They were so filled with love they could not live for themselves anymore. That is the greatest gift possible on this earth—to experience in our hearts this community with Jesus and with one another; we challenge one another to be awake and to have our lamps burning, to have oil.

We feel a very great love for the brothers in the West; it is today a bit over a year ago—the 7th of January—when God gave so much in the uniting. We love you brothers and sisters from Manitoba, South Dakota, Saskatchewan, Alberta,

Washington, or wherever there are Hutterian brothers; we love
you, and we also want to live for you. It should be our prayer
that this unity as it was given at Pentecost is given anew in our
time; that wherever oil is missing in the lamps, oil may be
given. We are very poor and needy. We all are lacking oil.
We all have to ask God for his compassion. Dwight sent us
these words in his own hand as a Christmas greeting: "To him
who loved us and freed us from our sins with his life's blood."
So we want to give our whole love to Jesus Christ, who
purchased us with his blood; and he offers to live in us. This
is what we need for each individual, and this is what we need
together as Hutterian brothers and sisters.

Samuel Kleinsasser of Sturgeon Creek Colony was one of the
brothers from Manitoba, Canada, who flew to Pennsylvania
immediately when they heard that Dwight Blough Vetter and
Jerry Kadish had been called into eternity. On his return home,
he wrote the following letter to Peter Tschetter Vetter of Mixburn
Colony, Alberta.

January 25, 1975

To our much beloved Peter Vetter with your Susanna Basel,
    We greet you with heartfelt warmth and wish you all that is
good, including sound health.
    We are having severe winter weather. We have already had
our second snowstorm. The first one was on the 11th, and now
another. Each time three or four communities were snowed in.
From Winnipeg they could not proceed any further: the police
would not allow anyone to go on. It has already been 23° below
zero, and a lot of snow has fallen.
    We are all in good health and spirits, thanks to God. We
have already slaughtered pigs for the second time. Before

Our beloved servant Dwight Blough was called into
eternity on December 30, 1974

Merrill Mow telling of "The Bruderhof's Struggle for Renewal"—1986

Christmas we slaughtered eleven and now eight more.

Now, dear Peter Vetter, I will tell you a little about my trip to Woodcrest. There were four of us servants who traveled from Manitoba: Fritz Vetter of Poplar Point with his daughter Anna, Michael Waldner Vetter of Milltown, Jakob Waldner Vetter of Parkview, and myself. Also Jake Kleinsasser Vetter, his sister Kate and her husband from Crystal Spring, and the three servants from South Dakota. All together there were ten of us. On January 1 at 8 a.m. we set out by plane from Winnipeg to Minneapolis and then on to Pittsburgh, Pennsylvania. God be thanked, we traveled safely and reached Pittsburgh about 3 p.m. The brothers were there waiting for us with two cars. They were very warm but also very sorrowful. Many tears were shed.

Then we set off for New Meadow Run, two hours away. When we arrived there, everything was quiet. We had phoned ahead from Pittsburgh, saying we did not wish any candles or other preparations to welcome us. They were glad because they were at a loss to know what to do. We got out of the cars and went inside. Heini Vetter and all the servants from Woodcrest and Evergreen were already gathered there. We greeted each other very warmly and with many tears. Hardly anyone could speak a word, for the sorrow was very deep and great.

After a while Heini Vetter said, "Dear brothers, we thank you for coming in this hour, this very serious hour, to stand by us. It is a great comfort to us; God must have sent you. Yes, dear brothers," he said, "God is speaking very seriously in taking our beloved brother and servant of the Word from us so suddenly into eternity."

Then there was much weeping, and many dear brothers and sisters came to welcome us, including many young people, girls and boys. It was heartrending.

How highly the whole community spoke of this man! He

shines like an angel of God. He must have been one of the very best, a man greatly gifted by God. The young people had a special love for him. Many who were new, or who had only been a year in the community, spoke, and I wish you could have heard what they said. Never in all my life have I wept so much. They took us to our rooms and said, "Have a good rest for an hour or so, and then we will come and take you to the meal."

Then we went into the dining room with them. Almost 400 people were already gathered as we came in. That was something! All had come from the world and were nicely dressed—much more simply than our people, in black, dark blue, brown, and grey. The women's skirts were eight inches from the floor; they all wore head coverings just like our women, and the little girls wore bonnets.

Oh, how loving, humble, and trusting all these people are. It seems to me that so much inner quiet and contentment is in them. I could not be more amazed and astonished. I found it all far, far beyond my expectations. My heart wept the whole time; I could not speak. It moved me mightily to see what God can bring about in people from the world. Such love and unity has to be the work of the good Spirit.

Now to the mealtimes. They do it differently from us—they sit in families. The parents sit with their children; but there is order, it is quiet and reverent. Then someone says, "To begin with let us sing such and such a song." And after the song he says, "We will sit in silence and thank God for food and drink and for his protection over us." And when that is done, he says, "Now we will all start eating." Later on we also spoke the prayer, the way we do it. After the meal all the people came and greeted us and thanked us for coming and sharing with them in this sad experience. There were many tears.

Many things among them are still different from the way we

have it, but it is not to be despised or rejected. This is the best journey I have ever made in my life. I can't even describe half of it to you, dear Peter Vetter. You will have to see it to believe and understand it! Just think: a thousand people from the world—they enter the church—they give up everything. Also their young people were so loving and trusting. The whole community was so united, trusting, and kind, and they mourned deeply for their servant of the Word.

We do not get a single soul visiting our communities—but visitors come to them daily. Some stay up to three weeks, living, working, eating, and singing with them. Many stay. They recognize it as the right way, they believe it sincerely, and they stand up after the prayer and speak out in a wonderful clear way. It is a miracle from God. It is not human doing; no man can create anything like that. I often wept bitterly when I thought of our cold, lukewarm people. It broke my heart. O great God, you alone can accomplish this!

The preachers from the States [South Dakota] said it was 50 percent better than what they had found last year.

Their whole operation is absolutely astonishing. It runs like clockwork.

Heini Vetter held the burial meeting. We were asked if we would like to take it. But we declined, as we wished to see how they conduct it. It was very much as we do it. Heini Vetter spoke for two hours. It was wonderful. At the end another song was sung, and then he was carried out to the grave. Many tears were shed by all, both young and old. All were shattered, saddened, and grieving because of their love.

The next day we went to the Evergreen Community, which is 600 miles away. We went by plane because the roads to Hartford were very icy. They paid for everything. From Hartford we had a two-hour drive by car to Evergreen. There we experienced the same. They were extremely kind and good to us. Here the burial meeting was held by Mark Kurtz Vetter. Twenty Jewish people from Boston came to this burial. Jerry was a Jew, so his parents, his wife's parents, and their brothers and sisters came. They were very humble, and they expressed their thanks and said their children were in God's hands.

Kurtz Vetter spoke a lot about Jesus as Savior of the world. He really rubbed it in. Oh, it was wonderful! We spent three days on each hof. On the first hof I wept continually. Here at Evergreen it was easier for me. The people are all the same. There is no difference.

Then we went to Woodcrest by car, a two-hour drive. Heini Vetter and the servants were all at home already. This is the largest hof. The playthings are sent here from the other places and are sold here, and the money all goes into a common purse.

Here I was immediately asked to take the prayer meeting, all in English. I was given the teaching on Micah 6. I took home with me fifteen teachings translated into English. They preach a lot from Jakob Hutter, also epistles of the forefathers, a great deal from the Bible, both the Old and New Testament, and many of our teachings. They speak well, clearly and plainly, also quite sharply. They sing often and beautifully. It shows that in the school there must be plenty of singing practice. Dwight Blough Vetter was an exceptionally good singer.

At each hof we also spent half a day in the school and in the children's houses for the smaller children. That was something! That needs a special setup. Everything is washed communally in the laundry. In the sewing room the sewing is done communally, and clothes are given out according to need. There is not such overabundance of clothing in the families, and selfishness is not encouraged. They have a watch repair man, a cobbler, a printing press, and a bookbindery. On each hof they have their own school teachers, five or six. Each hof has three or four nurses. They have a good doctor, who lives

"The parents sit with their children...it is quiet and reverent."

"...the children's houses for the smaller children. That needs a special setup."

in New Meadow Run, and he is also a servant of the Word—Dr. Milton Zimmerman, a very loving and humble man. He wears the Hutterian suit. Heini Vetter's daughter will soon have finished her medical training.

Church discipline and the ban are used just as with us. The discipline (shunning) is kept completely, not as superficially as with us. Dear Peter Vetter, I cannot tell you half of what I saw and experienced. Of course much could still be improved, but with us twenty times more so. No one should think that I want to overthrow or reject what we have. Oh, no. If only we would live according to our faith. Here in the church one can be blessed, if only we would live in real truthfulness, faithfulness, humility, and surrender to God. But our people lack this faith, love, unity, and the fear of God.

I will now close and remain your lowly friend,

Samuel R. Kleinsasser

P.S. Peter Vetter, one cannot describe everything. But these dear people have much, much, that is good. They also make great efforts with the young people. They have up to twenty-five young girls on each hof—such dear children.


Perhaps this is a good place to end this account, remembering our beloved ones who are now in eternity, especially our Heini and Annemarie and Dwight. In his dedication to Christ, Dwight would have gone through fire for Heini because he recognized that Heini served Christ. Both were loyal unto death. "He who is near to me is near to the fire."

The broad historical outline that I have tried to give in going over our history since 1935, all points to God, to the work of

God and the call of God. That is what is important. If human beings fail, this should *never* destroy or break down the inner commitment to God and his calling. In December 1975, one year after Dwight Blough was called into eternity, Heini put together a document entitled "The Covenant of the Lord's Supper," which is mounted on the wall in every brotherhood room. The points of this covenant cover the whole gamut of the problems we human beings have brought into our life together to block God's work. With this declaration on the part of the united brotherhood, we want from here on to declare war on these works of the devil. Something new has come to us; it is an affirmation made by each one at the time of baptism, after a serious disunity, or after a time away. In closing this report, I want to point to this declaration and to its importance. If there are questions about what our life stands for and what it does not stand for, this covenant of the Lord's Supper should answer them.

Covenant of the Lord's Supper
December 30, 1975

We declare ourselves in unity as under God's judgment and mercy of the last year, since December 30, 1974. We want and long to renew our covenant with God as we made it in baptism and ask God that we can take part in the Lord's Supper.

We vow that we want to live in reverence for God, for Christ, and for his Holy Spirit.

The Cross, where the forgiveness of sins can be found, is the center of our life.

We declare war against all irreverence toward God, his Christ, and his Church.

We declare war against all irreverence toward the childlike Spirit of Jesus as it is living in the children, and we want to fight for that for our children, because unfortunately there are some older children in whom the childlike Spirit has been partly lost.

We declare war against all emotional or physical cruelty toward children.

We declare war against all search for power over souls of people or over children. We seek the atmosphere of the Church and of the angels of God.

We vow to pray for the light of Jesus that all who are in bondage and all who are tormented by evil thoughts may be freed (that is, those who do not willingly give themselves to darkness but who are bound by demons), but that all those who serve darkness may be revealed and called to repentance.

We declare war against the spirit of Mammon and all false love connected with Mammon.

We declare war against all human greatness and all forms of vanity.

We declare war against all pride, also against all collective pride of our Bruderhofs.

We also want to declare war against all independence from the brotherhood and its services.

We declare war against the spirit of unforgiveness, envy, and hatred. To this belongs the spirit of comparing.

We vow to lay down before the Cross our own power and all our "greatness."

We stand in war against degrading people in any way, even if they have fallen into sin. We declare war against all cruelty toward anyone, even if he has sinned.

We declare war against all forms of magic or curiosity about satanic darkness.

We pray for the Holy Spirit and for the unity with the Upper Church. We do it in this moment in a special way, thinking especially of Dwight and Jerry. We pray for this unity with and for the whole Hutterian Church.

We pray for the great gifts that are described in the Beatitudes:

the need for God, the sorrow over the sin and injustice of the world, the gentle spirit, the hunger and thirst that right may prevail, the mercy of God, the pureness of heart, the making of peace between brothers and sisters.

We ask for courage to be willing to rejoice in suffering and persecution for the cause of right.

We ask for the forgiveness of our sins, because without Jesus we have no pure heart and no pure actions.

We pray to live for the world as Jesus expresses it in his last prayer in John 17: that all should be one as Christ is one with the Father, so that the world may believe that Christ was sent by the Father. We ask with Christ not to be taken out of this world, but for all to be protected from the power of evil.

So we ask Christ to consecrate our brotherhood through his truth. Christ's Word is the truth. In this sense we ask that he sends us into this world to be a light in the world.

# Epilogue

*The light of witnesses, shadowed by the darkness of betrayal, was always with us over the years—a continuing conflict of two atmospheres. The tragedy of Dwight's death on December 30, 1974, led to a separation of spirits and a cleansing judgment among us in the months and years that followed.*

*On July 23, 1982, our Elder Heini Arnold was called into eternity. Jacob Kleinsasser Vetter, Elder of the Hutterian Schmiedeleut communities, advised us at that time to appoint an Acting Elder immediately. We Eastern brothers and sisters did not listen, and that brought much harm to the church before and after Christoph Arnold was confirmed in the Elder's service on April 17, 1983. It was necessary to inform Jake Vetter (Jacob Kleinsasser) of envy and ambition on the part of some Eastern brothers. This sin, carrying with it critical thoughts, grumbling, and slanderous gossip about our Elder Christoph, was deliberately committed even by brothers entrusted with the service of the Word.*

*On September 17, 1985, every member of the Eastern brotherhoods signed a letter to Jake Vetter asking his forgiveness for our taking so long in our pride to heed his advice in July*

*1982. In Jake Vetter's reply of September 28, 1985, from Crystal
Spring, Manitoba, he writes of his question to us in the East,
especially to the servants of the Word. His letter below is followed
by Merrill Mow's answer to it.*

Beloved brothers and our dear Christoph Vetter,

I greet you all with the love of Jesus. Grace, peace, love, faith,
and victory I wish for you all from the bottom of my heart. If
only I could help you in your distress in the way I long to, if
only I could do enough for you to satisfy your hearts, I would
not hesitate a moment nor spare any effort. I pray to God our
heavenly Father to grant me my heart's desire for you because I
love you, and many times the joy I have in you is overwhelming.
I would like to help you. My heart is full of compassion for you,
especially for you, my dear Christoph Vetter.

My heart is filled with an overwhelming longing for you, and
I am pained right to my heart for your sake. But if such things
befall us for the sake of truth, we should know it means we are
not enemies of God but rather his friends and children. And what
a pain and hurt it is if we experience this from brothers; it is
painful enough when it happens to us from the enemies of truth.

How I would like to lay on your hearts what it means to reject
an Elder! Brothers and sisters, I cannot put it strongly enough
how important in the eyes of God is the appointment of his leaders
and elders among his people. How his wrath and judgment are
aroused and what a sin it is to reject, despise, and envy his
servants. Miriam and Aaron only criticized Moses (Numbers 12),
and the Lord heard what they said. Suddenly the Lord said to
Moses, Aaron, and Miriam, "I want the three of you to come
out to the tent of my Presence." From verse 6 on it says that the
Lord said, "When there are prophets among you, I reveal myself
to them in visions and speak to them in dreams. It is different
when I speak with my servant Moses. I have put him in charge

of all my people Israel. So I speak to him face to face, clearly, and not in riddles. He has even seen my form. How can you dare to speak out against my servant Moses?" It says the Lord was angry with them.

Oh brothers, when God departed from them, what a horrible judgment! Suddenly they were struck with a dreadful disease. And yet, when Moses cried out to the Lord to heal Miriam, the Lord answered, "If her father had but spit in her face, would she not have to bear the disgrace for seven days? So let her be shut out of the camp for seven days." We can learn from the Holy Word of God how greatly God is hurt when we reject and despise his election and especially when we are told in verse 3, "Moses was a humble man, more humble that anyone else on earth."

I thank God for you that he has given you a humble and loving Christoph Vetter as an Elder. Come out with the ointment of love and repentance to heal the marks of hurt that without doubt are not few, so that God may not turn against you and give you the Elder you deserve. My heart just aches and inwardly bleeds, hoping and wishing that God's wrath is not roused. I ask you all, beloved ones, to pray to the Lord God night and day for his mercy.

Furthermore, we can read in Numbers 16 that Korah rebelled against the leadership of Moses, saying, "You have gone too far. *All the members of the community belong to the Lord, and the Lord is with all of us.* Why then, Moses, do you set yourself above the Lord's community?" When Moses heard this, he threw himself on the ground and prayed. What more could Moses do, brothers? Then he said to Korah and his followers, "Tomorrow morning the Lord will show us who belongs to the Lord. He will let the one who belongs to him, that is the one he has chosen, approach him at his altar."

My dear brothers, the Lord was greatly grieved. His judgment should make us tremble. Moses said to the people, "The Lord has sent me to do all these things, and it is not by my own choice that I have done them." The Lord dealt in an unusual manner with this great sin. The earth opened up and swallowed them.

I do not mean these examples as a rebuke, but as a loving reminder to be more aware, out of love and as a protection to you all. We know and believe we are all only human. But as soon as we reject and despise or strive against those who are chosen by God and his church, it is not only human beings we oppose; we are opposing the ordinance of God and his holy will.

Beloved ones, I was shocked and hurt to my innermost heart that the devil in his cunning could hide so deceitfully. Had God allowed it to go any further, it could have meant the destruction of all that God has given in the last years. But praise be to God and his infinite love, God the Almighty had compassion so that that tyrant over our souls was not able to destroy us. May God be gracious to us and dwell with us forever. For his sake and for that of his church, I plead with you to accept these words and warnings, to take them to heart, for I have always testified to what I know and to the truth of God. From true fear of God I have never deceived you but with overflowing love reached out to you. I hate sin, I hate the devil, but I love God and the brothers. The devil, that raging lion, will not spare anybody. I just cannot stand it when the devil destroys a single brother or sister.

I would also think that we should take more seriously our calling and not take too much for granted that we live in community or that this is all we need. We will still face trials—to bring out what is truthfully in our hearts; otherwise, we are foolish and conceal or hide our evil. James pleads, "Count it all joy, my brethren, when you meet trials of every sort." Take comfort from these words, my beloved brothers and sisters, and remain valiant in the truth, for Christ says, "He who endures to the end will be saved." That means, fight loyally unto death for the truth.

*I do not want to overlook how you brothers repented. It moves my heart, and my love to you is not dead but gives me joy.* I only ask you to be eager always to do God's will, keep his commandments, and endure in his truth to the end, so that you may be blessed and rejoice with us eternally.

I also cannot express how grateful I am for the different letters of repentance I have received, even though some make my eyes water out of compassion and love. I have also received the letter with all the signatures, which nearly makes my heart break for joy and pain, appreciating God's judgment and also what a blessing it can be. Our beloved Heini Vetter, who lies in peace and rest, will be moved by it. My beloved ones, I can say with a clear conscience that I am more than willing to forgive you all. Only let us now stand together. I well remember how good I meant it for you right after Heini Vetter's passing away. If everyone had listened in sorrow to the good Spirit, much evil and hurt to brothers, to Christoph Vetter, and to the church could have been avoided.

I would very much like to touch upon the service of the servants of the Word, which I feel is not always accepted with trembling and in the fear of God because of the great responsibility that goes with it, but rather looked at as a promotion and great honor, which then results rather in irresponsible servants, servants of the flesh, instead of servants of God's holy Word or shepherds of the flock. Peter quite clearly describes this (1 Peter 5:1): "I who am an elder myself appeal to the church elders among you [meaning nobody else but the servants]. I who am a witness of Christ's sufferings, who will share in the glory that will be revealed, appeal to you to be shepherds of the flock that God gave you. Take care of it willingly, *as God wants you to*, and not unwillingly. Do your work not for mere pay but from a real desire to serve. Do not try to rule over those who have been put in your care, but be examples to the flock. Then, when the Chief Shepherd appears, you will receive the glorious crown that will never lose its brightness."

Now, what is it, brothers? Are you concerned to live and serve according to these wonderful instructions? Or do you want to be classed as false shepherds? Jesus speaks of himself as a good Shepherd who is willing to die for the sheep. But a hired shepherd, who is not a good shepherd and does not own the sheep, seeing a wolf coming, leaves the sheep and runs away. So the wolf snatches the sheep and scatters them. The hired shepherd does not care about the sheep.

In 1 Timothy 3, Paul says, "This is a true saying: If a man is eager to be a church leader, he desires an excellent work. But a church leader must be without fault, self-controlled, and orderly. He must not be a drunkard or violent, but gentle and peaceful. He must not love money. He must manage his own family well. If a man cannot manage his own family well, how can he take care of the church of God?" Brothers, if this is not true of a servant, there is a lack of faithfulness, and of responsibility and concern. There is spiritual emptiness, and soon, coldness and lovelessness. Beloved brothers, why is this evil spirit of coldness and envy and pride breaking out in so many of the servants? Please read the epistle to Timothy. This evil spiritual pride, betrayal, envy, and hunger for power and honor will not take root in all those who will believe and follow these instructions!

As we have sadly to admit, it comes again and again. There is already reason enough for us to tremble and to be fearful about this demon that so secretly creeps into the church and its servants. Such shame for us to call on the Lord Jesus, harboring this shocking spirit and enemy in our hearts! I believe that the real purpose of taking on the service of the Word is, simply said, just not taken seriously enough. If our hearts are empty and idle, the demons that were driven out once before can come back again and take possession. And true enough, as Christ says, then it is worse with such a person than it ever was before.

Beloved brothers, where does all this come from? I think first of all from disrespect to your Elder. In 1 Timothy 5:17 it says, "Let the elders that rule well be counted worthy of double honor, especially those who labor in the word and doctrine." Verse 19:

"Against an elder receive not an accusation except on the evidence of two or three witnesses." So, beloved brothers, consider how wrong it is to be resentful and envious behind a brother's back and in the darkness of deceit. It is completely the opposite of verse 17. It is surely not of the good spirit but of some evil spirit, which is only to be cast out of the heavenly place like Satan, who desired to rise above God, seeking the honor that did not belong to him. Therein lies a greater sin than we think. Whoever lacks discernment in this must have an unclean conscience and is blinded thereby. I think seeking for honor and power is a terrible sickness; only through the power of the Holy Spirit and through remorse and repentance can one ever be healed from it.

Beloved brothers, what love and strength we can see in Aaron and Hur when they supported Moses during the battle against the Amalekites (Exodus 17:12). When Moses' arms grew tired, Aaron and Hur brought a stone for him to sit on while they stood beside him and held up his arms, holding them steady until the sun went down and the battle was won. The Amalekites were totally defeated. Now, if Moses needed support, I believe our Elders today need it much more.

Beloved brothers and sisters, I have expressed my heart's desire. Let us leave behind all sin and evil and go forward together in peace and unity. We will be victorious against our enemies, even in our own bosom.

I, Jake Vetter, greet you even though with many concerns, yet a servant of the Lord through his grace. I hope to be a brother to you, your helping shepherd, and your companion in your suffering, trials, and tribulations. I am willing to endure in patience with you unto the day when we can all be gathered in the Upper Church with the many saints and martyrs. To God be the glory.

Your humble brother,

Jacob Kleinsasser

New Meadow Run
October 9, 1985

Beloved Jake Vetter,

I am so moved by the love and the truth from God in your
letter to all of us and especially to the servants of the Word. It
is so clear that all of this comparing, ambition, envy, gossiping,
and politicking comes exclusively from Satan, who wants to
destroy not only the Church but every one of us too. I have known
Numbers 12 and 16 and also Exodus 17:12, but I never before
saw so clearly how they apply directly to the Church right now
in our time.

Nine years ago, when we lived in Deer Spring, Heini Vetter
asked me to collect letters and documents and eyewitness accounts
about the struggle in our Eastern communities from 1932 onward.
That's the struggle between the God Spirit—God's Holy Spirit,
who called Eberhard Vetter to gather a faithful people together
in Germany—and the Satanic spirit of hate that always seeks to
destroy God's work. Joseph Kleinsasser Vetter, wrote to Georg
Vetter and Hardy Vetter on May 8, 1938, just after it had become
revealed that Hans Zumpe stood completely wrong and had
seriously misused the service of the Word to his own ends. The
English translation of the letter of Joseph Vetter (then Elder)
follows:

> The disappointment that was called forth among our people
> by him has not yet died down. Many indignant words are heard
> about this. To many it is a strange thing that a whole people
> could let itself be fooled by one man. And could be silent about
> it for so long.

Doesn't that express exactly your concern for us now, beloved
Jake Vetter. So it isn't a new thing among us. Since 1938, in
our little communities, confirmed servants of the Word have been
removed from the service (either temporarily or permanently)

more than forty times. Now during *most* of that time we were completely on the wrong track, and the faithful ones, like Heini Vetter, simply hadn't been listened to. But unfortunately this particularly devilish problem has continued right up to 1985. Why? What is it about us that opens just that door to Satan? And how can we find a way to slam it *shut* in the soul of *every* brother and sister?

I have sometimes wondered if a lack of *faith* and a *personal relationship to Jesus* isn't the root of the problem. No, I'm pretty *sure* that that really is it. With a living faith and a real personal relationship to Jesus, how can a person be envious or stand in opposition to those whom God has appointed? It is impossible.

Behind this problem I see stubborn selfishness, of course, but also a devilishly clever way of thinking that tends to make evil thoughts look good. So a person with an accusing spirit flatters himself to think that he is right and the other fellow is wrong; and his darkness is whitewashed. That's not new. It goes back to the third chapter of Genesis. But I wonder if it isn't especially strong in our modern world.

Many of us, like myself, were very liberal and humanistic in theology before we came to the Bruderhof. For years I doubted the virgin birth and practically all biblical miracles. I believed in natural evolution. And with all that came a "smart" way of thinking that was actually godless, yet at the same time I had a reputation for being a "Christian." People like this have their own humanistic sense of justice. They don't like it in the parable of the workers in the vineyard that those who came late got the same pay as those who worked all day (Matt. 20:1-16). And so they look at Heini Vetter or Christoph Vetter and anyone else who gives himself in a special way and they compare the "wages"—taking note of any love received, etc.

Many of us brought this godless and sinful way of thinking with us and have had to repent of it and turn away from it. That is understandable.

But that is not all. We also see it in people who were born and raised on the Bruderhof. They too have to repent, but why is it that they so easily catch this disease that shouldn't be at all present on any hof? It must be our education. And behind that our lack of faith and of a real relationship to Jesus, which I mentioned earlier.

I think we need help to find a deeper and more childlike faith and convey it early to our children so that the cleverness and the "science falsely called so" (I Timothy 6:20) that Paul rightly calls "profane and vain babblings" doesn't touch them and can't infect them during their school years, when all of the influences on them are directly *our* responsibility.

Beloved brother, I have expressed this very, very poorly. Mostly I want just to thank you with all my heart for your letter. May God grant that it marks a *turning point* in our life, to the honor and glory of God alone.

Now Christoph Vetter and all the others are in England and we eagerly await news of the baptism and of their return.

Much love, also from Kathy, to you and to your Mary Basel, your lowly brother,

                                                                Merrill

*The following letter has been added to the epilogue in the second printing of this book. It forms a fitting conclusion to* Torches Rekindled *and a direction for the future. Written by Heini Arnold in German to Johann Christoph Arnold in 1974, it was sealed in an envelope, to be opened only after Heini Vetter's death. This was done, and it was translated in August 1982.*

                                                          Woodcrest
                                                 June and July 1974

My very beloved son and brother Johann Christoph,

You, dear Christoph, have carried so very much with me in recent years, and so I have some thoughts to share with you for the time when I am no longer among you. What remains a basic direction for the future is your grandfather's last letters from Darmstadt, the one to Hans and Emi-Margret and the one to Oma. Let yourselves be guided by these always.

It has been led by God that since November 22, 1935 [the day on which Opa was called into Eternity], several have come to us whose influence on the Bruderhofs is a real gift from God. This is true of each genuine brother and sister, and especially for the English brothers and sisters. Those first English members who joined in 1934 and 1935, that is, in your grandfather's last year, brought him deep joy as well as much encouragement and stimulation.

Unfortunately nearly all our English members became guilty with us in the terrible deviation from the way of Jesus Christ. Of course this is true only of those who were in Paraguay or in Wheathill more or less from the start. It is not true of brothers and sisters who joined later. I am all the more thankful for each one who held out with us throughout the trial of those horrible years. How I love them all! A very particular leading from God, I feel, was the coming of brothers and sisters from the intentional communities (probably best translated as *Siedlungen* in German). The brothers and sisters from the Church of the Brethren and from the Quakers seem to me just as much a special gift from God. These groups of brothers and sisters take nothing away whatsoever from the significance of the Youth Movement for our feeling and attitude to life. On the contrary, they have enriched it and given it back to us.

It has been a real torment to me ever since 1963, I believe, when I realized that, through our unfaithfulness to Jesus as a Bruderhof, also the whole Forest River affair [*Handel*] was wrong and sinful. I saw no way of putting this sinful and disastrous state of affairs in order again before my death. We had sinned; but we had got too much used to unpeace, and because the brothers and

Heini and Annemarie Arnold on their fortieth wedding anniversary

Joseph Kleinsasser (Sunny Colony), then Schmiedeleut E visited Woodcrest with J Kleinsasser, present Elder, in

The crucial visit to Darvell in 1974 of all servants of the Word (*Left to right, front:* Hardy Arnold, Annemarie Arnold, Heini Arnold, Andreas Meier, Hans Meier, Ria Kiefer, Georg Barth. *Rear:* Don Alexander, Mark Kurtz, Merrill Mow, Christoph Arnold, Ben Zumpe, Dwight Blough, Milton Zimmerman, Glenn Swinger, Doug Moody.)

sisters who joined us from there were so genuine, I believed at first that the Hutterites were more in the wrong than we. We heard that some brothers had talked hatefully against us in the car. I believe there was much gossip at that time. Since the Hutterites demanded in the first place the return of all their baptized members, I knew no way to find a solution. The very suggestion on my part to send those brothers and sisters back to Forest River would have felt to me as if I were committing a grave sin and betraying them. I beseeched God in deep prayer to open up a way, and God answered the prayer. He gave much more than I would have dared to think or hope.

I now see the coming and the influence of the brothers and sisters from the Hutterites as a very special gift from God.

Never give way in questions of inner freedom and genuineness. Never deny God's greatness and God's kingdom on this earth. And always hold firm to the unanimity of the brotherhood, acknowledging that it comes from listening to God's uniting Spirit.

In all things hold fast to faith in God. Today we have the great grace of being able to live together in peace without any persecution from without. Should a time of persecution come, it will most likely begin with the fact that gradually less and less money comes in and our food and heating are difficult to maintain. Persecution mostly comes about by local feelings being aroused, and this can be spread abroad by radio and television nowadays, unlike the early Christian and Reformation times.

When this happens, remember your grandfather and how he began with nothing, especially at the Alm Bruderhof in Hitler's time. Believe that the prayers of the Upper Church as well as God's love through his angels will protect you and carry you through, even if there has to be imprisonment or martyrdom. Think especially of the whole Sermon on the Mount and of Matthew 6, verses 25-34. Think what a great grace from God it is to be allowed to suffer for Jesus. All the more the brotherhood must intercede for the children in prayer and ask that they be protected from evil. There too we can have complete trust for the children, even if it should cost their physical death. It must be our prayer that the children are protected in Jesus' arms. You know that Mama and I have twice experienced the loss of a child. Such a child can bring the kingdom of heaven nearer.

As a warning for you against the devil's tricks I want to give you a short survey of that part of the Bruderhof's history when Jesus was pushed almost entirely out of the brotherhood and many hardly noticed it. At the same time I want to emphasize that many remained faithful and suffered innocently, as Oma also did.

### How the life developed in a completely opposite direction from its beginnings in Halle and Sannerz

While your grandfather was still living, Jesus was already being increasingly thrust out of the brotherhood as a reality, Jesus as a real person. It is true that [in Primavera] Hutterian teachings were read; so were your grandfather's writings, as well as writings by Religious Socialists and others, including some Catholics, of whom Guardini is among the best, and also the martyr Alfred Delp. But the true Jesus, whom we want to love with all our heart, our soul, and being, was increasingly unwanted. And so it came about that the Bruderhof life gradually turned into the opposite of what it had been to begin with. I know I am expressing this very crassly. I will try to report the inner development and to do so without naming too many names. I think it will give a true overall picture.

There were some faithful souls who wanted to be faithful at first. Many saw it more as a greater or lesser deviation from our beginnings. But it had become the opposite, and I am speaking in such crass terms as a warning for your future. The twofold crisis in Darvell, originating each time in the Services and the will to power in those concerned, has had an important meaning for me. Your grandfather's Jesus-poems, many of which we sing now, were rejected already at the Cotswold Bruderhof, that is, long before the forties. Whenever I referred to my father, I was told that those poems were from his youth and that later in his life, your Opa did not stand by the personal experience of Jesus expressed in the poems. Some went so far as to say that your Opa had rejected that experience of Jesus and that personal love to Jesus. When Fritz lost two children within one year in the early Primavera time, he went through a deep shattering and experienced a change of heart. Under Hardy's leadership, Fritz as work distributor had your grandfather's poems printed. It was done also to give work to an old brother who was a printer. When I returned from my exclusion, these poems were in the outhouses as toilet paper.

When I speak of Jesus as a person, I don't mean an imaginary picture of Jesus, which any of us can have. It is not advisable to cling to such an imaginary picture. Of course one has a certain picture of Jesus born in a stable, of how later on he fasted and went hungry for forty days and nights in the wilderness, and how he wandered from one place to another without any place to call home or any sure way of earning a living; in this itinerant community women also took part. Even more striking pictures come to us on hearing the proclamation of the driving out of demons by the Holy Spirit, how lame people walked, blind men saw, lepers were cleansed, and even the dead awakened. In him, our Jesus, God's kingdom was already present.

I ask myself constantly: How was it possible for this community, founded in Christ, as represented as early as 1907 by Opa, Oma, and Tata, to develop that way and to be so thoroughly twisted into the opposite? From the very beginning it was obvious that no true Christian life in community could exist without a certain clear leadership. The misunderstanding of the meaning of leadership (which many rejected) and the power-seeking of some members was the root of the evil. How was it possible, after the beginning had been so clearly founded on Christ, that it was twisted so completely into the opposite later on?

It was clear right from the start that a truly Christian communal life cannot be a live organism unless there is a certain clear leadership. Even in marriage God created the husband to lead his wife and family. The ship of community needs a helmsman, who certainly must let himself be guided from above in a very humble way and must honor and respect the brotherhood. In Sannerz and at the Rhön Bruderhof any human leadership was absolutely rejected. It was recognized from the start that the helmsman of the ship of the Church, or the shepherd of his flock (remembering Peter), is an organic part of a true order and a genuinely brotherly life.

Beloved Johann Christoph, being led from above always means listening to the voice of the Holy Spirit as it speaks in the brotherhood. The servant of the Word must not isolate himself. By a very close cooperation with the brotherhood and its services in deepest humility, a perfectly clear direction in all matters can be given. This is true for matters of faith, for proclaiming the gospel, for all practical things, and for the overall inner attitude of a living brotherhood.

In the early life in community the little circle was deeply gripped by the love of Jesus, overflowing with love for one another. The burdens that this little group was able to bear were amazing. Even the children, because they too were filled with the love of Jesus, helped bear the burdens without realizing it and took it on to help beggars and other needy people in some way.

The contrast with the spirit of the beginning, especially in crises against the Arnolds and even against your Oma, was so crass and obvious that I am wondering now why I did not recognize it in all its horror. At this point I don't want to go into the historical details or the guilt, which we Arnolds certainly also shared.

The cry "royal family" went around; there was talk of the common people and the brotherhood. From now on the servant of the Word was no longer to have the leadership, but the people, the brotherhood. We were told on all sides, "From now on the rulership of men is to stop, and the people, the brotherhood, will rule." The "plain, simple" brother was now to have the leadership.

You can't imagine my astonishment the first time I took part in a Brüderrat or brothers' meeting after being in the Great Ban for three months. Very small matters were now being laid before the Brüderrat. I could hardly believe my eyes when I saw how every "simple" brother puffed himself up with his speech of agreement, long or short. You have no idea how proud it made them all that *they* were the ones to decide now. Even a witness brother shouted, "The voice of the people is God's voice!" This expression was too much even for the brotherhood of that time. It despises Jesus utterly. (Think of the people who shouted "Crucify him!") That expression pulled off the mask, and the true face could then be seen. So those words were slightly corrected.

All kinds of power cliques were now formed, consisting of "plain" brothers and sisters. Only one thing was broken up—the Arnold family. An Arnold was allowed to do the dirtiest work, and expected to serve in it with joy. But no Arnold ever had the chance to be recognized as a plain, ordinary brother or sister. After what I experienced in the Brüderrat I thought, "Well, that will soon break down; it can't last long." To my great astonishment a devilish miracle happened: the brotherhood believed that it was ruling; but in actual fact there was now, for the first time in Bruderhof history, a leader and dictators who ruled with a firm hand. At first I thought the brotherhood would not put up with this. But to my amazement, the brotherhood and the Brüderrat thought *they* were making the decisions, that the "plain" brother was deciding, and that the "royal family" was now finished with. And this was said many times.

The devil's trick was that from this point on one dictatorship kept replacing another. Wheathill had horrible experiences, culminating in 1948; yet none of that opened the brotherhood's eyes. The brotherhood actually believed it was setting the course. Majority vote was introduced. All this led the "simple brother" by the nose, and he was completely unaware of the dictatorship he was under. I tell you openly, the fact that it was the exact opposite of the way of Opa, Oma, and Tata did not dawn on me in its full horror until some time after 1961, and in a special way in the two Darvell crises through confessions that were made then. Jesus is driven out. Love is killed, and man—thrifty or extravagant—takes the reins in hand. Jesus' rule is over. Before 1961 the "plain brother" considered himself so good that I fear he no longer needed a crucified Christ. Repentance was scorned and was rejected as "emotional." The "plain brothers and sisters" did not need any of that.

Today, as this letter is being written, those former brotherhood members living outside in Germany and England (I mean, outside Darvell) are almost exclusively those who were particularly "plain brothers and sisters" of the Bruderhof. This is a great obstacle for them; it befogs their path. Their error is very difficult for them to recognize because it looks so good to them.

After my exclusions I worked with "plain brothers" in Loma Hoby, and I could feel what a high barrier this so-called plainness formed. As long as I live I shall make every effort to see that all of them become truly childlike brothers and sisters with us and that they all pass into the other world as such.

For all these brothers and sisters I want to fight constantly and pray to God. They have been blinded by a trick of the devil. Most of them, when they came to the Bruderhof, were quite simple people, plain in the true sense of the word, who had brought sin with them and who, as I believe, had been taken into the brotherhood by your Opa through the crucified Christ. This is what I long for for them all.

In the end we are all poor people, really very poor. Without the crucified Christ not one of us can find the way to God. That is our joy, our faith, our proclamation; and it is on this foundation that we experience the great world of Christ, the world for which he has the rulership over all powers and principalities in heaven and on earth because that is the Father's will.

Beloved brother and son Johann Christoph, in your service you will have to go through many needs from without and deep fears from within. Today the Bruderhofs are celebrating Woodcrest's twentieth anniversary, and I have just been thoroughly enjoying the children, their contests, and everything. Now I want to lay a few points on your heart.

1. What your Opa calls the Youth Movement in his last letter can be seen in children. The Youth Movement is now a piece of German and Swiss history. In my childhood it was still alive. Then came Hitler when I was a young man, and the Youth Movement died.

There was something of Jesus alive in the Youth Movement, and this was the main point of what Opa experienced there. The Youth Movement looked for what was genuine. They didn't ask first whether a thing was true, right, or good, but whether it was genuine. Of course that does not mean that evil was tolerated. They insisted on genuineness in religion. They would rather have someone innocently say something incorrect or awkward than listen to insincere religious speeches. They rejected that kind of talking and preaching very firmly. If something incorrect was said, they struggled to find the truth. Parrotlike religion was rejected.

From deep within people's hearts there arose a very new

approach to life and feeling for life, expressing itself in new forms
in all outward things. It was an inward urge that brought about
fellowship in settlements, and especially in hiking, singing, and
circle dancing. The circle around a blazing fire was felt as a deep
experience. The rhythmic movement in circle dances brought
something to expression from the depths of the heart. I have heard
that after the Lord's Supper the circle in Sannerz expressed what
they felt in this deep experience by a rhythmic dance.

This effort to give shape only to what was truly the heart's
experience came from rejecting all human pretense. Fashion, also
in clothing, was radically rejected. It was the inner experience
that gave vivid expression to all areas of life. Everything was an
expression of deep inner experience: the choice of songs, music,
dancing, hiking, communal meals, games and sports, as well as
clothing.

If we stay close to Jesus, we will find all this in its clearest
form. How sharply he speaks against the piety that tries to cleanse
from the outside. How clearly he tells us that the inside must first
be cleansed:

> "You blind Pharisee! first cleanse the inside of the cup and
> of the plate, that the outside also may be clean.
> "Woe to you, scribes and Pharisees, hypocrites! for you
> are like whitewashed tombs, which outwardly appear
> beautiful, but within they are full of dead men's bones and
> all uncleanness. So you also outwardly appear righteous to
> men, but within you are full of hypocrisy and iniquity."
>
> (Matthew 23:26-28)

Basically, we find in Jesus everything that Papa meant when
he spoke of the Youth Movement; unfortunately we will find it
seldom among Christians nowadays.

Let yourselves be guided completely by the Holy Spirit in

regard to the Hutterian brothers. It may be that in some things we are too worldly; let us be childlike and open. But it has to be genuine; it has to become alive from within. That is the only way to a rebirth. Sometimes I wish that more came from within in our life, that more were formed by Christ. But first and foremost I thank God for what he has given us after we had gone so far astray and now that we are a thousand souls or more.

2. JESUS CHRIST! He must remain the center at all times. The church is not the center. In Primavera and Wheathill the church occupied the central place. A body without a head is dead. That Christ is the head of the church is only a parable. Christ is the heart of God's throne. Another parable is that of the vine; in this parable the important thing is the cleansing, and most of all the bearing of fruit. This should be a fundamental concern in proclaiming the gospel to the souls entrusted to you and the other servants. The community needs constant renewal from within. By that I mean an ever new encounter with God and his Jesus Christ. This should happen in meetings as well as in each individual heart. Rebirth means the indwelling of the Father of our Jesus Christ, and it takes place through the Holy Spirit.

> "If you love me, you will keep my commandments. And I will pray the Father, and he will give you another Counselor, to be with you forever, even the Spirit of truth."
>
> (John 14:15-17)

> "He who has my commandments and keeps them, he it is who loves me; and he who loves me will be loved by my Father, and I will love him and manifest myself to him."
>
> (John 14:21)

Unless we have fellowship with Jesus, our soul dies. (John 15:4)

In his farewell speech in the Gospel of John, Jesus speaks of this indwelling. That is what I ask for each one of you: that Christ may dwell in you.

> "Abide in me, and I in you. As the branch cannot bear fruit by itself unless it abides in the vine, neither can you, unless you abide in me. I am the vine, you are the branches. He who abides in me, and I in him, he it is that bears much fruit, for apart from me you can do nothing. If a man does not abide in me, he is cast forth as a branch and withers; and the branches are gathered, thrown into the fire and burned."                                    (John 15:4-6)

What a priceless treasure—we in him and he in us. This deepest expression of mysticism depends absolutely on doing the will of Jesus.

When Christ dwells within us, it can happen (in holy moments) that we encounter him directly, and it seems as if the eyes of our hearts are seeing him. Only twice in my life has something like that happened to me. But a person's Christianity does not depend on the occurrence of a direct personal encounter of that sort. What happened to Paul on the road to Damascus is very rare, possibly unique. The same is true of the Revelation to John. But Jesus is not only head of the Church and dwells within the believers; he also sits at the right hand of power and shall come on the clouds of heaven.

> "Hereafter you will see the Son of man seated at the right hand of power, and coming on the clouds of heaven."
> (Matthew 26:64)

To regard Jesus as the bringer of a new religion is, I consider, an error into which Primavera fell in part or almost completely.

He himself is the inner life. Through the Holy Spirit he lives within the believer. That is why I love so very much the symbol he gives of eating his flesh and drinking his blood.

We experience Jesus as dwelling within us. That is our daily prayer. But he also rules, sitting at the right hand of the Father. He rules over angel-worlds, powers, and principalities as well as over his Church. We can only have an inkling of the supercosmic greatness of these mysterious but real facts. Let us have reverence. It will always be a mystery that Jesus tells his disciples in farewell that he is going to prepare a place for them. (John 14:2) It will always remain an awe-inspiring mystery what happens there in eternity, in the star-worlds, perhaps particularly in the angel-worlds and among the souls who have died in Christ. When Stephen was being stoned, he saw the heavens open and Jesus standing at the right hand of God. (Acts 7:55) John saw Jesus with flaming eyes. I believe that when Jesus comes again we will see him in person.

> While they were gazing into heaven as he went, behold, two men stood by them in white robes, and said, "Men of Galilee, why do you stand looking into heaven? This Jesus, who was taken up from you into heaven, will come in the same way as you saw him go into heaven." (Acts 1:10,11)

Your Opa describes on page 9 (English) of the book *The Early Christians* how some saw Jesus at the Lord's Supper and how the Church hears the heavenly choirs (on page 14 in the German). The father Blumhardt experienced something of the presence of heavenly choirs.

Because of the falling away by the community (from 1934 on) I am extremely fearful of empty religious words, of long speeches that try to present an abstract Christianity as if it were a philosophy. Jesus and his world is the greatest of all realities.

Without the cross an encounter with Jesus cannot be imagined. His person emanates the way of suffering, and his great love for all men floods our hearts and becomes an urge to go out to men, to save those who are in the grip of darkness. In deep encounter with Jesus the wish to suffer for him wells up quite naturally. I cannot imagine a meeting with Jesus unless there is a deep understanding of his way of suffering. Without the fire of love there is no experience of Jesus. To be sure, he often comes first only in judgment.

When you think of the person of Jesus, remember what your grandfather wrote in his last letter from Darmstadt: that Jesus' supercosmic importance has to be seen over and over again. Here we must begin with the living star-world. This brings the world of God's angels quite close to us, and also the terrible reality of Satan's angel-world. God's throne is in the star-world, and that is where the world of his angels is. We know from the times of the prophets and particularly from Jesus' life that some angels take on an almost human form, and others are like flames of fire. They too are created beings, and I believe we will be amazed one day when God's creation is made manifest to us.

I consider the last chapter of your grandfather's *Inner Land* of unusual importance. I believe the time will come when this book will have a crucial meaning for the whole earth, and I know that my father had the last chapter very specially on his heart; and that chapter speaks to me very much in the present hour. In "The Living Word" your grandfather wrote (beginning on page 516):

> Therefore when a man's life has been renewed through a common faith in Christ, he does not demand the appearance of Christ's body, as if it were necessary to bring Christ down from heaven or even up from the kingdom of the dead. Rather, he experiences the living presence of Christ's Spirit through the Word that has directly pierced his heart. The

life-giving Word, as the fullest expression of the experience of our hearts, is spoken out and confessed with our mouth. Faith in Jesus Christ and the confessing of his name are alive as soon as the Word, like a living seed, is planted directly into our innermost hearts. When the Word is near, it means that God is near. For the Word is Jesus Christ himself; out of his Spirit is born every sentence of the truth.

From the beginning, Jesus Christ is the revelation of the Father, which reached its culmination in history when he became flesh and dwelt among us. His life brought the Word among us as the will of God put into practice in actual life. Therefore, in the Word, Luther saw life and blessedness, forgiveness, and the sharing of a common life in God. Therefore, the keeping of the Word can be no blind, outward obedience such as a soldier pays to military orders. It is unity of life with Jesus Christ, the Lord and Bridegroom of the soul, energetically being put into practice here and now.

These words of your Opa's in *Inner Land* make it quite plain that we today should not expect to have his person appear to us in flesh and blood. I do believe, however, that when he comes again, we shall see Jesus in person. We can infer this from Acts 1, verse 11:

"This Jesus, who was taken up from you into heaven, will come in the same way as you saw him go into heaven."

I still want to lay on your heart, beloved Christoph, some more words out of Opa's "Living Word." On page 513 in the first full paragraph you will find the following:

In this relationship between the Word of God in the heart and the Word of God in the Bible, in this coming of the

Word of God, the life-giving Spirit is decisive. The living Christ himself is in this Holy Spirit, whom we can receive in no other way than through becoming one with the crucified Christ. This is the way God's truth is revealed.

I am absolutely convinced that to be disciples of Christ we must have a faith in which we are prepared to bear everything, and to give up everything, as the crucified Christ did. This utmost surrender struck me and called me to the depths in my childhood and youth, and I ask you to have this proclaimed over and over again and represented to the Church, to the new generation, and also to the other servants of the Word. On page 514 Opa says:

> What the Spirit says directly to the open and expectant Church cannot be said by any *man*. The divine will is made known to her by God himself. When that really and truly takes place, we are completely at one with the Bible of the prophets and the apostles.

For every Christian, then, Jesus' words in John 15:4 are of central importance: "Abide in me, and I in you." And on page 515 in *Inner Land*, at the end of the paragraph: "God's works proclaim the power of his Word."

The crucial thing is that God speaks in our hearts. And Jesus Christ promises this indwelling to us if we love him and keep his commandments. This love is what we must ask God for.

In the Book of Revelation Satan is called the Accuser, who accuses men to God and accuses God to men. I have experienced in a dreadful way what it means if a text in the Bible causes one to begin having doubt in Jesus Christ's great love. I was not faithful, after the great mercy God had shown me. Bible passages became veiled to me. (I tried to demonstrate from the Bible a philosophy for the masses, for all men.) Beware of that temptation;

it comes from Satan. To question God's love and his nearness leads to death for one who has already given him his life. We must be led to a deepening, an ever renewed deepening of our faith. It is good to recognize the evil in oneself. But we should never doubt God's great mercy, even in judgment. The least doubt leads to torments that make a person feel he is already in hell while in this life. Once a person starts yielding to that kind of temptation—woe to anyone who does that! I have done it; I searched in the Bible, and I suffered torments that I cannot describe.

I ask you to stand by any member who comes into such a temptation and always to lead him back to the way of the cross, the way of trust, the way of faith. Satan is cunning; and even Jesus, who never gave in to any of Satan's temptations, sweated drops as of blood in hours when he was tempted:

> And in anguish of spirit he prayed the more urgently; and his sweat was like clots of blood falling to the ground. (Luke 22:44, NEB)

We must pray to see Jesus just as he is!

Jesus Christ is very close to us at all our places. He comes near also in judgment. The deeper we experience the reality of Jesus, the more fruitful the life of the Bruderhofs and each of its members will become.

3. Please have it on your heart and lay it on the hearts of all the servants of the Word that each member should be used in ways that will bear fruit for Jesus Christ. It is of first importance for this that every heart burns for Jesus and for the greatness of his future. Each one must pause to consider that he does not know how long he will have the chance to bear fruit on this earth. We will all have to give an account one day.

So it is the task of all servants of the Word and those holding other services to help *every member to serve with joy*.

4. Yesterday we held the Lord's Supper jointly with Evergreen and for a large part of the time with New Meadow Run. Only the breaking of bread was held separately by the New Meadow Run brotherhood. The telephone really is a gift. The working together with the servants of the Word moves me deeply, and the fact that your father-in-law Hans is helping to carry the Service. What a miracle!

Now I want to lay *the children very specially* on your heart. In bringing up our children the real issue is that they find and experience a burning love for Jesus. They should be helped, too, to love and understand the Bible. I don't know if it is enough to go through the Old Testament with them in school. Certainly, the children have the wonderful opportunity of sensing God's greatness through the songs and choruses we sing, such as those from the *Messiah* or the *Elijah*. What seed is sown now in the hearts of our children and young people will be extremely important for the future of the Bruderhofs.

5. At this point I want to mention the subject of sports. My father loved sledding and encouraged us very much to sled on the steep Rhön hills; it went very fast and needed courage. He went with us, and at night he would work in the dark, often alone, to keep the track in order. Where the snow had been worn away he filled in the places and poured water on them so that next morning they would be covered with ice; that of course only increased the speed. He also built up little bumps that made the sleds fly in the air. He did these things to teach us bravery.

But Papa would not tolerate a passionate love for sports, games, or music, which filled a person's heart. He felt that was idolatry. I must tell you openly that I often am fearful that we are losing something in that area, and I shall call attention to this danger more and more.

My father had a deep love for life in creation and a deep love for his wife as a gift from God. But this was always under God, for God with his Christ is the Creator of all the marvels of creation; and music is one of these. To honor music for its own sake is idolatry. Everything must come under the Creator and be to his honor!! My father loved nature in the woods and meadows, the brooks and springs, and in one of these springs he held the baptisms of immersion. In this sense he was almost a romantic. Yet the moment anything created was held even slightly higher than the Creator, he resisted with his full authority. All that will be a question for the Hutterites.

With music there is basically the same problem as with anything created by God. God created music for the honor of his name, and no one must ever use it for any other purpose. If something leads to joy in the community, that is one way of honoring God, but it must not isolate.

We were too poor to have skis for everybody, but my father didn't like it if most of the children went sledding and one child went off by himself with the one pair of skis we had. For him the communal experience was extremely important, also in the children's education. We need to show the Hutterites that we take a sharp stand against any form of idolatry.

In clothing too, the honor of God should be quite genuinely shown; this was another part of our common experience in Sannerz and at the Rhön Bruderhof. Long before we were united with the Hutterites we wore our own unified clothing. In Sannerz and at the Rhön it was absolutely impossible for us to go along with fashion because the constantly changing fashions are determined mainly by mammonism and by impurity. The influence of fashion was ruled out. And everyone who came to Sannerz felt how unfitting it would be.

For you and your Verena and your beloved children I wish God's blessing on your future. Some day when I am no longer among you, you will be the head of our family. When the time comes that Mama cannot be so active anymore, she will find that very difficult. I believe, however, that a time of more inner quiet will have great importance for her inner life. I embrace you in great love as your father,

(Signed) Heini Arnold

# The Narrator

David Merrill Mow's life became part of our history. His
account of "The Bruderhof's Struggle for Renewal" was told to
the communities at various mealtimes and meetings from 1982
to 1986. He was born not far from Bombay on the west coast of
India on December 25, 1928. At the age of six he went with his
older brother and sister to Woodstock, a missionary boarding
school in the mountains. He was with his parents for only four
months of each year.

When he was eleven, his family moved to Chicago, where
Merrill spent his teen years with several others of our present
members who came from the Church of the Brethren. In
Manchester College he met Kathleen Fike. They were married
after her graduation and while he was attending Bethany Seminary
in Chicago. They were blessed with twelve children, all of whom
are at the Bruderhof.

During Kathy's last year in college, she and Bob and Shirley
Wagoner heard two brothers from Paraguay speak there. Bob and
Shirley then visited the Bruderhof in Primavera and returned to
tell how brothers and sisters were trying to live in accordance
with the teachings of Jesus. Merrill knew he had to visit and see
for himself. When the Woodcrest Bruderhof was started, the
Mows came to visit and found that the Christian life there rang
true to Jesus and his Sermon on the Mount.

Merrill and Kathy decided to join and with their growing family
spent Merrill's remaining thirty-one years at the Bruderhof. He

worked as storekeeper and shop foreman in early Woodcrest, and as witness brother and servant of the Word at each of our present communities except Pleasant View. For over twenty years they worked together as "parents" for the high school group. For many years Merrill led our various community choirs in directing a great variety of choral works and in the singing of solos. And directing the high school choir was a special joy for him.

Merrill had a deep love and respect for our brothers in the West, and they for him. During his last illness they reached out constantly to Merrill, Kathy, and the whole family.

Merrill's final illness became known in March of 1986, but he faced the future with a strong faith that his life was completely in God's hands, and this upheld him through all that he had to suffer. Again and again he gave all his strength. His last year included the marriage of his daughter Joyanna to Jonathan Zimmerman, an eight-week visit to Darvell, and visits to Deer Spring, Woodcrest, and Pleasant View. He also took part in making the film about early Woodcrest, and he worked with the New Meadow Run high schoolers on a singing production. In September he used all his strength for the trip to the Lancaster Conference (a meeting of Anabaptist churches), where he spoke to a large gathering. In December he made his last trip to Woodcrest to help with a baptism preparation group. He was very active and the meetings were quite intense.

On March 12, 1987, our beloved brother and servant Merrill was called home into eternity at the age of fifty-eight. He had known of his cancer for just one year. A month after hearing the diagnosis he said:

> If I have not much longer to live, that is within God's will, and my task is to find out what it means. . . . Faith doesn't depend on my having *my* way; faith depends on God having *his* way. This must be my highest joy and delight. Otherwise how can I pray, "Thy will be done"?

# Questions Our Novices Answer

1. Are you certain that this way of brotherly community, based on a firm faith in God and Christ, is the way to which God has called you?

2. Are you ready to put yourself completely at the disposal of the church community of Christ *to the end of your life*—all your faculties, the whole strength of your body and soul, and your entire property, both that which you now possess and that which you may later inherit or earn?

3. Are you ready to accept every admonition (where this is justified) and the other way around, to admonish others if you should sense within our community life something that should be clearer or would more fittingly bespeak the will of God, or if you should feel that something ought to be corrected or abolished?

4. Are you firmly determined to remain loyal and true, bound with us in mutual service as brothers and sisters, so that our love may be more burning and complete in the building of the church community, in the outreach to others, and in the proclamation of the gospel?

5. Are you ready then to surrender yourself completely and to bind yourself unreservedly to God, to Jesus Christ, and to the community?

# Chronology

1920    Beginning at Sannerz of the Christian community known later as the *Bruderhof,* the *Society of Brothers*, and familiarly the *"Eastern" Hutterites.*

1927    Rhön Bruderhof begun.

1930-31    Eberhard Arnold's journey to America and uniting with Hutterian Brethren.

1933    Adolf Hitler in power.

1934    Alm Bruderhof begun.

1935    Eberhard Arnold called into eternity.

1936    Cotswold Bruderhof begun.

1937    Visit of two Hutterian Brothers to Bruderhofs in Europe—Michael Waldner Vetter and David Hofer Vetter.

    Rhön Bruderhof closed by Gestapo.

1938    All Bruderhof members (the Eastern communities) gathered in England.

1941    Bruderhof found refuge in Primavera, Paraguay (1941-61).

1942    Wheathill Bruderhof begun in England.

1949-54    Mission journeys from Primavera to the United States.

1950    Visit of two Hutterian brothers to Bruderhofs in Paraguay—Samuel Kleinsasser Vetter and John Wipf Vetter.

1954    Woodcrest Bruderhof begun in New York State by some members of Primavera, Macedonia, and Kingwood communities.

1955    Bruderhof (the Eastern communities) involvement with Forest River Hutterian Colony and exclusion of Bruderhof from the Hutterian Church.

1957    Woodcrest Carriage House fire.

Bruderhof withdrew from Forest River Colony.

Oak Lake Bruderhof (later called New Meadow Run) begun in Pennsylvania.

1958    Macedonia Community became a Bruderhof.

Evergreen Bruderhof (later called Deer Spring) begun in Connecticut.

Bulstrode Bruderhof begun in England.

1959    Struggle for Miriam Way.

Hans Zumpe lost Service.

A turn in Bruderhof history.

1960    Near split—cable and correspondence.

1960-62 Primavera, Sinntal, and Wheathill Bruderhofs closed.

1962    Elder service of Heini Arnold confirmed.

1964    First journey West to seek reconciliation with Hutterian Brethren.

1965    New Meadow Run, new name for Oak Lake Bruderhof.

1966    Bulstrode community moved from England to U.S.A.

1971    Bruderhof returned to England—Darvell begun in East Sussex.

1973    Jacob Kleinsasser Vetter and Jacob Hofer Vetter's visit to Woodcrest.

1974    Second journey West, seeking and finding a reuniting with the Hutterian Brethren.

|      | Dwight Blough called into eternity. |
|------|-------------------------------------|
| 1975 | Lord's Supper Covenant. |
| 1980 | Emmy Arnold and Annemarie Arnold called into eternity. |
| 1982 | Heini Arnold called into eternity. |
| 1983 | Elder service of Johann Christoph Arnold confirmed. |
| 1986 | Pleasant View Bruderhof begun in New York State. |
| 1987 | Merrill Mow called into eternity. |
| 1988 | Bruderhof returned to Germany—Waldfrieden and Michaelshof begun in the Westerwald. |
|      | Building construction for Spring Valley Bruderhof begun in Fayette County, Pennsylvania. |
| 1990 | First residents move into Spring Valley. |
|      | Catskill Bruderhof begun in New York State. |

# Glossary and Names

**agouti**  Tropical American rodent about the size of a rabbit.

**Alm Bruderhof**  Small Bruderhof begun in Liechstenstein in 1934 as a refuge from Nazi teachers for our children and from military service for our young men. Closed in March 1938, when all moved to the Cotswold Bruderhof because of continued Nazi pressure on the government of Liechstenstein.

**Asuncion House**  Housing for an office of the Primavera Bruderhof, for students, traveling members, and guests, in Asuncion, port city and capital of Paraguay (1943-62). Display and sales outlet for Primavera turnery. Also called Bruderhof House, Asuncion.

**ban**  Most serious form of Hutterian church discipline.

**Basel**  Used with names of older sisters to show respect. (From *Base*, middle high German for aunt.)

**Blumhardts**  Johann Christoph (1805-1880) and his son Christoph Friedrich (1842-1919), pastors in southwest Germany (Württemberg).

**Bruderhof**  Eastern branch of the Hutterian Brethren or one of its communities. (From the German, home or place of the brothers.)

**Bruderhof House, Asuncion**  See Asuncion House.

**Bulstrode**  Bruderhof at Gerrards Cross, England (1958-66).

**Dariusleut**  One of three branches of the Hutterian Church. Originated in Russia under the leadership of Darius Walter. Settled in the U.S. and Canada. *Leut* is German for people.

**Darvell**  Bruderhof at Robertsbridge, East Sussex, England. Begun in 1971.

**Deer Spring**  Bruderhof in Norfolk, Connecticut. Begun as "Evergreen" in 1958.

**East-West**   East refers to the Bruderhof founded by Eberhard Arnold
in 1920 and to its communities in New York State, Pennsylvania,
Connecticut, England, and Germany. They have been referred to
in the West as the "new" Hutterites. West refers to the "old"
Hutterites, the Darius-, Lehrer-, and Schmiede-leut in Western
United States and Canada, whose origins go back to the 16th century
in central Europe. *Leut* is German for people.

**El Arado**   Small Bruderhof settlement near Montevideo, Uruguay
(1953-60).

**elder, Elder**   For 350 years the Hutterian Brethren had one leading
servant of the Word as Elder *(Vorsteher* or *Ältester)*, carrying the
main responsibility for the whole church. When they immigrated
to the United States in 1874, they settled as three groups and were
joined in 1930 by a fourth, the Bruderhof, each with an Elder. In
this volume any reference to these four Elders is capitalized, whereas
elders may refer to older servants appointed to support the Elder.

**Evergreen**   Bruderhof in Norfolk, Connecticut. Begun in 1958, later
renamed Deer Spring.

**family meeting**   Any meeting of the entire household (those able to
attend) from the youngest babies to the oldest members. The family
meeting most often referred to is on Sunday morning, when there
are songs, stories, or little plays given by or for the children.

**Gemeinde**   The church and the community together (from the German).
Seldom used by the Bruderhof, and therefore a German "n" is added
for the plural.

**Gemeindestunde**   Meeting for worship (in German, literally hour of
the church). Much used by the Bruderhof, and therefore an English
"s" is added for the plural.

**Gottliebin**   Surname Dittus. A young woman who suffered from demon
possession in Möttlingen, Germany. She was healed through the
prayers and the struggle (1842-43) led by Johann Christoph
Blumhardt.

**hof (hōf)**   1) Short for Bruderhof and interchangeable with "place."
2) Refers to central area of the communal buildings. "*On* the hof"
(in German *auf dem Hof*) often used to mean *at* or *in* the community.

**Hutterian Brethren**   An Anabaptist group which originated in the 16th

Century. While seeking a new home in Moravia in 1528, they began the community of goods that distinguishes them from other Anabaptists. From this group emerged the church of the Hutterian Brethren, named after Jakob Hutter, one of their foremost Elders (1533-36).

**Hutterisch** German dialect spoken by the Western Hutterian communities, related to the language of the Austrian Tirol.

**Ibaté** One of three Bruderhofs at Primavera, Paraguay (1946-61).

**Isla (Margarita)** One of three Bruderhofs at Primavera, Paraguay (1941-62).

**Kinderschaft** Room for or meeting of the children's community. (Coined from the German in early Woodcrest.)

**Koinonia** Christian community near Americus, Georgia.

**Lehrerleut** One of three branches of the Hutterian Church. Originated in Russia. Since their American settlement was led by Jacob Wipf, a teacher (*Lehrer*), they were known as "Lehrerleut." *Leut* is German for people.

**Loma (Hoby)** One of three Bruderhofs at Primavera, Paraguay (1942-60).

**Lotte Henze** Young woman in the Sannerz community who suffered from demon possession.

**lovemeal** Special communal mealtime to celebrate a meaningful experience or event.

**Lower Bromdon** Part of the Wheathill Bruderhof property in England.

**New Meadow Run** Bruderhof in Farmington, Pennsylvania. Begun as "Oak Lake" in 1957.

**Oak Lake** See New Meadow Run.

**Pleasant View** Bruderhof in Ulster Park, New York. Begun in 1986.

**Primavera** Collective name for the three Bruderhofs in Paraguay where brothers and sisters found a place of refuge during World War II. Originally the name of the large estancia purchased in March 1941 by the Bruderhof, which included finally three separate communities, Isla Margarita, Loma Hoby, and Ibaté (each named for its area of the Estancia "Primavera" — "Springtime" in Spanish).

**Reichslieder**   Hymns which came out of the revival movement of the 19th and early 20th centuries. (In German literally, Kingdom songs.)

**Reigen**   Singing circle games (from middle high German).

**Rhön Bruderhof**   Begun in 1927 by the Sannerz community and closed in 1937 by Gestapo. Situated in the Rhön hills of Hesse, West Germany.

**Sannerz**   Christian community, soon known as the Bruderhof, was begun in the village of Sannerz, Hesse, Germany, under the leadership of Eberhard and Emmy Arnold (1921-27).

**Schmiedeleut**   One of three branches of the Hutterian Brethren. Originated in Russia under the leadership of Michael Waldner. He was a blacksmith (*Schmied*) and this group was called "Schmiedeleut." *Leut* is German for people.

**servant**   See servant of the Word.

**servant(s) of the Word**   Minister(s), pastor(s). The brother(s) chosen by the whole church to care for the inner and outer well-being of the community. Authentic leadership in Christian community is service. Therefore the Bruderhof uses this old Hutterian designation. The words servant, deacon, and minister are all translations of the same word *diakonos* in the New Testament.

**service(s)**   Tasks in the church community, such as steward, work distributor, or servant of the Word.

**Shalom group**   Young people's group, unmarried, over 17.

**Sinntal**   Bruderhof in Germany at Bad Brückenau (1955-61).

**Society of Brothers**   An official name of the Eastern Hutterian Brethren (Bruderhof) adopted in England in May 1939 and used in Paraguay (Sociedad Fraternal Hutteriana) and in the U.S.A. until after the 1974 re-uniting with the Hutterian Brethren.

**Tracht**   The united dress of the Hutterian Church. (German for any traditional dress.)

**Upper Bromdon**   Part of the Wheathill Bruderhof.

**Vetter**   Used with the names of older brothers and servants of the Word to show respect. (From middle high German for uncle.)

**Wheathill**   Bruderhof in Shropshire, England (1942-61).

**witness brother(s)**   Brother(s) chosen by the whole church to support the service of the Word.

**Woodcrest**   First Eastern Bruderhof in the United States at Rifton, New York. Begun in 1954.

# Index of Names

Bold type indicates illustrations.

335

# RELATED BRUDERHOF TITLES

*Brothers Unite: An Account of the Uniting of Eberhard Arnold and the Rhön Bruderhof with the Hutterian Church,*
   edited by the Hutterian Brethren.

*The Chronicle of the Hutterian Brethren,* Vol. I.

*Community in Paraguay: A Visit to the Bruderhof,*
   by Bob and Shirley Wagoner.

*Confession of Faith,*
   by Peter Riedemann (Rideman), written in prison 1540-42.

*Inner Land: A Guide into the Heart and Soul of the Bible,*
   by Eberhard Arnold.

*Living Churches,*
   Vol. I, *Love to Christ and Love to the Brothers,*
   Vol. II, *The Meaning and Power of Prayer Life,*
   by Eberhard Arnold.

*Salt and Light: Talks and Writings on the Sermon on the Mount,*
   by Eberhard Arnold.

*Seeking for the Kingdom of God,*
   by Eberhard and Emmy Arnold.

*Torches Together,*
   by Emmy Arnold.


The above and catalog available on request from:

Plough Publishing House
Ulster Park, NY 12487

# SOME BRUDERHOF ADDRESSES

Woodcrest, Rifton, NY 12471 U.S.A.
Pleasant View, Ulster Park, NY 12487 U.S.A.
Catskill Bruderhof, Elka Park, NY 12427 U.S.A.
New Meadow Run, Farmington, PA 15437 U.S.A.
Spring Valley, Farmington, PA 15437 U.S.A.
Deer Spring, Norfolk, CT 06058 U.S.A.
Starland Hutterian Brethren, Rte 2, Box 133
     Gibbon, MN 55335 U.S.A.
Crystal Spring, Ste. Agathe, Manitoba ROG 1YO  CANADA
Darvell, Robertsbridge, East Sussex, TN32 5DR ENGLAND
Michaelshof, Auf der Höhe, 5231, Birnbach, WEST GERMANY